# ORDINATIO OXONIENSIS
# IN PRIMUM LIBRUM SENTENTIARUM

## DISTINCTIO 1, QUAESTIONES 8-9

**TEXTES PHILOSOPHIQUES DU MOYEN ÂGE**

*Collection fondée par*
Marie-Thérèse d'Alverny
et
Étienne Gilson

*dirigée par*
Joël Biard

DERNIERS TITRES PARUS DANS LA MÊME COLLECTION

XXVI. *De sex inconvenientibus. Traité anonyme de la philosophie naturelle du* XIV$^{e}$ *siècle*, édité par Sabine Rommevaux-Tani, 2022, 386 pages.

XXV. Jean de Reading, *Scriptum in primum librum sententiarum. Distinctio 1, Questiones 1-6*, édité par Francesco Fiorentino, 2018, 368 pages.

XXIV. Jean de Reading, *Scriptum in primum librum sententiarum*, édité par Francesco Fiorentino, 2011, 384 pages.

XXIII. Blaise de Parme, *Questiones super perspectiva communi*, édité par Graziella Federici Vescovini et Joël Biard, 2009, 356 pages.

XXII. Blaise de Parme, *Quaestiones circa tractatum proportionum magistri Thome Braduardini*, édité par Joël Biard, 2006, 240 pages.

XXI. Thomas d'Aquin, Super librum de causis expositio, édité par Henr-Dominique Saffrey, 2002, 224 pages.

XX. Blaise de Parme, *Questiones super tractatus logice magistri Petri Hispani*, édité par Joël Biard et Graziella Federici Vescovini, 2001, 432 pages.

XIX. Jean de la Rochelle, *Summa de anima*, édité par Jacques-Guy Bougerol, 1995, 298 pages.

TEXTES PHILOSOPHIQUES DU MOYEN ÂGE

XXVII

ADAM WODEHAM

# ORDINATIO OXONIENSIS IN PRIMUM LIBRUM SENTENTIARUM

DISTINCTIO 1, QUAESTIONES 8-9

*edited by*

SEVERIN V. KITANOV AND CHRISTOPHER D. SCHABEL

PARIS
LIBRAIRIE PHILOSOPHIQUE J. VRIN
6 place de la Sorbonne, V e

2025

*Imprimé en France*

ISSN 0495-3495

ISBN 978-2-7116-3220-6

*www.vrin.fr*

*In memoriam Girard J. Etzkorn*

# PRÉFACE

The distant origins of the present volume lie in our project to edit a long *Determinatio* by Master Richard FitzRalph from the 1331-1332 academic year at Oxford, in which he debated the Mertonian Bachelor William Skelton. In order to do so, we also had to transcribe related material from FitzRalph's *Lectura* on the *Sentences* for the background and edit the sections of Adam Wodeham's contemporary *Ordinatio Oxoniensis* in which Wodeham described the FitzRalph-Skelton debate and participated himself. To contribute to an understanding of the context, Schabel transcribed the two questions of Wodeham (book I, distinction 1, questions 8-9) edited below from the Sorbonne manuscript in the summer and fall of 2021.

In the fall of 2022 Kitanov decided to collaborate on the critical edition of these questions as part of a contribution to a collective volume edited by Monika Michałowska and Edit Anna Lukács. Late in 2022 and during his sabbatical leave from Salem State University in the spring semester of 2023, Kitanov collated the Mazarine and Tarazona manuscripts (images of the latter were kindly supplied by Ziang Chen), checked the transcription of the Sorbonne witness, compiled most of the apparatus fontium, and wrote the bulk of the doctrinal section of the introduction. While working under the aegis of Monica Brînzei's ERC project DEBATE-771589, Schabel collated the Vatican codex, spot-checked any anomalies in the collation of the Sorbonne, Mazarine, and Tarazona manuscripts, finalized the text and apparatus criticus, and compiled the philological section and initial historical part of the introduction. In the process it was learned via William O. Duba that Jerry Etzkorn had transcribed an anonymous related question from Vat. lat. 943, which Kitanov discovered to be a version of Richard FitzRalph's *Lectura*, question 10, article 2, so Schabel recollated and polished up Etzkorn's transcription for inclusion as an appendix. In addition, we are indebted to Olli Hallamaa for sending us his preliminary transcription of Roger Roseth's pertinent question 2, article 2, from his *Lectura* on the *Sentences*, which Kitanov double-checked against the manuscript where quoted below.

Understandably, the editors of the collective volume judged the result to be too long to be a chapter in a book, but we thank them for their support. In particular, we thank Monika Michałowska for sharing with us her forthcoming critical edition of Richard FitzRalph's *Lectura*, question 10, article 2. Although Schabel had transcribed the text as well, Michałowska identified and documented almost all of the source references in FitzRalph's article. For the text that Etzkorn had transcribed and the pertinent section of Wodeham's distinction 1, question 8, where he quotes from FitzRalph's article and deals with his sources, Michałowska's apparatus allowed Kitanov to locate the exact references to Augustine's *De Trinitate*, *Enchiridion*, and *De Genesi at litteram* as well as to Averroes' commentaries on Aristotle's *Metaphysics*, *Physics*, *De anima*, and *De caelo et mundo*, references that Kitanov then verified. During our work on the first question published below, Wodeham's *Ordinatio* I, distinction 1, question 8, Kitanov had already identified most of the references to Augustine's *De doctrina Christiana*, *De civitate Dei*, *De libero Arbitrio*, and *De duabus animabus* as well as to Lombard's *Sentences*, Anselm's *De casu diaboli* and *Cur Deus Homo*, Gregory's *Homiliae in Hiezechihelem prophetam*, and Aristotle's *Ethics*, *Physics*, and *Metaphysics*. On one occasion Michałowska's apparatus criticus was also consulted, but otherwise we employed Schabel's transcription from Paris, Bibliothèque nationale de France, lat. 15853.

After our happy collaboration with Vrin on an edition of some questions of Thomas Bradwardine's *Lectura* on the *Sentences* (which we hope to publish in full for this series), stemming from our work on FitzRalph's *Determinatio*, we decided to approach Joël Biard to consider publishing the present questions as a volume in his venerable Vrin series *Textes philosophiques du Moyen Âge*. Although these questions are part of a larger whole, that larger whole would require perhaps a dozen fat volumes to print and decades of hard work to accomplish. As will be clear in the introduction, the material presented here forms a distinct unit, more or less a separate treatise, and we thank Professor Biard, his anonymous reader, and the Librarie philosophique J. Vrin for accepting this volume for publication.

The spring of 2023 was a sad one for the field of fourteenth-century philosophy. In addition to Zenon Kałuża and Edith Sylla (whose scholarship is pertinent to the present volume), Jerry Etzkorn passed away while we were working on this book. Schabel is currently collaborating on the completion of a couple volumes of Jerry's other editions, but because of our inclusion of Jerry's transcription of what turns out to be an article by FitzRalph, we dedicate this publication to his memory.

14 July 2023
S.V.K., Salem
C.D.S., Aubervilliers

## INTRODUCTION

Before the Franciscan Adam Wodeham read the *Sentences* at Oxford in 1331-1332[1], Western theologians had been subjecting certain questions to mathematical analysis for many decades. In the late 1320s at Oxford a passion for this approach developed, grew into an obsession in the 1330s, and in the 1340s spread to Paris where it reached a feverish crescendo at the time of the Black Death[2]. Perhaps the *locus classicus* for mathematics in theology was the problem of the increase and decrease of grace in the human soul, traditionally treated in lectures on distinction 17 of book I. In the 1331-1332 academic year, « calculating grace », as Rega Wood once called it[3], became the most popular topic of discussion, along with the corresponding merit that grace helped one earn and their negative counterparts, sin and demerit. These issues expanded beyond not only the limits of their normal places in the *Sentences* but also those of the textbook itself. Wodeham was at the center of this great disputation, which involved his Dominican colleague Robert Holcot and a number of other bachelors reading the *Sentences* that year, who made grace, merit, sin, and demerit the focus of their principial debates, the first *principia* in Oxford for which we have substantial evidence[4]. Yet Wodeham and his *socii* also sparred with senior bachelors of the

1. For the date, see C. Schabel, « Ockham, the *Principia* of Holcot and Wodeham, and the Myth of the Two-Year *Sentences* Lecture at Oxford », *Recherches de Théologie et Philosophie médiévales* 87, 2020, p. 59-102.

2. See for example the classic studies of John Murdoch : J. E. Murdoch, « *Mathesis in Philosophiam Scholasticam Introducta* : The Rise and Development of the Application of Mathematics in Fourteenth-Century Philosophy and Theology », in *Arts libéraux et philosophie au Moyen Âge. Actes du quatrième congrès international de philosophie médiévale*, Montréal-Paris, Institut d'études médiévales-Vrin, 1969, p. 215-265 ; J. E. Murdoch, « *Subtilitates Anglicanae, in* Fourteenth-Century Paris : John of Mirecourt and Peter Ceffons », *in* M. P. Cosman and B. Chandler (eds.), *Machaut's World. Science and Art in the Fourteenth Century*, New York, New York Academy of the Sciences, 1978, p. 51-86.

3. R. Wood, « Calculating Grace : The Debate about Latitude of Forms According to Adam de Wodeham », *in* S. Knuuttila, R. Työrinoja, and S. Ebbesen (eds.), *Knowledge and the Sciences in Medieval Philosophy : Proceedings of the Eighth International Congress of Medieval Philosophy (S.I.E.P.M.), Helsinki 24-29 August 1987*, vol. 2, Helsinki, Luther-Agricola Society, 1990, p. 373-391.

4. See Schabel, « Ockham, the *Principia* of Holcot and Wodeham » ; C. Schabel, « The Genre in Adolescence. Adam Wodeham's Report of the Principial Debates at Oxford in 1331-1332 », *in*

Bible such as the Dominican William Crathorn, with the Franciscan inceptor John of Rodington, and with the new regent master Richard FitzRalph[1]. The exchanges continued the following academic year, 1332-1333, when Thomas Bradwardine and probably Richard Kilvington, Robert Halifax, and Thomas Felthorpe were *sententiarii* and Rodington was Franciscan regent master[2].

Among the tangential subjects treated mathematically was the temporal aspect of human willing, continuous and instantaneous willing, starting and stopping, and so on. For example, if someone in a state of grace fulfills the negative precept *Thou shalt not commit adultery* continuously for an hour, does that person merit? Would someone fulfilling the positive precept *Honor thy Father and Mother* continuously for a day merit more if she stopped and started that fulfilment a number of times, entailing more acts of willing? If so, is there a limit to how many times someone could stop and start willing? Such doubts led FitzRalph to ask in his *Sentences* lectures of 1328-1329, « Does an act of the will come about *subito* or in time? », in 1332-1333 Halifax wondered, « Can any act of the will be produced *subito* by the will », while in 1331-1332 Wodeham formulated two such queries, questions 8 and 9 of distinction 1 of book I : « Can the will produce *simul et subito* a voluntary act of meritorious and free love? » and « Can the will freely suspend its act or break off from an act it has *subito*? »[3]

It is these two questions that are edited below and contextualized in this introduction. The questions contain lengthy and complex discussions of primarily theological issues emerging from certain traditional Aristotelian assumptions about the divisibility of time and space, the determination of the limits of

W.O. Duba and C. Schabel, *The Rise of a New Genre of Scholastic Disputation : Principia on the Sentences, 1315-1350*, Turnhout, Brepols, forthcoming. We are currently critically editing the remnants of Wodeham's *principia* in his *Ordinatio*, but see C. Schabel, « Adam Wodeham's *Principium in II Sententiarum* in Vat. lat. 869. A Footnote to Onorato Grassi's Study of the Oxford Debates of 1331-1332 », *Studi sull'Aristotelismo medievale (secoli VI-XVI)*, 2 (2022) (= *Studi per Onorato Grassi*), p. 343-381, and, for Holcot, C. Schabel, « Robert Holcot's Principial Questions on Grace, Merit, and Sin : A Preliminary Edition of the *Determinationes* II and IV », *in* P. Bermon and C. Grellard (eds.), *Theologia modernorum. Recherches sur les questions théologiques inédites de Robert Holcot*, Turnhout, Brepols, forthcoming.

1. We are currently editing FitzRalph's main *Determinatio* on the subject, but see C. Schabel, « Richard FitzRalph vs William Skelton, 1331-1332 : The Attribution of the "*Determinationes*" in a Florence Manuscript », *in* M.W. Dunne and S. Nolan (eds.), *A Companion to Richard FitzRalph : Fourteenth-Century Scholar, Archbishop, and Polemicist*, Leiden, Brill, 2023, p. 207-270.

2. For pertinent texts, see S.V. Kitanov and C. Schabel, « Thomas Bradwardine's Questions on Grace and Merit from His *Lectura* on the *Sentences*, 1332-1333 », *Archives d'Histoire Doctrinale et Littéraire du Moyen Age* 89, 2022, p. 163-236 ; C. Schabel, « The Oxford Franciscan Robert of Halifax's Principial Debate over Grace and Merit with His Pelagian *Socius* and Other Colleagues in 1332-1333 », *in* M. Brînzei and W.O. Duba (eds.), *Principia on the Sentences of Peter Lombard : Exploring an Uncharted Scholastic-Philosophical Genre*, Turnhout, Brepols, 2024, vol. 1, p. 567-672 ; and, in the ongoing critical edition of the *Sentences* questions of Kilvington, the introduction to E. Jung and M Michałowska, *Richard Kilvington Talks to Thomas Bradwardine about Future Contingents, Free Will, and Predestination : A Critical Edition of Question 4 from* Quaestiones super libros Sententiarum, Leiden, Brill, 2023, p. 1-86.

3. These questions were first noted together in W. J. Courtenay, *Adam Wodeham : An Introduction to His Life and Writings*, Leiden, Brill, 1978, p. 33-34.

change, and the nature of qualitative change. The questions also form a part of Wodeham's extensive treatment of the will as a free power and a cause of its own acts[1]. The influence of key aspects of John Duns Scotus' and William of Ockham's voluntarism is evident throughout the treatment. In the context of questions 8 and 9, Wodeham's main debate companions are Richard FitzRalph, John of Rodington, and Richard Campsall. Wodeham is one of our main sources of information about the views of Rodington and Campsall, but FitzRalph's *Lectura* on the *Sentences* has been preserved, which is why we know much more about FitzRalph's opinions not only as reflected in Wodeham's work but also independently of Wodeham's extensive quotations. Although Master FitzRalph's bachelor lectures on the *Sentences* date to 1328-1329[2], there is evidence that the version surviving in most manuscripts is the *Opus correctum*, perhaps put in final form during the debates surrounding and following his inception in mid-1331, probably in part as a result of exchanges with Wodeham[3], who cites the *Opus correctum* in the questions edited below [twice in 9.2. 83][4]. Nevertheless, Jerry Etzkorn once transcribed an anonymous question in Vat. lat. 943 that, as we shall see, may be from the early version of the pertinent question in FitzRalph's extant *Lectura*, so we have corrected Etzkorn's transcription, printed below in an appendix.

## I. Texts and contexts

The human will exists in time and so do all of its spontaneous and premeditated choices. Medieval scholastic investigations into the nature of the will's activity – whether we think of it as instantaneous or continuous and successive – are tied in general to the fundamental metaphysical problem of the possibility of change of various kinds (e.g., local motion, substantial transformation, qualitative and quantitative alteration). Understanding how change is possible, however, is also necessarily bound up with understanding the nature of time and space, and

1. On this see S. V. Kitanov, « Adam Wodeham's Analysis and Defense of Free Will », *in* M. Michałowska and R. Fedriga (eds.), *Willing and Understanding : Late Medieval Debates on the Will, the Intellect, and Practical Knowledge*, Leiden, Brill, 2023, p. 232-273.

2. K. Walsh, *Richard FitzRalph in Oxford, Avignon, and Armagh : A Fourteenth-Century Scholar and Primate*, Oxford, Clarendon Press, 1981, p. 4 and 44. Courtenay, *Adam Wodeham*, p. 76, had hypothesized 1326-1327, but Walsh found documentary evidence.

3. For the *Opus correctum*, see Courtenay, *Adam Wodeham*, p. 77-78, although giving the date of the *Opus correctum* as 1330-1331 because earlier, p. 75-76, he dated FitzRalph's inception to before 24 May 1331 and by October 1330, when in fact it was after 24 May 1331, and he also believed that Wodeham lectured on the *Sentences* in 1330-1332 (or 1330-1331 and 1332-1333), when it was simply in 1331-1332. Thus Courtenay's dating of the *Opus correctum* must be shifted forward to the 1331-1332 academic year, his first year as regent master. See Walsh, *Richard FitzRalph*, p. 4, Schabel, « Ockham, the *Principia* of Holcot and Wodeham », and Schabel, « Richard FitzRalph vs William Skelton, 1331-1332 », p. 213.

4. We cite the questions edited below in square brackets according to question, article, and paragraph.

specifically with the question of the infinite divisibility of time and space[1]. Since the human will is a faculty of the incorporeal soul and is therefore not spatially extended, its changes – such as beginning and ceasing as well as continuous motion over time – must be conceived primarily in qualitative terms even though the kinematic model of explanation applicable to moving bodies was also seen as applicable to the will, with time representing the duration of a given volition and intensity understood in terms of the varying degrees of intensity of the volition at a single instant[2]. The point of the departure for early fourteenth-century discussions of change against the background of the possibility of different kinds of indivisibles is provided by Aristotle's *Physics*, VI. 5 and VIII. 8, so it is to be expected for discussions of the nature of the will and the will's activity, even in a theological context, to be deeply rooted in the scholastic interpretation of Aristotle's natural philosophy. In scholastic terminology, the human will is a permanent entity (*res permanens*) insofar as by its very constitution the will represents a unity much like Socrates' existence. But we can also talk about the will's activity as a successive entity (*res successiva*) or a process very much like Socrates' running[3]. Thus, one aspect of understanding the will and its activity is related to the so-called *limit-decision* problem, which is about determining how permanent and successive entities begin and end, a problem that scholastic authors articulated and resolved well beyond Aristotle. The other aspect is inseparable from the problem of the composition of the continuum and takes us straight into the heart of the great scholastic debate about the metaphysical status of indivisibles (i.e., atoms, points, lines, surfaces).

Wodeham's own *Tractatus de indivisibilibus* represents a major witness to the debate between British indivisibilists (Robert Grosseteste, Henry of Harclay, Walter Chatton, and William Crathorn) and divisibilists (John Duns Scotus, William of Ockham, William of Alnwick, and Walter Burley)[4]. As Rega Wood's

1. See J. E. Murdoch, « The Analytic Character of Late Medieval Learning : Natural Philosophy without Nature », *in* L. D. Roberts (ed.), *Approaches to Nature in the Middle Ages : Papers of the Tenth Annual Conference of the Center for Medieval & Early Renaissance Studies*, Binghamton, NY, Center for Medieval and Early Renaissance Studies, 1982, p. 171-213, at p. 176-177 : « For the later books of the *Physics* deal with motion, and, as Aristotle says at the very outset of his investigation of this topic, with all those things that are necessarily involved in or follow from motion, that is, with what it is to be continuous, with how the infinite presents itself in the continuous, and with place, void, and time as the presumably necessary conditions of motion ».

2. The idea was that the total quantity of motion (but also of any kind of quality in general) can be calculated on the basis of its temporal duration and velocity. Nicole Oresme even introduced a two-dimensional geometrical model to represent the quantity of motion with a horizontal line standing for time and a vertical line intersecting the horizontal perpendicularly for describing the velocity of acceleration or deceleration. See O. Hallamaa, « Introduction », *in* Roger Roseth, *Lectura Super Sententias, Quaestiones 3, 4 & 5*, ed. O. Hallamaa, Helsinki, [University of Helsinki], 2005, p. 40-41.

3. For the distinction between permanent and successive things, see Murdoch, « The Analytic Character of Late Medieval Learning », p. 185-186.

4. For a summary of the debate between indivisibilists and divisibilists as reflected in Wodeham's treatise, see R. Wood's « Introduction » to Adam Wodeham, *Tractatus de Indivisibilibus*, ed. R. Wood, Dordrecht, Kluwer, 1988, p. 3-27, at p. 3-14. For the contents of the work, including the question on the continuum, see p. 14-19.

critical edition of the treatise shows, Wodeham quotes extensively from the works of Scotus, Harclay, William of Alnwick, Chatton, and Ockham. According to Wood, the *Tractatus* was written after 1323 and before 1331, but likely closer to 1323[1]. Since, however, an excerpt from FitzRalph, whose view of instantaneous volitional causation is presented and discussed in great detail in Wodeham's own question on the subject, is also found in Wodeham's *Tractatus*, and Wood found parallels between Wodeham's treatment in the *Tractatus* and in Crathorn's questions on the *Sentences*, which have now been dated to 1330-1331[2], it is also possible that the *Tractatus* was composed after the fall of 1330. Wood's *terminus ante quem* of 1331 is based on the fact that in the *Tractatus* Wodeham cites FitzRalph as *Hybernicus*, whereas William J. Courtenay remarked that after FitzRalph became a master of theology (in the late spring or summer of 1331) Wodeham labelled him *quidam doctor*. Nevertheless, Courtenay also recorded how marginal references to FitzRalph in Wodeham's *Ordinatio* stemming from after the fall of 1331 still call FitzRalph *Hibernicus*[3], and this is true in two manuscripts for question 8 edited below [8.1. 67, 8.1. 87, 8.1. 90, 8.2. 2]. Finally, there are four references in questions 8 and 9 edited below to a future treatment of indivisibles and the continuum[4], suggesting that Wodeham's *Tractatus* in final form may actually postdate his Oxford lectures on the early part of book I and could have been originally either a later part of those same lectures or planned as a separate work from the start[5].

1. Wood, « Introduction », p. 15-16.

2. Wood, « Introduction », p. 8 ; Schabel, « Ockham, the *Principia* of Holcot and Wodeham », p. 61-66.

3. Courtenay, *Adam Wodeham*, p. 77 n. 144-145.

4. See below [8.1. 16] : « Sed impossibile est quod instans immediate succedat instanti vel mutatum esse unum in eodem motu continuetur alteri vel unum indivisibile alteri situetur immediate ab eodem distincto – immo hoc includit repugnantiam, *ut satis patebit* in materia de non-compositione divisibilis ex indivisibilibus ». [9.2. 70] : « ... instans instanti sine medio succedere includit repugnantiam, sicut et indivisibile indivisibili in continuo, *ut alias demonstrabo* ». [9.2. 71] : « ... et sic haberemus unam moram vel durationem compositam ex indivisibilibus consequenter se habentibus, cuius oppositum evidentissime, ut aestimo, *alias in materia de continuo demonstrabo* ». [9.2. 71] : « ... si valet ratio Philosophi contra indivisibilia in continuo consequenter se habentia. Immo quia valet, ut *alias declarabo*, valet et mea, quae omnino similis est de indivisibilibus succedentibus sicut de indivisibilibus permanentibus ».

5. Courtenay, *Adam Wodeham*, p. 35-36, notes that both manuscripts of the *Tractatus* contain works dating to after 1328 and accompany the *Tractatus* itself with works from after 1334. Nevertheless, an apparently earlier version of the *Tractatus* exists, published *in* J. E. Murdoch and E. A. Synan, « Two Questions on the Continuum : Walter Chatton, O.F.M. (?) and Adam Wodeham, O.F.M. », *Franciscan Studies* 26, 1966, p. 212-288, which, along with certain statements in the *Tractatus* itself, informs us that Wodeham worked on the problem for a very long time. If Oxonian *sententiarii* at the time followed the Parisian sequence in lecturing on the four books, I-IV-II-III, then we might hypothesize that Wodeham spoke about the problem in his lectures on book IV, which would account for the colophon to book II, quoted in Courtenay, *Adam Wodeham*, p. 36 n. 69 : « Explicit secundus liber, alias enim multas quaestiones secundi de motu, de tempore, de continuo et de individuatione et similibus alias seriosius pertractavi ». In the previous note, p. 36 n. 68, Courtenay quotes Wodeham to the effect that Walter Chatton was lecturing on book II before and after Easter, 11 April 1322, which would imply a I-IV-II-III sequence, with lectures on book IV beginning in January.

Wodeham's account of instantaneous volitional production and cessation or interruption in questions 8 and 9 demonstrates clearly how the *limit-decision* and continuum/indivisible problems are entangled with the conception of the will as a psychological faculty. Question 8 asks whether the will can produce an act of meritorious and free love all at once and suddenly (*simul et subito*). The title of the question is by no means exceptional. We find similarly phrased questions from roughly the same time period in the *Sentences* commentaries of Richard FitzRalph, Robert Halifax, and Roger Roseth as well as in the anonymous text in manuscript Vat. lat. 943 (fols. 49r-50v). FitzRalph asks whether the act of the will occurs suddenly in the *Lectura* on book I, question 10 (*Utrum amor procedat ab aliqua notitia*), article 2 (*Utrum actus voluntatis fiat subito*). The material of this article is of utmost relevance to our investigation since Wodeham quotes extensively from it in his effort to provide a faithful and complete account of FitzRalph's position. In question 8, article 1, several arguments in defense of Wodeham's claim (expressed in Wodeham's fifth thesis) that the will can cause a meritorious volition instantaneously are taken verbatim from FitzRalph together with some of FitzRalph's own rejoinders [8.1. 66-67, 8.1. 69, 8.1. 76-79, 8.1. 82, 8.1. 84, 8.1. 87, 8.1. 89-90]. Moreover, question 8, article 2 features an entire barrage of 16 arguments borrowed directly from FitzRalph [8.2. 2-11, 8.2. 14-19, 8.2. 21-23]. Wodeham even presents FitzRalph's own abstract of the arguments buttressing his position [8.2. 23]. In Wodeham's own question, the arguments are arranged as objections to his fifth thesis. In FitzRalph's question 10, article 2, they occur at the very beginning of the treatment and are explicitly targeted at the claim that the will can have a first instant of willing, which is also how FitzRalph conceives of the problem of instantaneous volitional production in the initial wording of the principal question (*Et intelligo utrum vel sit aliquod primum instans actus voluntatis*). In Wodeham's text, FitzRalph's arguments appear in a somewhat abbreviated form and with a slightly different ordering. Finally, and as we shall see below when we focus on the details for Wodeham's own position, Wodeham offers a comprehensive summary of FitzRalph's view as it is in effect developed in FitzRalph's own response to the principal question. Wodeham knows FitzRalph's position thoroughly. He reports it accurately and disagrees with it on certain key points.

Anneliese Maier proposed the hypothesis that the anonymous question in Vat. lat. 943, *Utrum actus voluntatis fiat subito in instanti vel fiat in tempore*, may have been authored by Wodeham. Her evidence was a reference in the text of the question to a past treatment of the division and composition of the continuum (*quaere in quaestionibus de divisione et compositione continui, quia ibi tractavi istam materiam*)[1]. Courtenay pointed out that there were several other authors who wrote on the same subject matter after 1329, thus making the definitive

1. A. Maier, *Ausgehendes Mittelalter I. Gesammelte Aufsätze zur Geistesgeschichte des 14. Jahrhunderts*, Rome, Edizioni di Storia e Letteratura, 1964, p. 252 n. 42.

attribution of the question to Wodeham problematic[1]. Curiously, though, the same reference appears in question 8 although in a future sense (*ut satis patebit in materia de non-compositione continui ex indivisibilibus*) [8.1. 16]. A closer inspection of the contents of the anonymous witness reveals, however, that the text can be attributed with some certainty to FitzRalph. The text represents a shorter and unfinished version of FitzRalph's question 10, article 2, perhaps from a *reportatio* of his lectures in 1328-1329. The author first presents 18 arguments against the thesis that the act of the will can take place in an instant. Almost all of these arguments are found verbatim and with a slightly different ordering in question 10. The author then articulates 14 arguments in defense of the contrary thesis, namely that the act of the will can occur instantaneously. These arguments are also given in the body of question 10, article 2. Most importantly, the position defended by the anonymous author is clearly that of FitzRalph as developed in question 10, article 2. The gist of FitzRalph's position is that entities like intellection, volition, sensation, and pleasure can be said to be perfect or complete in an instant but not in the sense that they are instantaneously generated in their totality. Rather, they are generated and intensified successively to the point where their total being is completed or made perfect in the sense that the soul or potency that produces them is brought to rest. This claim is then supported on the basis of the authority of Aristotle and Averroes. According to the authority of the Philosopher and the Commentator, neither pleasure nor vision is an instance of movement or generation; they are perfect or complete in their species in an instant and without any kind of prior diminished action :

| FitzRalph, *Lectura super Sententias*, I, q. 10, a. 2, Paris, BnF. 15853, fol. 66rb-va | Anonymous, Vat. lat. 943, fol. 50va |
|---|---|
| Sed quia argumenta contra hanc partem multa sunt et difficilia, ideo pro quibusdam argumentis est notandum quod intellectio, sensatio, volitio, et delectatio dicuntur perfici semper in instanti, quamvis per aliquod tempus intendatur ex ali<qu>a causa, sicut scilicet quod postquam sensatio intenditur per aliquod tempus vel intellectio vel volitio vel delectatio, tunc in termino illius temporis dicitur sensatio esse perfectior quam prius, et similiter est de intellectione, volitione, delectatione. Ista enim postquam sunt in augeri per aliquod tempus et non ultra, tunc in fine istius temporis et aliis instantibus | Respondeo primo ad argumenta statim superius posita quae probant quod actus voluntatis fiat in instanti. Est tamen advertendum quod intellectio, volitio, sensatio, et delectatio dicuntur perfici subito et in instanti non quia quodlibet eorum generetur et intendatur quantum ad totum suum esse quod habetur subito in instanti – immo potest quodlibet eorum generari et intendi successive in tempore, sicut suo modo forma caloris in aqua, licet non ita perceptibiliter, apponatur de tempore – sed quodlibet eorum dicitur fieri et perfici subito in instanti quia quando esse completum et totaliter intensum cuiuslibet |

1. Courtenay, *Adam Wodeham*, p. 33-34, who gives the date as 1327 based on the view that FitzRalph read the *Sentences* in 1326-1327 rather than 1328-1329.

| | |
|---|---|
| sequentibus dicuntur esse perfecta in sua specie, quando est in anima perfecta quies. Et ideo ista omnia pluries dicuntur a Philosopho fieri <in> [et] indivisibili, et quod sunt actiones perfectae, propter hoc scilicet quia quando sunt perfectae in suis speciebus, tunc non coniunguntur cum aliquo motu vel cum actione diminuta, sed magis perficiuntur per quietem animae ab omnimoda transmutatione, secundum quod patet per Philosophum et Commentatorem, VII *Physicorum*, commento 20. Econtrario cuilibet verae alterationi quomodo dum est perfecta in sua specie in aliquo instanti in quo subiectum eius quiescit, quia tunc ipsa alteratio non est. | istorum fuerit in aliquo instanti terminante tempus suae factionis, tunc anima et potentia habens eum quiescit. Unde totalis et completiva perfectio intellectionis et cuiuslibet eorum quattuor sit in quiete vel cum quiete subiecti habentis eam. Ita quies subiecti et instans ultimatae perfectionis cuiuslibet illorum stant simul. Sed non sic est de forma quae proprie acquiritur per motum et alterationem, sicut est calor in aqua, immo ultimata perfectio formae alterabilis in subiecto coniungitur in ultimo instanti quo habetur ultimum complementum motui praecedenti in tantum quod alteratio non est quando cessat motus. Nam forma alterabilis intenditur et perficitur per motum ; sed intellectio et volitio et sensatio et delectatio perficitur magis per quietem ; tamen non sequitur « ergo subito in instanti », immo potest perfici et fieri cum quietae in tempore. |
| Et haec est ratio Philosophi, X *Ethicorum*, capitulo 4, ad declarandum, quia delectatio non est vera generatio nec verus motus, sicut nec visio, quia delectatio perfecta est in instanti, sicut visio perfecta est in instanti. Simili modo loquuntur Philosophus et Commentator, VII *Physicorum*, commento 18, probantes quod in virtutibus moralibus non est motus, quia virtutes sunt perfectiones et consistunt in indivisibili, quia esse perfectum virtutum consistit in quiete et in indivisibili, <scilicet> [p] in instanti, et similiter quaecumque actio perfecta virtutis. Secundum hunc modum loquitur Philosophus III *De anima* et Commentator, commento 28, ubi dicunt quod intellectio et similiter visio sunt actiones perfectae et fiunt in non-tempore. Nec eas praecedit actio diminuta. Hoc est quod sensatio et intellectio sunt perfectae in suis speciebus in instanti. Nec tunc requirunt actionem successivam immediate praecedentem, sed certe in perfecta quiete animae et corporis maxime perfecta sunt. | Et ista est ratio Aristotelis, X *Ethicorum* capitulo 4, ad ostendendum quod delectatio non est motus nec est vera generatio sicut nec visio, quia delectatio est perfecta in instanti sicut visio. Similiter Philosophus et Commentator VII *Physicorum*, commento 17, dicunt, probantes quod in virtutibus moralibus non est motus, quia virtutes sunt perfectiones et consistunt in indivisibili pro quanto esse perfectum ipsarum virtutum consistit in quiete et in indivisibili, scilicet instanti. Et isto modo loquuntur Aristoteles et Commentator III *De anima*, commento 28, ubi dicunt quod intellectio et similiter visio sunt actiones perfectae et fiunt in non-tempore, nec eas praecedit actio diminuta. Hoc est quia sunt perfectae in suis speciebus in instanti. Nec tunc requirunt actionem successivam immediate praecedentem, sed sunt in perfecta quietae animae et corporis, et tunc maxime sunt perfectae. |

The text of the anonymous author quoted on the right side of the table refers also to the example of the intensification of heat in water. The argument is that, unlike in the case of volition, forms such as heat are acquired, intensified, and perfected through movement rather than rest. The very last moment of the heating of water is still part of the process of alteration so that water is still said to be in motion. In the case of intellection, volition, and sensation, however, the subject undergoing the change is at rest. Although the comparison with the heat of water is not part of the exact passage of the text of question 10, article 2 quoted on the left side of the table, the comparison can be traced to another portion of FitzRalph's response to the principal question where he raises explicitly the issue of the multiple meanings of whether the faculty of the will can have a first instant of willing. It is in this context that he asks whether there is a first instant in which water undergoes alteration and argues that there is no such first instant[1].

All we know about Roger Roseth is that he was an English Franciscan who became a doctor of theology. His only surviving work – the *Lectura super Sententias* – was being copied in late 1337 and must have been composed shortly after Wodeham's *Ordinatio* on Book I since Roseth cites and criticizes Wodeham's famous view of the soul's finite capacity for grace based on the analogy with a vessel that cannot take in more liquid without a miraculous divine intervention. Two explicit citations of Thomas Bradwardine indicate a firm *terminus post quem* of the fall of 1332[2]. According to Hallamaa, it is unclear whether the *Lectura* originates from lectures delivered in a university classroom. The only evidence of a connection with Oxford, besides the citations of Wodeham and Bradwardine, is Roseth's explicit use and development of the methods of analysis characteristic of the Oxford calculators[3]. In fact, what makes the *Lectura* remarkable is the tendency of its author to deal with problems that appear to have little to no bearing at all on the traditional theological subject matter of Lombard's *Sentences*[4]. The issues that motivate Roseth's treatment are tied primarily to natural philosophy and logic so much so that the two long questions on the augmentation of charity (q. 4 : *Utrum caritas possit augeri*; q. 5 : *Utrum caritas augeatur per opera meritoria*) contain only two references to the Bible (Genesis 22 : 12 and Job 19 : 27), one reference to Hugh of St. Victor's *De sacramentis Christianae fidei*, and three to Augustine (*De Trinitate*, *De immortalitate animae*, *Epistola* 186).

1. Richard FitzRalph, *Lectura super Sententias*, I, q. 10, a. 2, Paris, Bibliothèque nationale de France, lat. 15853, fol. 65va-b : « Et potest articulus aliter intelligi sic quod quaerat utrum sit aliquod instans in quo ipsa potentia volitiva vult quando ipsa vult aliquid postquam non voluit illud. Et isti intellectus multum sunt diversi. Sic si quaeratur utrum sit aliquod primum instans certi <caloris> [valoris], scilicet *a* vel *b*, sed ex quo in quolibet instanti est alius et alius calor totalis, sicut dictum fuit in articulo de intensione formarum accidentalium, patet quod cuiuslibet caloris est aliquod primum instans. Potest autem ista quaestio sic intelligi quod quaerat utrum sit aliquod primum instans in quo alteratur ista aqua. Sic non est aliquod primum instans in quo habet calorem, et hoc supposito quod ista aqua patiatur tota simul, ita quod sit primum motum in ista alteratione ».

2. For the 1337 date and the citations of Bradwardine and Wodeham, see Courtenay, *Adam Wodeham*, p. 120-121 and n. 10-11.

3. Hallamaa, « Introduction », p. 6-8, 15-18.

4. Hallamaa, « Introduction », p. 15.

We bring up the contents of Roseth's *Lectura* here for two reasons : first because it epitomizes the method of calculatory analysis that is likewise characteristic of the works of FitzRalph and Wodeham, and second because Roseth's question 2, article 2 deals with the exact same problem addressed by both FitzRalph and Wodeham and upholds a view at odds with that of Wodeham as developed in question 8. Roseth denies the possibility of instantaneous volitional causation. In his first thesis, Roseth argues that the will causes all of its acts successively[1]. The second thesis states that no created agent can create something (*aliquod totum*) all at once and instantaneously[2]. The third thesis determines that no indivisible entity can be caused by a created agent[3]. And the fourth thesis contends that nobody can merit precisely for an instant, because all acts of the will are caused successively and in time[4].

If Roseth lectured on the *Sentences* at Oxford, it was probably after 1332-1333, since Schabel has argued that Robert Halifax was most likely Bradwardine's Franciscan *socius* that year. The subject of instantaneous volitional causation is broached in question 5 of Halifax's commentary on the *Sentences* (*Utrum aliquis actus voluntatis possit esse subito productus a voluntate*). The division of the question is interesting insofar as its first article is devoted to the issue whether the act of the created will can be made more intense or remiss. It is in the body of the second article that Halifax answers the principal question after formulating several propositions concerning intensification and remission. Especially relevant are conclusions 3 and 7 of sub-article 2. Conclusion 3 states that nothing that is produced by a finite potency is produced suddenly and instantaneously. Conclusion 7 says that every act of the will, which, as conclusion 6 notes, is produced by a finite potency, is produced in time[5].

1. Roger Roseth, *Lectura super Sententias*, q. 2, a. 2, Oxford, Oriel College 15, fol. 232ra : « Prima conclusio est quod voluntas quando causat actus suos solum causat [*iter.*] illos successive et nullo modo <in> instanti ita quod sit dare aliquem actum voluntatis quem actum voluntas causat [totum *add. sed del.*] totum simul et non per partem ante partem ».

2. Roger Roseth, *Lectura super Sententias*, q. 2, a. 2, Oxford, Oriel College 15, fol. 273va : « Secunda conclusio est quod nullum agens creatum potest aliquod totum [potest *add.*] simul et instantanee causare, quia si [*s.l.*] aliquis posset, hoc maxime foret de angelo vel de anima respectu proprii effectus, puta respectu volitionis vel intellectionis, quia talia agentia minimam vel nullam patiuntur resistentiam in agendo. Sed probatum est modo in conclusione praecedente quod nec angelus nec anima possent tales actus subito sive instantanee causare, ergo etc. »

3. Roger Roseth, *Lectura super Sententias*, q. 2, a. 2, Oxford, Oriel College 15, fol. 273va : « Tertia conclusio, quod nulla res indivisibilis non habens partes potest causari ab agente creato, quia talis res non potest nisi instantanee causari ex quo non habet partes ; in tali modo non potest agens creatum causare ».

4. Roger Roseth, *Lectura super Sententias*, q. 2, a. 2, Oxford, Oriel College 15, fol. 273va : « Quarta conclusio, quod nullus potest praecise mereri per instans ita quod non per tempus, quia nullus potest mereri nisi mediante actu voluntatis, et tales actus non causantur instantanee praecise sed successive et per tempus ».

5. See on question 5 the detailed *tabula* of *quaestiones*, *articuli*, *conclusiones*, and *propositiones* in Schabel, « The Oxford Franciscan Robert Halifax's Principial Debate over Grace and Merit », p. 640-672.

Thus, similarly to Roseth, Halifax rejects the will's instantaneous causation. The human will is a finite power and all its acts occur in time. If Roseth's and Halifax's agreement expresses the widely accepted position, then, as we shall see below, Wodeham's position represents a nuanced view that seems to allow the possibility of instantaneous causation although not instantaneous ceasing.

## II. Question 8, Article 1

Let us turn our attention now to the contents of Wodeham's question 8, article 1. Before we begin our exposition, however, we must make a brief terminological remark. We translate « *simul* » as « at once », « *subito* » as « suddenly », and « *in instanti* » as « in an instant ». For the most part, Wodeham is very precise and consistent in his use of this terminology. As we shall see below, he clarifies exactly how he understands the notion that something is caused at once (*simul*). It also seems that Wodeham treats the terms « *simul* » and « *subito* » as synonymous. As for the term « *instans* », it will become clear in our discussion that Wodeham understands it to mean an atemporal slice analogous to a mathematical point. An instant of time is an abstraction without any kind of foundation in reality. Time can be sliced indefinitely, and it is never the case that we can reach an absolutely simple and indivisible atom of time.

The principal argument against the claim that the will can produce an act of love instantaneously is that if each moment of time (i.e., with duration) contains an infinite number of instants, then one could merit by an infinite amount of equal merits, which means that one could merit infinitely in the given moment of time. Assuming an infinite number of instants, one merits either in every instant or in none. Since it makes no sense to merit in some instants of that moment but not in others, it follows that one merits in every instant of that moment [8.1. 2].

Wodeham proposes without asserting (*quam non assero*) the following conditional thesis in response to the question : « If an angel or our will or an angelic will is not causing (*non causat*) love at this very (*hoc*) instant, then it cannot without an interval (*sine medio*) after this very (*hoc*) instant suddenly and at once cause any love » [8.1. 5]. He defends this thesis by pointing out that if we say that an act of love is caused *at once* (*simul*) in the sense of *instantaneously*, we mean that it is not caused part by part but indivisibly. If one considers instants to be indivisible measures succeeding each other in time, however, then if a last instant of its non-being precedes this love, then there would be a series of adjacent instants without any intervening time (*esset instans instanti immediatum*) [8.1. 6]. Wodeham repeatedly contests the claim that any instants are conjoined to each other without a temporal span or gap between them.

Wodeham also resorts to Aristotle's denial of an intrinsic limit to the ceasing of permanent entities in *Physics* VIII, which would have been understood immediately by an audience that had heard lectures on that text in Franciscan *studia*, but which is more opaque to most modern readers. Wodeham argues – by parity of reasoning – that just as permanent entities have no last instant of being (rather, according to Aristotle, such entities have a first instant of non-being but not a last instant of being), so there is no last *indivisible* instant wherein the given entity or any part of it does not exist [8.1. 7].

The key point in Wodeham's defense of his first thesis is that there cannot be two or more immediately adjacent instants. Wodeham denies that instants have any thickness or duration, and so if one insisted that there were no temporal span between two instants, then in fact they would be one and the same instant and indistinguishable[1]. Just as when one slices a loaf of bread in half at one point, that point does not contain any bread, an instant does not contain any time, so one cannot stack any number of instants or add them together to produce any duration at all. Moreover, taking any two of these absolutely indivisible yet dimensionless instants, there are always an infinite number of instants in between them, no matter how close they are in time. Thus if one were to move immediately from one instant to any other instant, this would involve a jump, which would undermine the continuity of motion, or, in this case, volition. So take any instant of the temporal duration of an act of the will. If at this particular instant the will does not cause love, then it cannot do so at any other instant without some span of time in between, because there is no such thing as the « next » instant.

There are several issues that converge in Wodeham's account. The first is whether the will is capable of causing an act of instantaneous and sudden volition. As is clear from Wodeham's fifth thesis, the answer to this question is affirmative. The second issue is whether Wodeham believes that time is made up of instants defined as absolutely indivisible units (i.e., points). The answer to this question is negative, for as we learn from Wodeham's *Tractatus de indivisibilibus*, Wodeham rejected indivisibilism and defended Ockham's non-entitism, which is the view that indivisible entities such as atoms and points have no reality whatsoever[2]. The third issue is tied to Aristotle's puzzle about the present instant or about things that last only for an instant[3].

The first thesis is met with eight theological counter-arguments linked to God's power [8.1. 8-15]. Recall that the thesis, which, again, Wodeham takes care to say he is not asserting, holds that if some will is not willing *x* at point or instant

1. In the *Tractatus de indivisibilibus*, for instance, Wodeham argues that if two indivisibles were added to each other, then there would be an increase in quantity, which, according to Aristotle, would entail that indivisibles must touch each other and are therefore continuous. See Adam Wodeham, *Tractatus de indivisibilibus*, q. 1, a. 1, ed. Wood, p. 34.11-36.5. Most of the Oxford calculators embranced an ontology of continuous magnitudes according to which latitudes and grades are infinitely divisible. Such magnitudes could not have extended parts or be composed of atoms because then any transition from one part to another would entail a discontinous leap. Continuity is possible only on the assumption that latitudes and grades are similar to geometrical points. Since points by definition have no extension, no two points can be contiguous. Between any two points in a given magnitude one can imagine a potentially infinite number of points. See Hallamaa, « Introduction », p. 42-43.

2. See Wood, « Introduction », p. 10-11 ; Murdoch, « The Analytic Character of Late Medieval Learning », p. 178.

3. This issue is explicitly addressed and solved in Walter Burley's *Physics* commentary. See C. Trifogli, « Walter Burley on the *Incipit* and *Desinit* of an Instant of Time », *Vivarium* 55, 2017, p. 85-102, at p. 88-92. See also Aristotle, *Physics* IV, c. 10 : 218a8-29.

*y* in time, then it cannot suddenly and at once will *x* after point or instant *y* in time without an intervening span of time after point or instant *y*. The first objection is that God could annihilate the whole world immediately after this instant such that it would cease to be at once. The reason is that God in fact created the world at once, and there is no reason why God could not do what is easier, destroying in this way, than what God in fact did in creating the world [8.1. 8]. Other arguments assert that God can make it so that something exists for only one instant, for example an angel that God makes and at once ceases to exist : in this case God has the power to make it so that an instant is indeed immediately adjacent to an instant, contrary to Wodeham's general claim [8.1. 9]. Another example : God could cease cooperating with the sun's illumination of the medium for one single instant, or create an obstacle blocking the sun's light and immediately annihilate it, so for that instant the sun would not illuminate the medium, although immediately afterwards and at once it would do so, without « any cause of succession there » (*non esset ibi causa aliqua successionis*) [8.1. 10-11].

These objections accept that instants can be adjacent to each other and also imply that an instant is more than just a mathematical point, since they assume that something can exist or not exist or happen or not happen *per unum instans*, as if an instant is a duration or some sort of measure. Wodeham prefaces his rebuttals by insisting that « according to the truth instants are not a kind of measure that some people imagine, as I will declare on book III », perhaps a reference to question 11, « Whether Christ's soul is able to see distinctly in the Word to which it is united the smallest of parts inhering in him or the smallest particles of the body that it informs ». Rather it is impossible for instants or indivisibles to follow or be adjacent to each other immediately such that they make up a continuum [8.1. 16]. All of the arguments for the other side either assume something impossible or claim that something can happen in an instant that actually can only occur successively. For example,

> If it is assumed absolutely that God could, immediately after the present instant, in which it is supposed that the world exists, annihilate the world at once (*simul*), it must be said that this is not doable, but includes a contradiction (*repugnantiam*), because it entails that something that would come about at once or would be destroyed at once, and consequently instantaneously, would not come about or be destroyed at once nor instantaneously, because an instant cannot succeed an instant immediately. But it does not follow from this that God is not able to destroy the world at once just as he was able to create it at once. Rather he is equally able to do the one just as the other. But if he wills to annihilate the world at once, this will not be immediately after the last instant of its being. Rather then it would not have a last instant of its being [8.1. 18].

Similarly, for the light example,

> Positing that entire case, that in this way just for an instant the sun would not illuminate the medium, it is not along with this doable that the sun immediately afterward at once (*simul*) illuminates the medium, but in parts (*particulariter*) and successively it does indeed happen.

Wodeham thus meets these challenges head on. After responding to each argument, Wodeham formulates and defends four additional theses. The second thesis states that, « if an angel in this instant is not causing love, and yet it will cause love immediately after this instant, this love will be caused successively and not suddenly » [8.1. 30]. Wodeham specifies that this thesis follows from the previous conditional thesis, which, to recall, tells us that if the will is not willing *x* at this instant, then it cannot will *x* immediately afterwards at another instant without a temporal span in between.

Wodeham asserts in his third thesis that some love can be caused successively. He proves the thesis on the ground that every form that is subject to intensification and remission can be caused by God successively. Love is such a form, and we even experience in ourselves that we love the same object more or less intensely at different times. Besides, if habitual charity can be intensified, so can actual charity [8.1. 31-32].

The fourth thesis proposes that love can be caused by an angel or by the human soul in a successive sort of way [8.1. 34]. This claim aligns well with that of the second thesis. The proof is that the angel or the human soul cannot cause love without the mediation of the cognition of the lovable object, which must be understood as a partial cause or co-cause with the will (*concausa*). Yet this cognition varies in degrees as the object of cognition affects the angel's cognitive power differently in proportion to the object's proximity to that power [8.1. 35]. This leads to interesting arguments against there being a maximum distance an object can be from the angel's cognitive power and still affect that power, along with parallel arguments concerning vision [8.1. 36-40].

Wodeham's response to an intriguing argument directed at theses 3 and 4 reveals a key aspect of his understanding of the nature of the act of the will, and, perhaps, of any act of any other potency. According to some, the act of love is simply indivisible and cannot be said to have any parts. Otherwise, if the act of loving God were infinitely divisible into more and more remiss parts, then some part would be more perfect than the act of loving a fly, some part perhaps equally perfect, and maybe eventually some part lesser or less perfect than the act of loving a fly. But since every part of the act of loving God is itself love, it would follow that a certain act of loving God would be less perfect than an act of loving a fly [8.1. 40]. By the same logic, a little stench would be more perfect than the act of loving God [8.1. 41]!

On the contrary, Wodeham holds that every act of created love is divisible and has parts, and he explains that even if some act of loving God is *quantitatively* less perfect than the act of loving a fly, insofar as by intrinsic goodness the perfection of the act of loving a fly could be *quantitatively* greater than that of loving God, *qualitatively* speaking any act of loving God is by nature *qualitatively* more perfect than any act of loving something else [8.1. 50]. As for the small stench argument, Wodeham resorts to breathtaking ridicule. The strength of this argument, Wodeham says, amounts to no more than the great abomination expressed in its terms. Wodeham mocks the opponent's effort to reduce to vulgar absurdities doctrines that are known even to simple people to be of the most certain and catholic truth :

> What is to be done if such a person glories in reducing the respondent to the absurdity that God is in the ass of a donkey or in the dung of a dog? In order to avoid this should one deny the article of faith about divine immensity by which all saints know that the true God is in all places? But I would say this only to shame those who on account of the lack of an effective argument resort to the support and testimony of lay people [8.1. 53][1].

But if the act of love is divisible, then we may ask whether it is divisible into subdivisible parts and so indefinitely or if it is divisible into absolutely indivisible entities. We already know that, like most scholastics, Wodeham rejected the existence of atoms in physical spatio-temporal reality. Since the act of love is something immaterial, however, because it is caused by an immaterial soul, the question is whether given the act's divisibility – which as we have already seen Wodeham grants – the parts of the act are each absolutely indivisible or not[2]. Wodeham is clearly opposed to the view that there are absolutely distinct and indivisible instants :

> But these [objections] notwithstanding, without any assertion I hold as before, that it is the same – for me and many others – to come about instantaneously or in an instant, according to the correct understanding, and to come about at once such as not to come about part before part. For according to the truth instants are not a kind of measure that some people imagine, as I will declare on book III. But it is impossible that an instant follows an instant immediately, or that one changed being in the same motion is continued after another, or that one indivisible is situated immediately adjacent to another that is distinct from it – rather this includes a contradiction, as will become clear enough in the subject-matter of the non-composition of the divisible from indivisibles [8.1. 16].

An act of the will can therefore be divided indefinitely into smaller and smaller discrete parts, but these parts are never indivisible by nature and there are always smaller parts within any given part. This is consistent with Wodeham's addition account of qualitative change. According to this account, the intensification of an act of love occurs by means of the addition of parts in such a way that the

1. Curiously, the issue of escape by way of vulgarity appears also in the *explicit* of Wodeham's *Ordinatio*, book III, q. 12. Here, « the pious ears are horrified by the comparison of God's greatest gift to Christ and the blessed with the dung of a fly ». Wodeham explains that an escape by way of vulgarity is a disguise for the absence of a good argument and is meant to provoke shock, as when someone argues against the doctrine of divine omnipresence that it entails that God is in the dung of a dog. See Courtenay, *Adam Wodeham*, p. 195-196.

2. On this particular issue, Walter Chatton held the view that an indivisible entity such as the soul cannot have compound accidents. In other words, spiritual qualities such as volitions are indivisible and their change cannot be explained in terms of additions and subtractions of parts. Chatton therefore favored a version of the admixture theory of the augmentation of forms that explained change in physical qualities in a manner consistent with the addition theory but change in spiritual qualities in a manner consistent with the succession theory. See Wood, « Calculating Grace », p. 382-383.

previously existing parts and the newly added part taken together constitute a greater whole[1].

The fifth and final thesis, which responds directly to the principal question, is that « the will can cause a meritorious volition at once and suddenly » [8.1. 61]. Wodeham believes that this is sufficiently established on the ground that if there is neither formal nor virtual repugnance nor any kind of resistance or contrariety on the part of the passive subject – presumably the will itself taken as a passive recipient of the act – then a cause that is close enough acts suddenly, so the will must be capable of causation. Causal temporal succession is only required either when the passive recipient is somehow indisposed, or there is a continuous approximation of the agent toward the patient, or there is some kind of impediment that takes time to surmount [8.1. 62, 8.1. 65]. In the case of the will, these obstacles can be removed, so the will is capable of causing suddenly an act of meritorious love.

Furthermore, if the intellect is capable of sudden causation or activation, then the will must also be capable of such. Since at least with respect to the first act of the intellect there does not have to be anything contrary, such as some habit, passion, or something similar in the intellect, there is thus no intrinsic or extrinsic resistance, and the intellect acts suddenly. Remarkably, this particular argument is supported on the basis of Averroes' explication of Aristotle's argument against motion in a vacuum in *Physics* IV [8.1. 63][2]. If in the absence of external or internal resistance the will were unable to act suddenly, but necessarily acted in time, by the same token a natural agent such as light or heat would act in time absent any resistance in the medium. Yet even Wodeham's opponents admit that if an agent of a given strength produces an effect in a certain amount of time on account of some resistance, then an agent that is twice as strong must produce the same effect in half the time, and so on proportionally, until we reach a situation in which an agent facing resistance and an agent facing no resistance would cause the exact same effect in the exact same amount of time, which is false, according to the common medieval doctrine [8.1. 64].

The decisive authoritative argument in defense of sudden causation, however, is based on Averroes' interpretation of Aristotle's account of intellection and sensation in the *De anima* III. This argument is a commonplace in the debate about sudden causation and is discussed by both Richard FitzRalph and Roger Roseth. According to Averroes, intellection and sensation are perfect actions that take place in an instant and are not preceded by any kind of process [8.1. 66]. It is at this point that Wodeham reports and criticizes FitzRalph's interpretation of

1. See Wood, « Calculating Grace », p. 376-377, 379 and 381.

2. The exact number of arguments that Aristotle raised against the possibility of motion in a vacuum in *Physics* IV has been a matter of debate since antiquity. But the principal argument relevant to our discussion is a *reductio ad absurdum*, which shows that since motion in a vacuum bears no ratio to any motion in a plenum, motion over any kind of distance in a vacuum must take place in an infinitesimally short time that has no ratio to any finite time. See T. Kouremenos, « Aristotle's Argument Against the Possibility of Motion in the Vacuum (Phys. 215b19-216a11) », *Wiener Studien* 115, 2002, p. 79-110, at p. 80-84, esp. p. 84.

Averroes' text. As we pointed out earlier, FitzRalph's view is that intellection, sensation, and volition are caused and intensified successively but made perfect in an instant. Wodeham adds that what FitzRalph says must apply to all forms that are acquired by alteration. In this sense, a form acquired in any instant of a process of alteration is more perfect than the form that was had beforehand [8.1. 67-68]. Wodeham then details FitzRalph's twofold evasion of the problem that this consequence generates. On the one hand, one can say that forms do not attain the perfection of their own species until a certain quantity has been amassed at a certain instant. On the other, one can say that forms such as intellection, sensation, and volition are not said to be perfect when understood as involving a corporeal and spiritual transmutation. Rather, they are perfected when the soul comes to rest apart from any transmutation. Thus, according to the Philosopher and the Commentator, the moral virtues are not movements but perfections that consist in something indivisible and are perfected in an instant [8.1. 69].

In response to FitzRalph's twofold evasion, Wodeham stresses the difference between relative and absolute species with respect to both quality and quantity. For instance, in the rotation of the foot of a compass, at any instant one can say of the arc or line generated by the movement of the foot « *A* line and arc has been caused » with respect to the absolute species of quantity, but it becomes a perfect circle only at the instant in which the foot has completed a 360° turn. Any other prior arc or line cannot be considered a circle [8.1. 70][1]. It is likewise in the case of an entity taken absolutely in itself and in relation to something else. Since virtue consists in the intermediary state between two extremes, what is considered virtue with respect to the temperate person is not virtue in the case of the akratic person who merely happens to resist a strong passion. In general, the state of being virtuous does not manifest the presence of the absolute species of the form of the given virtue and is always a matter of degree [8.1. 71]. And just as in the case of health and beauty we speak in relative terms about health being compromised as a result of an excess of humor and beauty being undermined because of some disproportion, so also in the case of a virtuous choice a disordered passion can undermine the integrity of that choice [8.1. 72]. More importantly, no bodily perturbation or passion of the soul can prevent the

1. The basic structure of the mariner's compass as used in the Middle Ages involved a magnetized pointer floating in a bowl of water, sometimes in the form of a needle put through a straw in the form of a cross before set to float in the water. This structure is called the ur-compass. The first reference to the device comes from a Chinese source (ca. 1040), and the first European references to it date from the late twelfth century. The first documented use of the ur-compass by Arabs in the Mediterranean world dates to 1240 : B. M. Kreutz, « Mediterranean Contributions to the Medieval Mariner's Compass », *Technology and Culture* 14, 1973, p. 367-383, at p. 368-369. The device described by Wodeham seems more sophisticated. It has a fixed silver pointer (maybe dry-pivoted) and a ground plate, and it may have been self-contained. The first reference to a self-contained and portable device comes from the early fourteenth century in the Tuscan lawyer-notary Francesco da Barberino's *Documenti d'amore* (ca. 1315) : Kreutz, « Mediterranean Contributions », p. 373-375. Divisibilists used the geometry of the compass against the indivisibilists to demonstrate that there are no two points immediate in position in the same continuous line. See Adam Wodeham, *Tractatus de indivisibilibus*, q. 1, a. 1, ed. Wood, p. 52.10-31, and n. 52 for the accompanying diagram on p. 281.

soul from understanding or willing once an intellection or volition has informed the soul according to its corresponding intrinsic perfection. Bodily perturbation and spiritual passion can prevent the awakening of specific acts of understanding or volition, but they cannot undermine them once they have taken hold of the soul. Perhaps one should not call such intellection and volition felicity or virtue until the bodily perturbation and passion of the soul have been subdued. Once in place, however, these acts enable the soul to understand and to will without any hindrance [8.1. 74].

Further arguments from FitzRalph are given and then addressed in the remainder of the first article of the question. These arguments support the thesis of the sudden causation of the act of the will, but they are also presented by Wodeham conjointly with FitzRalph's responses to them in tandem with Wodeham's own critical responses. For example, if, as Aristotle and Averroes maintain, corporeal vision occurs suddenly, volition can be caused by the will suddenly as well [8.1. 76]. According to Aristotle's account in *Ethics* X. 4, pleasure comes about in an instant and not in time [8.1. 77]. According to Peter Lombard, Christ merited at the first instant of his conception [8.1. 78]. Finally, if the will could not cause love suddenly, then if someone suddenly at some instant first saw God, that person by nature would not love God at that time nor experience the delight of this vision. This is false, as Augustine testifies, because the presence of the object of love necessarily brings delight with it. Moreover, as Averroes notably argues, pleasure follows apprehension just as a shadow follows a body. And if the shadow follows the body at the same instant, so does pleasure accompany apprehension at the same instant [8.1. 86].

Especially informative is Wodeham's rejoinder to FitzRalph's response to the case of seeing God clearly yet failing to love God and experience delight. FitzRalph claims that there are in fact two acts, the first act of seeing God and the second of loving God. Thus even if a person saw God clearly in the first instant of existence, that person could not have the second act in that same instant and, therefore, could not experience delight at that point either [8.1. 87]. Wodeham characterizes FitzRalph's response as deficient and points out that if God were to create actual love in that instant, then delight would follow naturally. He also notes that FitzRalph himself holds the view that a person cannot fail to love and enjoy God in the beatific vision [8.1. 88]. Thus, in essence, FitzRalph contradicts himself[1].

In sum, in book I, distinction 1, question 8, article 1 of his Oxford *Ordinatio*, the Franciscan Adam Wodeham argues at great length that nothing lasts an instant,

1. For further discussion of FitzRalph's views on beatific enjoyment in relation to the beatific vision, see M. W. Dunne, « Richard FitzRalph on the Beatific Vision : *Delectatio* and *Beatitudo* in His Oxford Lectures on the *Sentences* (1328-29) », *Irish Theological Quarterly* 80, 2015, p. 327-343, and S. V. Kitanov, « Is It Better for the King of England to Be a King of England than a Duke of Aquitaine ? Richard FitzRalph and Adam Wodeham on Whether Beatific Enjoyment Is an Act of the Intellect or an Act of the Will », *in* M. W. Dunne and S. Nolan (eds.), *Richard FitzRalph : His Life, Times and Thought : A Conference to Commemorate the 650th Anniversary of His Death*, Dublin, Four Courts Press, 2013, p. 56-78, at p. 64-69.

because for him an instant has no duration and does not really exist. Yet the will is able to cause a volition suddenly : although Wodeham has not asserted that the will always does so, at least in certain circumstances, analogously with a medieval view of vision and intellection, it can. This assertion will be tested in article 2.

## III. Question 8, Article 2

In question 8, article 2, Adam Wodeham's fifth, final, and principal thesis is subjected to numerous counter-arguments. The list of these counter-arguments is explicitly attributed to Richard FitzRalph both in the corpus of the text as well as in the margins of the manuscript witnesses. But in the course of the dialectical investigation, arguments from John of Rodington appear as well. FitzRalph's first ingenious argument, if it was indeed developed by him originally, is that the will cannot elicit an act of meritorious love suddenly, because otherwise it could also sin suddenly in the first instant of its existence. If in that first instant someone has the knowledge of good and evil infused by God, a necessary and sufficient condition for willing evil (or good) and for the freedom of choice, then on Wodeham's account, it seems, the person can freely will evil (or good) in that first instant, which FitzRalph considers false. FitzRalph reasons that the first sinful act must corrupt the will, but since corruption requires the pre-existence of some good in the will that is destroyed or corrupted, the will itself must exist prior to the first act of sinning, and « consequently the instant in which the will first sins is not the first instant of the will's existence » [8.2. 2]. FitzRalph supports the argument by an appeal to Augustine's demonstration in the *City of God* XII. 6 that an evil volition is not contemporaneous with the will in which it exists [8.2. 3]. Furthermore, if the evil angels had sinned in the first instant of their existence, then their nature would already have been corrupted at their creation, in which case they sinned by their nature, which is no sin at all. FitzRalph refers to the *locus classicus* of Augustine's *City of God* XI. 15, where Augustine refutes the Manichaean interpretation of the biblical claim that « The devil sinned from the beginning » (Isaiah 14 : 12). For Augustine, the biblical sentence cannot mean that the devil's nature was evil from the start of its existence. Rather, it was through the devil's first sin that his nature was corrupted [8.2. 4].

All of the remarkable theological arguments recorded by Wodeham can be traced to the text of FitzRalph's question 10, article 2. One of the arguments is that a repercussion of Wodeham's view is that two individuals could merit equally although one of them merits for an instant (*per instans*) whereas the other merits continuously over time, in which case continuing to act meritoriously would be useless. FitzRalph gives the example of two people who merit under the exact same conditions except that one does so for an instant and the other for an hour. Obviously the one who merits for an hour has more merit, yet the ratio between that person's merit and the merit of the one who only merits for an instant is a finite ratio, because neither is the merit of one hour infinite nor is the merit of one instant equal to zero. FitzRalph suggests as an example that the ratio of their merits is 2 : 1, although it could just as easily be a million to one. If so, then suppose that a third person in identical conditions, except for the duration, merits for 30 minutes (or one millionth of an hour) : this third person's merit would equal the merit of the person who merits instantaneously, which is absurd [8.2. 9]. Indeed, although FitzRalph does not say so here, a fourth person who acted meritoriously for just 15 minutes would merit only half as much as the person who merited for an instant.

Another argument highlights the possibility that God would be powerless to reward sufficiently one's instantaneous merits or to exact a sufficient punishment for one's instantaneous demerits. FitzRalph declares that every will is finite and can undergo only a certain maximum pain or punishment (or there is a pain or punishment so great that it cannot undergo it, to cover both opinions on limits). If that person commits one instantaneous mortal sin, the corresponding punishment must be in some finite proportion to the maximum punishment that will can undergo. Again FitzRalph chooses a 2 : 1 ratio as an example, but it could be any finite proportion. Since FitzRalph, like Wodeham, is not an indivisibilist, he claims that in any amount of time, no matter how small, an angel, at least, could sin ten or a hundred times (or any number) as gravely as it sinned in one instant, by stopping and resuming the sinful action that many times, so that the amount of punishment deserved for those sins would equal and exceed the maximum punishment the angel could undergo. In this case God could not punish the angel sufficiently. A similar argument could be made for rewards for meritorious action. Since the conclusions are absurd, so is the premise that one can sin or merit in an instant [8.2. 10].

There are also purely philosophical objections. For instance, how could the will's sudden action come about without any kind of immediately preceding movement or change? It is absurd to think that a sudden change in the will can occur by itself, i.e., without this change being the endpoint of a prior successive transmutation [8.2. 14]. An argument in the realm of ethics is that if we take an individual who gets the maximum merit concerning one object by loving continuously for an hour, according to Wodeham's fifth thesis about the will causing a volition suddenly, it follows that the same person could merit tenfold by switching the act of loving back and forth between two objects over the same period of time. If this were possible, then it would never be rational to choose to love one thing continuously when one can love multiple things consecutively or two things in turn. But this consequence must be false because it goes against the grain of Aristotle's contention in *Ethics* X. 8 that happiness is the most continuous operation [8.2. 18].

Wodeham sums up FitzRalph's overall position by saying that FitzRalph denies that there is a first instant in which the will wills but accepts that there is a first instant in which this or that volition exists. Wodeham outlines all the specifics of FitzRalph's argument as delivered in the secular master's question 10, article 2. If there were a first instant in which the will willed, then this would be the case either with respect to a volition that is freely caused by the will or with respect to a volition that follows necessarily upon some apprehension. It could not be the first instant in which the will willed a freely caused volition, because such a volition can only be the result of a prior transmutation, since, as the Philosopher and the Commentator declare, every sudden change is the endpoint of a process of successive transmutation. Nor could it be the first instant in which the will has a volition as the natural outcome of an intellectual apprehension, both because there would have to be a prior instant in which the intellect actually contemplates beatitude or something else enjoyable, and because there is not even a *first* instant in which the intellect contemplates that object. In order for the intellect to have a new thought, this thought must either be caused freely, which again would require a prior process of volition, or be generated naturally by a species contained in the imagination.

At this point, FitzRalph's reasoning takes a very intriguing turn. There either is a species of minimum force such that it can engender a thought in the intellect or a species of maximum force that cannot do so. But there cannot be a species of minimum force, because if a species of a certain force can move the intellect, then a slightly weaker species can move the intellect. FitzRalph draws an analogy here with physical forces and velocities[1] : for the secular master, one and the same body can have a slower and slower velocity through the application of a lesser and lesser amount of force, such that there is no minimum force that can move that body [8.2. 21]. Also, if there were a first instant in which a species in the imagination caused thinking, then let it be granted that it causes it in the present *now*. This species must act naturally and must now be for the first time sufficiently forceful to cause thinking, otherwise it would have acted earlier. If it acts now for the first time, then it must be the species of the minimal force that can do so. But there is no such species, as previously shown. Thus, the present instant is not the first instant in which a species in the imagination acts on the intellect, and so

1. FitzRalph's terminology of maximum and minimum force reflects his familiarity with the attempts of the Oxford Calculators to determine the conditions of local motion in connection with various active and passive powers. In the works of the founders of this tradition – Richard Kilvington and Thomas Bradwardine – we find clear formulations of the conditions of motion in terms of minimum and maximum excess of active power over resistance for both the initiation and continuation of motion as well as specifications of the limits of active and passive powers. See E. Jung, « The New Interpretation of Aristotle : Richard Kilvington, Thomas Bradwardine, and the New Rule of Motion », *in* D. A. Di Liscia and E. D. Sylla (eds.), *Quantifying Aristotle. The Impact, Spread and Decline of the Calculatores Tradition*, Leiden, Brill, 2022, p. 37-79, at p. 54-58. See also E. Jung and R. Podkoński, *Towards the Modern Theory of Motion. Oxford Calculators and the New Interpretation of Aristotle*, Łódź, Wydawnictwo Uniwersytetu łódzkiego, Centrum Filozofii Przyrody, 2020, p. 57-67. Kilvington, in particular, differentiated between two aspects of action-passion processes. See Jung, « The New Interpretation of Aristotle », p. 58 : « Although he did not explicitly formulate general rules concerning different types of division, his debates reveal that he approved the following conditions for the existence of limits. First, there must be a range in which the potency can act or be acted upon, and another range in which it cannot act or be acted upon. Second, the potency should be capable of taking on a continuous range of values between zero potency and the value that serves as a boundary, and no other values ». See also Jung and Podkoński, *Towards the Modern Theory of Motion*, p. 67.

« there is no first instant in which the intellect thinks when its thinking naturally comes about by a species imaginatively » [8.2. 22].

In response to FitzRalph's first argument, Wodeham states that the will of an individual equipped with pre-existing cognitions required for sin can sin in the first instant of its existence, which sin would thus damage the will [8.2. 25]. Wodeham then engages in a prolonged exegesis of Augustine. He argues, for instance, that those whom Augustine opposes claimed that nothing makes an evil volition, but rather, for them, an evil volition always existed. But as Augustine clearly says, an evil volition must exist in some nature, and if it exists in that nature, then it must have corrupted it, in which case the will was not evil beforehand, when it had something good that the evil volition could destroy [8.2. 26]. Wodeham then proposes several different ways in which a sin of commission or omission can be said to take away a created nature's inherent goodness (*ademptio boni*) [8.2. 28-30].

Wodeham replies to FitzRalph's denial of sinning in the first instant of the being of evil angels by differentiating between a *de facto* and a *de possibili* interpretation of this state. According to Wodeham, Augustine opposes not those who believe that the angels could have sinned (*ponentium angelum potuisse peccare*) but those who say – like the Manichaeans – that the angels actually did sin (*tenentium angelum peccasse*) in the first instant of their existence because they had bad natures from a bad *principium* (in which case they would not even have sinned). Logically speaking, Wodeham explains, Augustine did not see a contradiction for the cause of sin and the effect of sin to be coeval. The cause of sin and the effect of sin can be coeval just as the imprint of a foot can be causally dependent on yet coeval with the foot and the splendor of fire causally dependent on yet coeval with the fire. As Wodeham notes, Augustine had famously used the imprint-foot and splendor-fire examples against Arius' exegesis of the generation of the Son from the Father. Thus, one could say that the angels could have sinned from the first instant of their existence. This was not the case, however, because no creature can sin in the first instant of its existence left in its state of nature and given God's general influence, because under these conditions sin requires deliberation, and deliberation requires time. Hence, the evil angels did not sin in the first instant of their existence [8.2. 31]. In order for them to have done so, God would have had to infuse their intellects with the moral knowledge presupposed by wicked choices, as Wodeham acknowledges [8.2. 36].

At one point Wodeham brings in John of Rodington's response to FitzRalph[1]. Despite the appearances in what follows, it must be noted that Rodington seems to have believed that no act of the will can occur instantaneously and that it requires time. He asks specifically whether an act of the intellect or the will can last for an instant. After citing several arguments in defense of the view that volition

1. The most detailed analysis of the textual tradition and various redactions of Rodington's *Sentences* commentary is found in C. Schabel and R. L. Friedman, « Trinitarian Theology and Philosophical Issues III : Oxford 1312-1329 : Walsingham, Graystanes, Fitzralph, and Rodington », *Cahiers de l'Institut du Moyen-Âge grec et latin* 74, 2003, p. 39-88, at p. 42-44.

requires time, Rodington refers to Richard Campsall's question, discussed below, whether one can act against one's conscience, and he sums up in a single sentence Campsall's argument that the denial of instantaneous volition threatens the freedom of the will. In his response, Rodington claims that volition necessarily requires time but not a definite time, because time can be divided indefinitely [1].

Wodeham's reference to Rodington is given in the body of question 8, article 2, as a rejoinder to FitzRalph's seventh argument, which is about the comparative value of merit generated instantaneously with respect to merit accumulated gradually over the course of one hour. As discussed above, according to the specifics of the argument, two individuals exert equal moral effort and experience love of equal intensity. The individual who upholds the act of love for the entire hour must acquire greater merit than the individual whose act of love occupies only an instant of time. Since the quantity of this merit can only be finite, let it be granted that it is double the amount of the merit amassed instantaneously. Suppose then that there is a third individual who merits in half an hour. This third individual's merit must then be half of the hourly-accrued merit and yet equal to the amount of the instantaneous merit. The third individual's merit is also equal to the second individual's merit in the first half of the hour as well as in the second half of the hour if there is an interruption in the second individual's act [8.2. 9].

Rodington's rejoinder to the aforementioned argument is that if the hourly merit is double the amount of the instantaneous merit, then one should not concede that it doubles the amount of the first half of the hour, but only in some other proportion, because there is a different amount of merit in the second half of the hour than in the first half [8.2. 60]. Part of Rodington's reasoning requires that the merits of the first half and of the second half of the hour are not distinct, as FitzRalph's argument supposes : « Therefore I say that the person merits more in the second half than in the first, but these merits are not totally distinct » [8.2. 61] [2].

Wodeham begins gently in his objection to Rodington – a senior Franciscan who was about to incept – by saying that his argument is cautious but neither true nor sufficient, because in effect he concedes the problematic inference of FitzRalph's *reductio ad absurdum* : as soon as Rodington admits that the merit of an hour exceeds in some finite proportion the merit of an instant, he thereby accepts that a merit of some lesser duration would be equal to the instantaneous merit, no matter how he combines or separates those two merits. Rodington's arguments entail that the continuation of a meritorious act does not always make

1. John of Rodington, *Lectura in Sententias*, I, d. 1, q. 4, a. 2, dub. 9, Città del Vaticano, Biblioteca Apostolica Vaticana, Vat. lat. 5306, fol. 43rb : « Ad istud dicitur quod ista volitio necessario requirit tempus, et tamen nullus tempus determinatum necessario requirit, et dico quod in <medietate> [mente] illius potest rescindere actum suum et in medietate medietatis in infinitum. Unde opinio male imaginatur quod voluntas necessario requirit tempus in quo minori non posset fieri. Et quando arguitur 'igitur voluntas non est libera', nego consequentiam ».

2. Although we have not found this particular argument in Rodington's *Sentences* questions, it must be noted that in his *Quodlibet*, q. 5, a. 3, Rodington rejects the view that a person whose meritorious act continues for an hour merits more than in the first instant of that hour : Schabel, « The Oxford Franciscan Robert Halifax's Principial Debate over Grace and Merit », p. 574-575.

a difference [8.2. 62-63]. Indeed, if Wodeham's presentation of Rodington's position is fair and accurate, the senior Franciscan put forth something « false and totally irrational », as Wodeham labels Rodington's further contention that the merits of the first and the second half of the hour should not be seen as totally distinct. After all, if the individual who attempts to sustain an act of love for an hour dies after half an hour, then his merit cannot be augmented any further and must therefore be distinct from the hourly amount of merit he would have earned [8.2. 64].

The dialectical dissection of the remaining arguments from FitzRalph with other occasional rejoinders by Rodington continues and deepens the complexity of Wodeham's treatment. The difficulty increases especially around the issue of someone (a human being or an angel) being asked to obey a divine command in some special circumstances that strain the limits of the will. In the case of sensation there is a minimum we can sense and a maximum we cannot sense. For example, when we look at a clock, the hour hand rotates, but we cannot perceive this by watching it, because it is below the minimum velocity we can sense or the maximum velocity we cannot sense. It this way also in the case of the will being asked to perform tasks that require minute temporal discriminations. Just as we cannot immediately perceive the rotation of the hour hand of a clock or discern the movement of the sun in the sky, so there is a minimum time span that we can switch from willing to not willing or nilling and a maximum time span within which we cannot :

> For since one now wills that act to be, one wills it to be... and as long as one wills it to be, one will not have nilling through which it is removed, by which it quasi commands, « Now don't will », and it will not be able to do this freely before the lapse of that minimum time *quod* or the maximum time *quod non.* Therefore, since it cannot freely remove this act except though such an imperative nilling or something similar, it follows that it is not in the power of the will not to have the act that it now wills to have and which it now thereby causes until the end of that time [8.2. 70].

In other words, after all this discussion of mathematical limits, Wodeham comes to an important practical conclusion about the mechanics of actual human free willing. Regardless of the fact that instants do not exist, or that they have no duration and nothing can last an instant, although things can happen at an instant, some time is necessary for free willing :

> Thus let someone try as quickly as one can according to the present dispositions to abandon (*dimittere*) an act that one now wills to be. And since one cannot abandon it immediately afterwards, there will be a time within which one cannot abandon the act by oneself freely, since one cannot distinctly discern every instant.

Naturally, one does not gain any additional merit via this sort of continuation of an act either, so to that extent, if there were instantaneous merit, it would be equal to the merit of the act continued for the time it takes to abandon it [8.2. 71].

## IV. Question 9, Article 1

In question 9, Wodeham asks whether the will can freely suspend its act or cease from an existing act in a sudden sort of way (*subito*). The question is divided into two articles. Article 1 captures Wodeham's response to the principal question, and article 2 debates two *dubia*. According to a marginal note in Vat. lat. 955, « these arguments are Rod(ington's) », but it is not clear whether only the argument « contra » with its subordinate arguments is meant [9.1. 3-9] or also the single argument « quod sic » [9.1. 2-9]. It also appears that the difference between these two sides is quite subtle. The principal argument in defense of the affirmative thesis starts from what Wodeham has already determined in question 8, article 1. Since the will can freely cause an act suddenly, it must also be able to cease freely and suddenly from such an act that has been caused. The metaphysical principle employed as a premise in this argument is that it is easier for an agent to destroy than to build something if the agent can do both [9.1. 2].

There is one principal counter-argument with six proofs of the falsity of its consequent. The main argument proceeds by process of elimination, but then surprises us with a confusing reversal :

> [An act] produced instantaneously cannot at the same time altogether (*simul totus*) cease in the instant in which it exists, because the act would then exist and not exist at same time (*simul*). Nor can it cease immediately afterwards, because then an indivisible would succeed another indivisible immediately, from the proofs of the first thesis of the preceding question. Therefore only mediately afterwards could the will cease from the instantaneously elicited act, and consequently it would not be in the power of the will, if it suddenly caused in itself a volition, not to will afterwards for some time before it suspended its act fully or before it fully ceased from that act. But the consequent seems false, therefore so does the first antecedent [9.1. 3].

But what is this first antecedent ? It is that the act produced instantaneously cannot cease in the same instant, in which case Rodington would be arguing that such an act can in fact cease in the same instant ? It seems so, because when Rodington goes on to explain why the last consequent is false, he begins thus : « It is proven that the will can suspend its act in such a way that he wills only for an instant ». Otherwise the will would continue its act unwillingly ; for that extra time it would be unable to will in conformity with the judgment of the intellect advising it not to continue ; the will would necessarily merit or demerit for that time ; the viator could not do penance for that time ; the will could not be corrupted for that time ; and, lastly :

> It would follow that in that case volition would be with respect to the unknown, because let it be posited that in the middle of that time the person goes mad (*fiat homo demens*), such that the cognition with respect to that object is corrupted, and since the volition will still endure further, the point follows [9.1. 4-9].

If the opening argument claimed that one can cease willing freely and *subito*, is the counter-argument distinguishing between *subito* and *instantanee*? If so, perhaps this is why, in response to the principal question, Wodeham differentiates between two senses of suspension or ceasing. In the first sense, if the will has an act in this instant, then it *will* have this act or a part of it. This is Wodeham's first thesis and he labels it as the *quasi* converse of the first thesis of question 8, article 1 [9.1. 11-12]. The proof of the thesis is that otherwise there would be two instants adjacent to each other. If the will ceases to act, then it must cease to act either in the same instant in which it has an act, in which case the act both exists and does not exist, or in the immediately adjacent instant, and no such thing exists, or at a later instant, in which case it will remain in the intermediate time (*per tempus medium*), which is what Wodeham ultimately aims to prove [9.1. 13].

In the second sense, the act's ceasing is preceded by an interval of time in such a way that at the endpoint of this interval the will neither has the initial act nor any part of it. At this point, the will can be said to have ceased from acting. This is the second thesis. In this sense, the will's ceasing to act amounts to the absence of the initial act that the will intended to suspend, but this absence is always preceded by a prior time when the will has an act of will not to have the initial act. Wodeham explains that this involves intellectual discourse and deliberation leading to the judgment that what is currently willed is bad and must not be willed. Thus, the will can cease to love or hate instantaneously or suddenly but only given some prior time at the end of which the will can be said to have stopped loving or hating and to have done so instantaneously [9.1. 14].

What follows is a fascinating set of remarks on the difference between actions one is commanded to carry out or not and choices that conform or do not conform to the dictates of practical reason[1]. In the case of the latter, it is not difficult for the will to endorse freely dictates that are rooted in evident or firmly believed judgments even when there is a temptation to act contrary to those dictates. In the case of the former (different kinds of loves, hatreds, and acts of willing against something), however, it is much more difficult for the will to go along with the dictates that enjoin or prohibit them. One must work hard to find motivating reasons to obey such dictates. « For example », Wodeham says, « when I judge that I must love someone whom I hate or vice-versa, or that I must love God more fervently than I do, I cannot always will it or do it suddenly ». I must prepare myself conceptually first. I must tell myself that the person I hate is one of God's creatures who is destined for a supernatural good and has been redeemed through Christ's blood. The Stoic background of Wodeham's distinction

1. This is very reminiscent of the distinction between first- and second-order volitions, which can be traced back to Augustine and was systematized by John Duns Scotus, William of Ockham, and Walter Chatton. For a detailed account of the development of the notion, see M. Michałowska, « Second-Order Volitions », *in* R. Fedriga and M. Michałowska (eds.), *Safeguarding Free Will : William Ockham, Walter Chatton, and Richard Kilvington on the Will*, Kraków, Księgarnia Akademicka, 2022, p. 115-131.

is unmistakable[1]. Indeed, it is through self-consciously and reflectively examining and strengthening the moral grounds of one's choices that one can tame one's spontaneous reactions and harness one's desires and aversions [9.1. 15-16].

Among Wodeham's conversation partners in the context of the dialectical examination of the arguments opposed to instantaneous ceasing we find Richard Campsall, who had become master of theology at Oxford about a decade earlier. Katherine H. Tachau notes that Campsall is cited here as denying that voluntary acts require time[2]. More precisely, Wodeham tells us that Campsall's arguments are intended to prove that the will can freely will for only one instant, otherwise the will would not be free [9.1. 23]. Tachau has traced the five arguments that Wodeham paraphrases to the second article of Campsall's question titled « Whether one can act against one's own conscience » (*Utrum homo possit agere contra conscientiam suam*) [the odd numbers 9.1. 23-31]. It is unclear from Wodeham exactly what view Campsall is defending, but if we look at the contents of the second article of Campsall's question on conscience, it becomes apparent that Campsall is concerned with preserving the will's efficient causality with respect to its own acts. If the will cannot act instantaneously and is bound to continue its act for a certain amount of time, then the will cannot be genuinely free[3]. Campsall's overall take on the denial of the will's instantaneous ceasing is also confirmed by Rodington[4]. With this context in the background, we can see that each of Campsall's arguments as documented by Wodeham aims to draw a problematic consequence of denying the will's ability to act instantaneously. Rather than simply assert that there is no such thing as something happening for just one instant, Wodeham seems to give Campsall a more sympathetic reading, but nevertheless responds to his arguments. So, for instance, Campsall argues that if I cannot will for just one instant (*praecise per instans*), then I have no free will and I am even coerced to sin. If I must will for a minimum duration, the argument goes, let us say that my intellect judges that it is bad to will that object in the

1. For the Stoic background of medieval scholastic discussions of the passions and the reconceptualization of the passions primarily by Franciscan authors as forms of willing or affections of the will rather than as strictly movements of the sensitive appetite, see P. King, « Dispassionate Passions », *in* M. Pickavé and L. Shapiro (eds.), *Emotion and Cognitive Life in Medieval and Early Modern Philosophy*, Oxford, Oxford University Press, 2012, p. 9-31.

2. K. H. Tachau, « Richard Campsall as a Theologian : New Evidence », *in* B. Mojsisch and O. Pluta (hrsg.), *Historia Philosophiae Medii Aevi : Studien zur Geschichte der Philosophie des Mittelalters. Festschrift für Kurt Flasch zu seinem 60. Geburtstag*, vol. 2, Amsterdam-Philadelphia, John Benjamins, 1991, p. 979-1002, at p. 986.

3. Richard Campsall in Tachau, « Richard Campsall as a Theologian », p. 993 : « Prima consequentia patet, quia si voluntas non haberet actum suum per unum instans tantum, sed oporteret quod teneat actum suum per tempus, tunc – ut videtur – esset aliqua causa cogens voluntatem ad morandum per tempus in actu suo. Et sic non esset causa tota efficiens nec libera sui actus, nec posset contrahere et rescindere suum actum libere sicut vellet. Hoc patet de sole, quia illuminat medium subito, sed libere hoc faceret ; hoc posset facere pro libito in uno situ tantum et non in alio ».

4. John of Rodington, *Lectura in Sententias*, I, d. 1, q. 4, a. 2, dub. 9, Vat. lat. 5306, fol. 43rb : « Contra : quia voluntas elicit actum manentem tantum per instans, aliter cogeretur ad peccandum etc. ; require in quaestione de Campsale utrum possit facere contra conscientiam suam ».

second half of that given time. In this case, either I can cease to will at that point, in which case there can be no span of time no matter how small that I cannot cease to will the object before its end; or I cannot cease to will at that point, in which case I am coerced to will [9.1. 23]. In response, Wodeham says that if an intellect were to judge at the beginning of the given time by clearly differentiating one half from the other, then the time was bigger than should have been granted. If instead this judgment were made anew, either from another source or from outside, then one retreats from the terms of the arrangement to which one has committed by accepting the hypothetical scenario [9.1. 24][1].

## V. Question 9, Article 2

The two *dubia* articulated in article 2 of Adam Wodeham's question 9 raise bewildering challenges. The first *dubium* asks whether it follows that if Socrates merits in this instant, then Socrates will merit immediately afterwards. The first argument denies this consequence on the ground that if the will cannot rescind its own act so that it ceases to exist after that instant, then it is much easier for us to retract a finger than to stop our own will from willing, which goes directly against Augustine's thesis that nothing is as much in the power of the will than the will itself [9.2. 1-2].

On the contrary, as Wodeham's first thesis of question 9 declares, if the will has an act in this very instant, then it *will* have that act or part of it, so if Socrates merits in this very instant, he *will* merit, because if the will cannot cease all at once, neither can Socrates cease to merit immediately in the instant after he merits. Wodeham thus concurs that the aforementioned consequence is true and follows logically from his first thesis [9.2. 7]. Accordingly, Wodeham rejects the argument that it is easier to retract one's finger than refrain from willing. One can tie one's finger and make it impossible to be moved by the will, but one cannot so restrain the will. The opponent may say that I can retract my finger at any time. This is true, Wodeham says, but only insofar as the case grants it, since the movement of the finger results from the impetus of the will absent any obstacles. If I must voluntarily abstain from moving my finger while in motion, I must do so by means of another act of the will that is more immediately under the control of my will [9.2. 8-10]. Another way of responding to the argument is by pointing out that God can stop the movement of one's finger at any time, but not in the very instant in which it is moving, since when it is moving, it *will* still be moving [9.2. 11]. Or one can concede that it is easier for the will to retract a finger than it is to rescind its own act. The causation of the act of rescinding, however, is most certainly within the power of the will [9.2. 12].

1. The missing context for understanding the case as a kind of pact or vow is provided by Campsall's response to an argument originally presented possibly by Thomas of Hothum. See Tachau, « Richard Campsall as a Theologian », p. 999 n. 25.

The target of the second *dubium* is Wodeham's second thesis of question 9. If, as the thesis states, the will can cease suddenly after some time of deliberation and decision, then if Socrates is commanded to cease an act of willing suddenly before (*citra*) the instant *t1* of midday and Socrates fails to do so, then it follows that Socrates both first sins and does not first sin at this very instant *t1*, which is contradictory. Socrates sins in *t1* because between any prior instant *t-1* and *t1* there is some interval of time and consequently an infinite amount of instants, and Socrates could have ceased at any instant in between *t-1* and *t1*. Since Socrates has not done as commanded, therefore Socrates has sinned. Socrates does not sin at *t1*, however, because he was commanded to cease before *t1* and not at *t1* [9.2. 19].

Wodeham says that this argument is commonly used with respect to instantaneous acts and summarizes it as follows : suppose that God commands me to cause an act prior to *t1* and yet I omit to do it until after *t1*. The absurd consequence is that I both sin and do not sin. I sin because I disobey God when I do not elicit the act until after the instant when I was supposed to elicit it. And yet, I sin neither prior to *t1* nor at *t1* nor after *t1*. I sin neither in *t1* nor after *t1* because I am not commanded to act at *t1* or after *t1*. But neither do I sin prior to *t1*, because – as the case holds – I was never obliged to act at any instant prior to *t1* [9.2. 20]. As Tachau notes, this particular argument had become the test case that reveals the problem of understanding the will's acts as instantaneous[1].

One possible response to the arguments is that they hold against those who falsely posit that such acts can be caused or suspended suddenly by the will, but not against those who claim that they can only be caused successively by the will [9.2. 21]. Wodeham thus proposes a third argument form aimed specifically at the latter group. According to this modifed argument, Socrates can begin to cause (*potest incipere causare*) such an act at some instant in such a way that he does not cause that act at this instant *t1*, but rather immediately afterwards, whether suddenly or successively. In other words, he begins to cause the act at *t1* but does not complete it until *t2*. Thus, suppose that God commands Socrates to begin to love God above all things at *t1* but that he in fact does not begin to do so at *t1*. Then the time passes (*cedat tempus*). In this case, Socrates sins because he has not done as commanded. Yet, Socrates did not sin at *t1*, because he was only commanded to begin loving at *t1*, not to love at *t1*. But neither has Socrates sinned after *t1*, because he was not commanded to begin to love after *t1* [9.2. 22].

Wodeham formulates three theses in response to the case presented in the second *dubium*. The lengthy remainder of the second article of the question is devoted to the defense and painstaking analysis of the objections to each thesis. The first thesis is this :

> Socrates, who has been commanded to cause an act before *t1*, or to abandon an act had before *t1*, or to begin to do something before *t1*, and who does not do it or carry it out before *t1*, does not first sin at *t1* [9.2. 24].

1. Tachau, « Richard Campsall as a Theologian », p. 988, and p. 999.257-1001.302 for Campsall's own response to the argument.

This is because at *t1* Socrates neither commits nor omits something contrary to what God has commanded him to do, because God has not commanded him to will or cease from willing at *t1* [9.2. 25]. Furthermore, it can also be argued that it is impossible for Socrates to do what he has been commanded to do. Suppose that Socrates' intellect has been divinely infused with the knowledge that he will not do or begin to do what he has been commanded to do prior to *t1*, or perhaps Socrates knows this naturally. He could thus feel remorse and sadness about this before *t1*, in which case Socrates could have grace at *t1*, so he does not first mortally sin at *t1*, because grace and sin are incompatible [9.2. 27]. Or the entire case can be modified in such a way as to say that Socrates died at *t1* but miraculously retained this use of free choice until *t1*. In this case, Socrates cannot have first sinned at *t1*, because no one sins who is not in this life, although he would have been worthy of eternal punishment, since he was not obedient at *t1*, having neither done nor begun to do what he should and could have done before *t1* [9.2. 28]. In a sense, the book of Socrates' sins is now closed and nothing else can be added to it.

The second thesis is that the following compound proposition is not true, if formed : « Socrates has sinned before *t1 and* yet never before *t1* or at no instant before *t1* would it have been true to say 'He sins'» [9.2. 51]. Wodeham explains that this self-contradictory proposition is upheld in different ways by different people. Some say that Socrates has sinned at no instant although he has sinned at some instant. Others say that Socrates has sinned not at any given instant but in the whole temporal interval that extends to *t1* when the term « whole » is taken categorematically [9.2. 52].

In defense of his thesis, Wodeham develops an argument that he says applies to all those who uphold the abovementioned contradictory compound proposition. He argues that – on the assumption that Socrates does not commit a mortal sin other than the one specified by the case – Socrates is continuously in grace up until *t1*, according to those people, because he was in grace beforehand and did not sin mortally before *t1*. If Socrates has lost his grace before *t1*, then between this instant *t-1* and *t1* there was some intermediate time. This is the case whether one grants a last instant of the existence of grace or a first instant of its non-existence. And if Socrates has fallen from grace anywhere in between or in the total time in between, then it is true that Socrates was at fault before *t1*, and it was true to say at some instant and in fact in an infinite number of instants : « He sins » [9.2. 53].

The third thesis is that, positing the case above, Socrates sinned prior to *t1* and that for some time and for an infinite number of instants of this time Socrates was a sinner before *t1* [9.2. 73]. This follows because we already know from the first thesis that if Socrates does not first sin at *t1*, then he must have sinned prior to *t1*. Likewise, we know from the second thesis that it is impossible for Socrates to sin prior to *t1* without sinning at some instant prior to *t1*. And if Socrates did not do what he was commanded to do in the temporal interval between *t-1* and *t1*, and since this interval contains potentially an infinite amount of instants, then Socrates perseveres in sin for a potentially infinite amount of instants [9.2. 74].

One of the notable features of Wodeham's critical analysis of the case of omitting to obey a divine command before a specified instant of time is his extensive dialogue with William of Auxerre (†1231)[1]. Wodeham labels Auxerre a *doctor antiquus* and includes him with a group of *doctores moderni* who hold the opposite of Wodeham's view with respect to the first thesis. In particular, Wodeham cites a case treated by Auxerre that occurs in the context of Auxerre's discussion of the suppression of venial sexual movements before they become mortal sins, concerning a person who has been commanded to think about God before the end of a given day but has failed to do so. The person is not culpable prior to the end of the day, because she could always have done as commanded at any instant between the instant when the command was given and the instant the day ends. Neither can the person be said to have incurred the stain of omission (*macula omissionis*) until the instant the day ends [9.2. 30]. Wodeham responds that Auxerre's argument fallaciously assumes that the person can freely delay or will to delay until the exact instant they see fit by stretching the limit of the time needed to act. This requires deliberation, and deliberation requires a precise amount of time proportionate to the nature of the will and the intellect and the circumstances of the case at hand, which requires action before a certain instant [9.2. 31]. Wodeham warns that one must be very cautious not to stretch the limit of time beyond what is humanly possible to perceive because one can then no longer freely and knowingly do what has been commanded [9.2. 33]. He also adds that Auxerre spoke under the assumption that the created intellect can cognize distinctly every slice of time in the process of infinite division towards the minutest slice. On this assumption, Wodeham states, « I could not see a better escape than his [Auxerre's] unless perhaps one said that such a creature has simply chosen not to do as commanded ». If one always wills to delay, however, then one sins by risking a delay until it is too late to act [9.2. 34].

Ultimately, as Wodeham observes, Auxerre did not in effect adhere firmly and decisively to his initially proposed solution of the case. Wodeham cites with precision and in detail what Auxerre writes about the limits of contrition in the given case. Auxerre concurs that one sins by not repenting at the specified instant of time but holds that one cannot be held liable for not repenting at this instant, because it is impossible for one to have repented without taking the time to think about one's own sin, eternal punishment, and God's justice. God gives everyone time for deliberation, but nobody can tell exactly how much time they have. Thus, if one does not repent during the time of deliberation or at the moment

1. Courtenay, *Adam Wodeham*, p. 42, says that « Wodeham rarely cites authorities between Lombard and Scotus. He had great fondness for early twelfth-century authors, principally Anselm, whose interest in linguistic logic endeared him to many fourteenth-century authors. But, with the exception of William of Auxerre, one seldom finds mention of *doctores* active between 1160 and 1280 ». What may explain Wodeham's interest in Auxerre is the latter's use of geometrical and mathematical reasoning in the treatment of theological problems. Auxerre was among the pioneers of what John Murdoch called the new languages of the intension and remission of forms, proportions, and degrees of latitude. See C. Baladier, « *Intensio* de la charité et géométrie de l'infini chez Guillaume d'Auxerre », *Revue de l'histoire de religions* 225, 2008, p. 347-391, at p. 349.

when the time for deliberation has lapsed, then one has incurred the stain of omission. Hence, one is to blame, but this is because one has failed to repent during the grace-period (*in tempore indutiarum*) when one ought to have repented. As Auxerre himself testifies, if contrition requires time, because many things must happen first before one becomes contrite, one does not commit the sin of omission at the end of the time required for contrition but at the instant when one has first become unable to repent. « There is a general teaching », Auxerre says, « that if one is held to do some action on this very day, if this action does not require time for its completion but can be done in an instant, then one incurs the [sin of] omission neither at the end, nor near the end [of time]. If, however, the action requires time for its execution, then the [sin of] omission is incurred not in the end but near the end [of the time], at the instant at which one has firstly become unable with regard to this action on this very day » [9.2. 36].

Wodeham's defense and analysis of objections to his three theses proceeds with thoroughness and exactitude that test one's patience and stamina for exhaustive logical discrimination. No stone is left unturned. We see Wodeham in penetrating dialogue with Rodington and FitzRalph and learn specifically about Rodington's own interpretation of the contradictory compound proposition denied in Wodeham's second thesis [9.2. 66] as well as about FitzRalph's peculiar understanding of the sin of omission as a pure privation of an act [9.2. 83].

## VI. Conclusion

The history of the Oxonian debate over issues related to the problem of sudden and instantaneous willing, which migrated to Paris in the 1340s[1], cannot be told in full until more texts by Adam Wodeham, Richard FitzRalph, John of Rodington, and a number of other influential philosophers and theologians active at Oxford in the late 1320s and 1330s have been edited. Fortunately, much editing work is now underway for the above figures and Robert Holcot, Thomas Bradwardine, Richard Kilvington, and others, which will eventually allow the further contextualization and expansion of our discussion of Wodeham's views as expressed in the two questions edited below. For now, we believe that we have captured sufficiently the gist of Wodeham's position and provided the reader with the necessary information to understand and appreciate Wodeham's contribution to a debate that was still in its emerging phase.

In conclusion, for medieval academics, what the will can and cannot do is determined, on the one hand, by its own metaphysical limitations and, on the other, by the conditions of the world, which impose various restrictions on its action and choices. We learn through experience what the will can do, but theory and possible-world analysis can help us understand to some degree how the will

1. The long-term impact can be seen in the late-1350s : C. Schabel, « The Forgotten *Principia* of a Forgotten Theologian : Jean de Moyenneville, 1356-1357, and Parisian Theology in the Late 1350s », *in* M. Brînzei and W.O. Duba (eds.), *Principia on the Sentences of Peter Lombard : Exploring an Uncharted Scholastic-Philosophical Genre*, Turnhout, Brepols, 2024, vol. 1, p. 261-36, at 312-319.

works and what metaphysical limits it has. As is evident from the contents of the two questions, Wodeham thinks of the will as a power capable of acting suddenly. His dominant concern in the context of these questions is with resolving multiple theological and philosophical problems entailed by Aristotelian assumptions about change and time. The will can produce an act of meritorious love suddenly, but ceasing from an occurrent act requires time and cannot take place instantaneously.

## VII. The edition

Questions 8-9 of distinction 1 of book I of Wodeham's *Ordinatio* survive in at least ten manuscripts, not including at least fifteen manuscripts and the 1512 printing of Henry Totting of Oyta's so-called *Abbreviatio* (*A*)[1]. William J. Courtenay argued that only four witnesses contain the full redaction of the *Ordinatio* for book I[2] :

*M* = Paris, Bibliothèque Mazarine, 915 (parchment, 14th c., 229ff.)
*S* = Paris, Bibliothèque Interuniversitaire de la Sorbonne, 193 (parchment, 14th c., 233ff.)
*T* = Tarazona, Archivo Biblioteca de la Catedral, 7 (parchment, 14th c., 204ff.)
*V* = Città del Vaticano, Biblioteca Apostolica Vaticana, Vat. lat. 955 (parchment, before 1350, 217ff.)

Courtenay reasoned that the *Ordinatio* in *MST* was in final form before news of the death of Pope John XXII in Avignon on 4 December 1334 reached England. Courtenay found that the base text in *V* matches that in *MST*, but « lacks their polished, finished form » and contains later marginalia from an abbreviated second redaction, the so-called *Collectio Brevis*, in the following witnesses[3] :

*B* = Bruges, Bibliothèque de la Ville, 172 (parchment, 14th c., 146ff.)
*F* = Firenze, Biblioteca Nazionale Centrale, Conv. Soppr. B VII 1249 (parchment and paper, 14th/early 15th c., 174ff.)
*P* = Paris, Bibliothèque nationale de France, lat. 15892 (parchment, 14th c., 174ff.)

It should be noted that in book IV (not contained in *V*), where Courtenay saw the *Ordinatio* in *BMST* and the *Collectio Brevis* in *FP*[4], Marilyn McCord Adams and Rega Wood found in their edition of question 10 that *FP* (*P* being a copy of *F*, they argued) carried the same redaction as *BMST* and not an abbreviation[5].

1. See the appendices in Courtenay, *Adam Wodeham*, p. 183-228. Transcriptions of some questions from the *Ordinatio* have been made available by Jeffery C. Witt on the Lombard Press : https://scta.lombardpress.org/text ? resourceid=http://scta.info/resource/wodehamordinatio

2. See Courtenay, *Adam Wodeham*, p. 7-34, for the redactional issue and its history, and p. 186-187 for descriptions of and bibliography on the four manuscripts.

3. Courtenay, *Adam Wodeham*, p. 202-203.

4. Courtenay, *Adam Wodeham*, p. 186.

5. M. M. Adams and R. Wood, « Is to Will It as Bad as to Do It ? The Fourteenth-Century Debate », *Franciscan Studies* 41, 1981, p. 5-60, at p. 30-34. See also R. Wood, « Introduction », *in* Adam Wodeham, *Lectura secunda in librum primum Sententiarum. Prologus et distinctio prima*, ed. R. Wood with G. Gál, St. Bonaventure, NY, Franciscan Institute, 1990, p. 33*-34*.

Whatever the case with book IV, in book I, on which Courtenay concentrated, *BFP* do have a shorter text. For example, of the first 29 paragraphs in question 8, article 1, edited below, *P* omits nine of them : 7, 13, 15, 21-22, 25-27, and 29.

For book I of the *Ordinatio*, Courtenay considered *S* and *T* the best witnesses. For a certain section of text, he concluded that occasionally *ST* agree against *M*, *MS* frequently read against *T*, and *MT* never go together against *S*; that each of *S* and *T* have omissions *per homoeoteleuton* not in the other and hence they are independent; and that *M* commits all the omissions *per homoeoteleuton* of *S* plus several more of its own. Thus Courtenay advised ignoring *M* except where *S* and *T* are hard to read, but in the cases of disagreement between *S* and *T*, where the correct reading is not obvious, he noted that « the second redaction and the Oyta abbreviation, independently of one another, were based on a copy of the archetype that was at least as good as the Tarazona manuscript if not better ». Courtenay thus recommended appealing to those other redactions, singling out *P*, from which he gave an example[1].

Unlike Wodeham's truncated *Lectura secunda*, which has been published in three volumes[2], as far as we know the only parts of book I that have been critically edited and published are numerous passages from Wodeham's first *principium* disguised as the two questions of the Prologue and the first question of distinction 1, by Onorato Grassi[3]. Grassi did not have access to *T*, but collated *SMV* along with *FP* and occasionally appealed to the edition *A* and three manuscripts of the Oyta *Abbreviatio*. Grassi generally followed *S*, but he reported several omissions *per homoeoteleuton* in *SM*, as expected, with several more in *M* alone (a couple corrected in another hand in *S*), and one in *S* alone (p. 114.6-7), proving that the scribe of *M* had access to another manuscript. *PF* share a couple of such omissions, but *P* has several more alone, whereas Grassi only recorded two for *F*. *V* has just one of its own, but sometimes corrects those in *SM* in another hand.

The question is whether access to *T* would have made the collation of *FP* and any appeal to *A* unnecessary. We will eventually edit the entirety of the first three questions from which Grassi edited fragments, but Courtenay also warned that there was evidence that Wodeham's *Ordinatio* was copied by the pecia system, which implies that his conclusions about the manuscript tradition may not hold for all sections of the text. This being the case, for questions 8-9 of distinction 1, i.e., questions 10-11 overall of the *Ordinatio*, we have done a full collation of *MSTV*, all four manuscripts of the *Ordinatio*.

Generally for works in repetitive scholastic philosophy, given a sufficient amount of text, omissions *per homoeoteleuton* provide a reliable statistical basis

1. On the manuscript tradition of the *Ordinatio*, see Courtenay, *Adam Wodeham*, p. 26-30.

2. Adam Wodeham, *Lectura secunda in librum primum Sententiarum*, ed. R. Wood with G. Gál, 3 vols., St. Bonaventure, NY, Franciscan Institute, 1990.

3. O. Grassi, « Il problema della conoscenza di Dio nel commento alle *Sentenze* di Adam Wodeham (Prologo e q. 1) », *Medioevo* 8, 1982, p. 43-136, at p. 89-136, apparently reprinted with German translation in D. Perler, *Satztheorien : Texte zur Sprachphilosophie und Wissenschaftstheorie im 14. Jahrhundert*, Darmstadt, Wissenschaftliche Buchgesellschaft, 1990, p. 266-331.

on which to construct a tentative stemma, which is normally supported by less obvious sorts of errors. With roughly 28,000 words of text, our data is rather trustworthy. Our findings confirm that *S* and *T* are independent from each other and that *M* is by far the worst witness of the three, but as in the case of the section that Grassi edited, in this section *M* cannot have derived solely from *S*, since *S* commits an omission *per homoeoteleuton* that *M* does not.

In fact, where there are no corrections, each of *MSTV* commits large unshared omissions *per homoeoteleuton* of five words or more, *M* having 10, *S* 1, *T* 3, and *V* 2 :

8.1. 52 : actu diligenti – imperfectior] *om. hom. M* (15 wds)
8.2. 8 : producibilis – simul] *om. hom. M* (9 wds)
8.2. 21 : vel est – intellectum] *om. hom. M* (16 wds extra)
8.2. 22 : nunc – agit] *om. hom. M* (8 wds)
9.2. 31 : causare ipsum – praecipitur] *om. hom. M* (15 wds)
9.2. 35 : nec prius – instanti] *om. hom. M* (12 wds)
9.2. 47 : nec in a – actum] *om. hom. M* (12 wds)
9.2. 70 : secundum quam procedit – legem] *om. hom. M* (11 wds)
9.2. 78 : et nihil est – fac nunc] *om. hom. M* (12 wds)
9.2. 85 : ita etiam ad interiorem – exteriorem] *om. hom. M* (12 wds)

8.2. 26 : bonum – nocuit] *om. hom. S* (6 wds)

8.1. 38 : secundum totum vel – alia] *om. hom. T* (18 wds)
8.1. 73 : et nunc – intellectionem] *om. hom. T* (5 wds)
9.2. 54 : ultimo habuit – ante a] *om. hom. T* (9 wds)

8.2. 51 : distincte – perceptibilis] *om. hom. V* (5 wds)
9.1. 23 : aut igitur – dati] *om. hom. V* (11 wds)

In our questions, moreover, where there are no corrections, *M* shares few large omissions *per homoeoteleuton* with *S* or *T* against the others :

8.2. 76 : cum nolitione – non] *om. hom. MT* (12 wds)
9.2. 65 : inferendum – praeterito] *om. hom. MS* (8 wds)
9.2. 67 : interceptum – temporis] *om. hom. MT* (7 wds)

What is striking is that *MST* share 8 large omissions *per homoeoteleuton* against the original text in *V* :

8.1. 21 : quo posito – instans] *om. hom. MST* (8 wds)
8.1. 51 : nisi – muscam] *om. hom. MST* (7 wds)
8.2. 9 : aequale – est] *om. hom. MST* (14 wds)
9.1. 11 : nunc – post] *om. hom. MST* (6 wds)
9.2. 20 : igitur numquam – post a] *om. hom. MST* (13 wds)
9.2. 36 : non citra – termino] *om. hom. MST* (16 wds)
9.2. 47 : dupliciter – omissio] *om. hom. MST* (9 wds)
9.2. 52 : et quod – peccavit] *om. hom. MST* (7 wds)

Putting aside *M*, which is very poor and may switch exemplars, we thus have two families represented by *ST* and *V*, so normally the agreement of *SV* against *T* or *TV* against *S* is followed in the edition below. The question becomes what to do in cases where *ST* agree against *V*. If we take into consideration only the large omissions *per homoeoteleuton* in the original uncorrected texts, *V* is far superior to *ST*, which share 8 such omissions against only 2 for *V*.

The situation is much more complicated, however, because each of the four manuscripts has been corrected extensively. Before those corrections were made, mostly in the margins in the case of omissions *per homoeoteuton*, *M* committed 3 other unshared *homoeoteleuta*, *S* 1, *T* 2, and *V* no fewer than 22 :

8.1. 32 : intensibilis – etc.] *mg. (hom.) M* (14 wds)
9.2. 13 : huic – praeponatur] *mg. (hom.) M* (8 wds)
9.2. 24 : causet – a] actum et dimittit actum praehabitum quod ante a *mg. (hom.) M* (10 wds)

8.1. 88 : sed illud – delectatio] *mg. (hom.) S* (15 wds)

8.2. 31 : nec etiam – esse] *mg. (hom.) T* (11 wds)
8.2. 71 : ex primo ostensis – esse] *mg. (hom.) T* (8 wds)

8.1. 20 : sed – medium] *mg. (hom.) V* (14 wds)
8.1. 42 : et imperfecte – imperfecte] *mg. (hom.) V* (10 wds)
8.2. 6 : si autem – cedatur] *mg. (hom.) V* (6 wds)
8.2. 9 : et pari ratione – tertii] *mg. (hom.) V* (15 wds)
8.2. 31 : in primo – peccare] *mg. (hom.) V* (11 wds)
8.2. 45 : per tempus – exspectabit] *mg. (hom.) V* (7 wds)
8.2. 61 : in secunda – meretur] *mg. supra (hom.) V* (12 wds)
8.2. 69 : certe hoc – et] *mg. (hom.) V* (26 wds)
8.2. 71 : percipere – percipere] *mg. (hom.) V* (5 wds)
9.2. 3 : hoc sequetur – igitur] *mg. (hom.) V* (23 wds)
9.2. 4 : potest deus – instans] *mg. (hom.) V* (18 wds)
9.2. 18 : etiam non – movebitur] *mg. (hom.) V* (8 wds)
9.2. 34 : et per illum – differre] *mg. (hom.) V* (17 wds)
9.2. 37 : igitur si – praecepti] *mg. (hom.) V* (17 wds)
9.2. 55 : impleat – dandi] *mg. (hom.) V* (10 wds)
9.2. 56 : et si non – praeceptum] *mg. infra (hom.) V* (19 wds)
9.2. 57 : sed ab – praeceptum] *mg. (hom.) V* (10 wds)
9.2. 60 : iste est – fuit] *mg. (hom.) V* (10 wds)
9.2. 65 : fuit igitur – peccans] *mg. (hom.) V* (13 wds)
9.2. 72 : et tamen – a] *mg. (hom.) V* (5 wds)
9.2. 74 : probatum est – a] *mg. (hom.) V* (15 wds)
9.2. 74 : et tamen – a] *mg. (hom.) V* (19 wds)

This means that before any such marginal corrections were made, the total number of unshared omissions *per homoeoteleuton* in *M* was 13, in *S* 2, in *T* 5, and in *V* 24. If we take into consideration the 8 shared *homoeoteleuta* of *MST*, in terms of these sorts of omissions before corrections, *V* was still only about as reliable as *M* and rather less than *S* and *T*.

More significantly, on 6 occasions *V* has a marginal correction of what must have been an omission *per homoeoteleuton* that had been shared by *MSTV* but which remains in *MST*, 5 simple ones and a more complicated instance in which *MST* shared a *homoeoteleuton* within a larger *homoeoteleuton* in *V* that was later corrected, where the scribe of *S* seems to have recognized the problem and attempted a conjecture :

8.1. 93 : et non – fieri] *om. hom. MST*; *mg. V* (7 wds)
9.2. 36 : sed in instanti – indutiarum] *om. hom. MST*; *mg. V* (12 wds)
9.2. 60 : quia mortaliter – damnabitur] *om. hom. MST*; *mg. V* (19 wds)
9.2. 78 : fac nunc quoniam – tale] *om. hom. MST*; *mg. V* (15 wds)
9.2. 81 : primo peccat – ante] *om. hom. MST*; *mg. V* (17 wds)

9.2. 59 : sed de nullo qui ante c fuit dignus paena aeterna potest in c fieri quod ipse non fuerit dignus poena aeterna] *om. hom. MT*; igitur non potest esse quin caruerit gratia (*ut corr. om. hom.?* ) *S*; (*mg. V*) (21 wds) || sed de nullo – poena aeterna] *mg. (hom.) V* (37 wds)

Otherwise, on one occasion *S* has a marginal correction of what had been a shared omission *per homoeoteleuton* in *MSTV* :

9.2. 47 : non compatiuntur – eum] *om. hom. MTV*; *mg. infra S* (15 wds)

Courtenay suspected that *V* contains « marginal notations and additions » in « Wodeham's own handwriting » or at the very least following his directions, and that some of these additions were found incorporated into the later redaction, from after 1334, represented by *P*. Courtenay concluded that while the original text in *V* contains frequent errors, the additions are exceptionally clean[1]. In our questions, however, there are very few actual additions in *V*, but rather the original text has frequently been corrected with the same redaction, even if someone, probably Wodeham himself, has also tweaked the text in minor ways. That is to say, in our questions most marginal corrections in *V* are not additions to the text, but rather restorations of the text that Wodeham had originally. The 6 instances of shared omissions *per homoeoteleuton* of *MSTV* later corrected in *V* and the one later corrected in *S* also reveal that before corrections *MSTV* stem from a common exemplar below the archetype, which could verify Courtenay's suspicion that both the later redaction and the Oyta abbreviation derive from an independent branch or branches of the stemma.

If we examine the omissions *per homoeoteleuton* in the *MST* branch of the stemma before corrections, we find that *MST* shared another 7 before they were corrected, with 4 corrections in both *M* and *S*, leaving *T* with 4 unshared *homoeoteleuta*; with 3 further corrections in *S* alone, leaving *MT* sharing

1. Courtenay, *Adam Wodeham*, p. 20-23.

3 *homoeoteleuta*; and with one correction in *M* alone, leaving *ST* sharing one *homoeoteleuton* :

8.1. 18 : immo – esse] *mg. M*; *om. hom. ST* (7 wds)
8.2. 2 : et libertatem – male] *mg. MS*; *om. hom. T* (13 wds)
8.2. 4 : in instanti – peccasset] *mg. M*; *mg. infra S*; *om. hom. T* (16 wds)
8.2. 39 : sed tunc – partem] *mg. M*; *mg. infra S*; *om. hom. T* (17 wds)
8.2. 68 : secundum istam responsionem – horae] *om. hom. MT*; *mg. infra S* (48 wds)
9.2. 75 : perseveravit sortes – aliquod] *om. hom. MT*; *mg. infra S* (12 wds)
9.2. 83 : et sine medio – peccato] *om. hom. MT*; *mg. infra S* (9 wds)

Finally, before corrections *MS* shared 6 other omissions *per homoeoteleuton*, but no further ones are recorded for *MT*, so *M* does seem to have been closer to *S*. Of these 6, 5 are corrected in *S* and the sixth is corrected in *M* :

8.1. 69 : unam – pertingunt] *mg. M*; *om. hom. S* (19 wds)
8.2. 43 : oporteat – indispositum] *om. hom. M*; *mg. infra S* (14 wds)
8.2. 61 : horae in principio – medietate] *om. hom. M*; *mg. infra S* (30 wds)
8.2. 64 : non totaliter – ipso] *om. hom. M*; *mg. infra S* (31 wds)
9.2. 19 : praeceptum – in a] *om. hom. M*; *mg. S* (9 wds)
9.2. 22 : sortes peccavit – formetur] *om. hom. M*; *mg. S* (18 wds)

The upshot of all of this is that, while before corrections *MST* and *V* represented two divisions of one branch of the stemma of the once extant manuscripts of Wodeham's *Ordinatio*, of which the *MST* division was superior to the *V* division, after corrections we have found that the resulting text in *V*, where it differs from that in *MST*, is normally superior to that in *MST*. We have thus generally accepted *V*'s extensive corrections. These corrections have also allowed us to omit collating manuscripts from the shorter *Collectio Brevis* and later abbreviation by Henry Totting of Oyta, although we have appealed to *P* and report its readings on occasion. In the future we will attempt a broader analysis of the tradition of those other redactions in conjunction with that in *MSTV*.

Where there is no correction, and there is no clear superiority in meaning, syntax, or grammar, we have sometimes gone with *MST* against *V*, simply because, *ceteris paribus*, the reading in *MST* was more likely to be what Wodeham's medieval readers saw, even if Wodeham himself went through *V* carefully and approved its text.

In order to reduce the size of the apparatus criticus, we have ignored the differences between *igitur* and *ergo* and between forms of *illa* and *ista*. We have also decided not to report minor corrections in any individual codex that result in the readings shared by the other manuscripts. *MS* share frequent notations in the lower margins, which may have been in the common exemplar of *MST*, but which the scribe of *T* may simply have ignored; these are reported in the *apparatus criticus*. Where the manuscripts report minor divisions of the text in the margins we have not recorded these, except that when the manuscripts have numbered the arguments, we have placed these numbers within parentheses in bold, e.g., **(3)**, after the paragraph numering, e.g., [100] **(3)**.

Orthography has been standardized and classicized for clarity. In the *apparatus criticus*, different readings are separated by a semi-colon, for example : est] et *M*; erat *S* (instead of *est*, *M* reads *et* and *S* reads *erat*). To save space, different treatments of the same reading are separated by a comma, for example : est] et *M*, *a. c. mg. S* (instead of *est*, *M* reads *et* and *S* also reads *et* before it was corrected to *est* in the margin). Here are the abbreviations employed in the *apparatus criticus* :

*a. c.* = ante correctionem (x] y *a. c. A* = ms *A* had y before correcting to x)
*add.* = addidit (x] y *add. A* = ms *A* added y after x)
*add. sed del.* = addidit sed delevit (x] y *add. sed del. A* = ms A added y after x and then crossed it out)
*add. sed exp.* = addidit sed expunxit (x] y *add. sed exp. A* = ms *A* added y after x and then signalled its removal by putting points or dots beneath it)
*a.m.* = alia manu (in another hand)
*codd.* = codices (the manuscript witnesses)
*coni.* = coniecimus (our conjecture)
*def.* = deficit (x] *def. A* = ms *A* does not have the x because of a larger variant or omission)
*i.l.* = infra lineam (x] *i.l. A* = ms *A* has x below the line)
*iter.* = iterat (x] *iter. A* = ms *A* repeats x)
*mg.* = in margine (x] *mg. A* = ms *A* has x in the margin)
*mg. (hom.)* = in margine (hom.) ( *A* corrects an omission *per homoeoteleuton* in the margin)
*om.* = omisit (x] *om.* A = ms A omits x)
*om. hom.* = omisit per homoeoteleuton
*p. c.* = post correctionem (x] *p. c. A* = ms *A* has x only after correction)
*scr. sed del.* = scripsit sed delevit (x] *scr. sed. del.* A = ms *A* has written x but crossed it out)
*s.l.* = supra lineam (x] *s.l. A* = ms A had x above the line)
*tr.* = transposuit (x y] *tr. A* = ms *A* has y before x)
<x> = x is a word or words added by editors
* = lectio incerta

ADAM WODEHAM

# ORDINATIO OXONIENSIS IN PRIMUM LIBRUM SENTENTIARUM

## DISTINCTIO 1, QUAESTIO 8

[M 31vb, S 37vb, T 26vb, V 51r]

[1] Utrum voluntas possit simul et subito[a] producere actum voluntarium meritoriae et liberae[b] dilectionis.

[2] Videtur quod non, quia tunc in momento temporis posset mereri meritis aequalibus[c] infinitis in infinitis instantibus eius[d] : cum[e] non sit[f] maior ratio quod voluntas possit producere meritoriam dilectionem in uno instanti quam in alio de dicti[g] momenti instantibus infinitis, igitur in quolibet vel[h] nullo.

[3] Contra : principia activa alicuius effectus in passo summe dis|posito[i] in **T 27ra** quo nulla est resistentia impeditiva subitae[j] causationis possunt[k] instantanee[l] in[m] eo praesente, si sint sufficientes et nihil desit ex concausis, causare effectum in ipso ab eis causabilem ; sed voluntas est tale passum circumscriptis impedimentis omnibus, et ipsa etiam est causa activa respectu eius cum aliis ; igitur omnibus positis subito causabitur talis actus.

[4] In ista quaestione primo ponam aliquas conclusiones et probabo eas et solvam instantias[n]. Secundo principaliter fient[o] dubia contra principalem conclusionem.

(a) simul – subito] *tr. V* || (b) voluntarium – liberae] meritoriae *V* || (c) aequalibus] essentialibus *V* || (d) in – eius] instantibus eius *a.c. mg. M* ; *om. T* || (e) cum] *s.l. M* ; tamen *S* ; *p.c. T* || (f) sit] fit *S* || (g) dicti] dicta *MT* || (h) vel] in *add. S* || (i) summe disposito] *tr. V* ; et *add. V* || (j) subitae] in *add. V* || (k) possunt] causari *add. sed. del./exp. MT* || (l) instantanee] instantiari *p.c. T* || (m) in] *scr. sed. exp. T* || (n) et probabo – instantias] et solvam instantias *MT, a.c. S* ; et probabo eas et solvam instantias aliquas parvas *p.c. mg. infra S* || (o) fient] fieret *M*

## PRIMUS ARTICULUS[a]

### PRIMA CONCLUSIO[b]

[5] Pro primo articulo[c] prima conclusio est ista, quam non assero : quod angelus vel voluntas nostra vel angelica, si in hoc instanti non causat dilectionem, non potest sine medio post hoc[d] instans subito et simul causare dilectionem aliquam.

[6] Hanc probo, quia[e] eo ipso quod illa[f] dilectio causaretur simul, non per partem ante partem, instantanee et indivisibiliter[g] causaretur, et hoc est causari[h] in instanti. Si[i] enim sunt instantia indivisibiles mensurae succedentes in tempore distinctae[j] a permanentibus, et immediate praecessisset aliquod ultimum instans sui non-esse, ex dato, igitur aliquod[k] instans instanti immediatum.

[7] Praeterea, non potest contingere quod aliquid[l] nunc[m] sit ultimum[n] secundum se et quamlibet eius partem, propter idem medium. Et quia secundum Philosophum, VIII *Physicorum*[1], non est dare ultimum rei permanentis in esse, igitur pari ratione non est dare ultimum indivisibile in quo res aliqua et quaelibet eius pars ultimo non[o] sit.

### *<Contra primam conclusionem[p]>*

[8→5] Sed contra hanc conclusionem argui potest, primo sic : quia[q] Deus immediate post hoc instans posset, si vellet, totum mundum adnihilare, ita quod modo esset et immediate post simul non esset; sed[r] simul desineret esse, alioquin

(a) primus articulus] *mg. MS* ; *om. TV* || (b) prima conclusio] *mg. MTV* ; *om. S* ; ponitur prima conclusio quod si aliqua res non sit in hoc instanti non potest immediate post hoc esse simul tota **a** *add. mg. infra MS* || (c) pro – articulo] primi articuli *V* || (d) hoc] huius *T* || (e) quia] *om. V* || (f) illa] *s.l. M* ; *om. T* || (g) indivisibiliter] divisibiliter *a.c. s.l. SV* || (h) causari] causare *MST* || (i) si] non *MV* ; cum *T* || (j) in tempore distinctae] in tempore distinguo *a.c. V* ; in successione distinctae *p.c. mg. V* || (k) aliquod] esset *add. S* ; *om. V* || (l) aliquid] aliquod *M* || (m) nunc] non *MT* ; *post* ultimum *mg. S* ; *iter. post* ultimum *a.c. V* || (n) ultimum] ultimo *MV* || (o) non] *scr. sed exp. T* || (p) conclusionem] contra hanc conclusionem arguitur 8 mediis **b** ad quae respondetur **c** *mg. infra MS* || (q) quia] cum *add. S* || (r) sed] si *M*

1. Aristoteles, *Physica*, VIII, c. 8 : 263b9-16, *Translatio vetus*, ed. F. Bossier et J. Brams (AL VII. 1.2), Leiden 1990, p. 325.6-12.

S 38ra non | videretur ita potens ad destruendum mundum[s] sicut ad producendum ipsum simul; igitur eadem ratione posset facere econtra quod modo[t] non esset et immediate post[u] totus simul esset; igitur a simili in proposito.

[9] **(2)** Praeterea, posset Deus[v] facere unum angelum[w] qui praecise esset per instans, et ille angelus illo casu posito simul desineret esse, igitur instans instanti immediatum, per tuum modum arguendi.

[10] **(3)** Praeterea, praecise per unum instans posset[x] Deus[y] nolle[z] cooperari[a] soli ad illuminationem medii summe dispositi. Quod[b] si fieret, in illo instanti sol non[c] illuminaret medium, et tamen statim[d] post illuminaret et simul, quia non esset ibi causa aliqua successionis.

[11] **(4)** Praeterea, Deus[e] obstaculum aliquod impeditivum illuminationis interpositum inter solem et medium posset instantanee adnihilare, et illo casu posito sol immediate post illud instans illuminaret medium sine successione, quia non esset ibi[f] causa successionis.

[12] **(5)** Praeterea, in quacumque mensura potest creatura[g] successive agere aliquam rem simul factibilem, Deus potest eam simul et subito producere, quia rem simul[h] factibilem simul fieri nullam includit contradictionem[i]; sed creatura potest immediate postquam talis res non est nec aliquid eius agere successive talem; igitur Deus potest immediate post instans in quo[j] aliqua[k] res[l] non est nec aliquid eius simul eam producere; igitur nulla apparet repugnantia quin etiam sic fieri posset[m] volitio a voluntate.

M 32ra [13] **(6)** Praeterea, Deus immediate | post hoc instans potest totam rem
V 51v aliquam et quamlibet | eius partem conservare; sed divina[n] conservatio est vera productio; igitur Deus potest immediate post hoc instans aliquid simul producere et totaliter. Ita etiam sol, si staret immediate post hoc instans, conservaret radium quem nunc[o] producit; et conservare ut prius est producere[p], etc.

[14] **(7)** Praeterea, omne illud cui non repugnat simul esse immediate post hoc instans potest Deus immediate post hoc instans[q] simul producere, *quia non erit* ei[r] *impossibile omne*[s] *verbum*[1]; sed nulli[t] creaturae[u] permansivae repugnat simul esse immediate post hoc instans, quia omnis talis de facto erit secundum se[v] immediate post hoc instans vel aliquid eius[w]; igitur omnem talem poterit[x] Deus immediate post hoc[y] instans producere simul, etiam dato quod nunc non sit[z].

(s) mundum] *mg. MV* ; *om. ST* || (t) econtra – modo] quod *a.c. mg. M, a.c. mg.* (econtra) *et s.l.* (modo) *S, T* || (u) post] *s.l. M* ; *om. ST* || (v) posset deus] *tr. V* || (w) angelum] a simili in proposito *add. S* (*cf. supra*) || (x) posset] potest *a.c. M, ST* ; posset *p.c. s.l. M* ; *post* praeterea *mg. V* || (y) deus] *om. V* || (z) nolle] quod *add. sed del. MT* || (a) cooperari] posset *add. sed del. MT, add. sed exp. V* || (b) quod] et *MT* ; *mg. S* || (c) non] *mg. MT* || (d) tamen statim] *tr. S* || (e) deus] *om. MT* ; *mg. S* || (f) non – ibi] ibi non esset *MT* || (g) creatura] causa *a.c. M, ST* || (h) quia – simul] quia simul esse et *a.c. M, T* ; quia rem simul *p.c. mg. M* || (i) contradictionem] repugnantiam *MT* || (j) quo] qua *T* || (k) aliqua] *om. MT* || (l) res] nunc *add. S* || (m) posset] possit *V* || (n) divina] dei *MS* || (o) nunc] non *a.c. s.l. M, T* || (p) producere] igitur *add. S* || (q) potest – instans] *om. hom. M* ; potest deus *mg. M, S* || (r) ei] ibi *ac. mg. M, T* ; sibi *S* || (s) omne] *i.l. MV* ; *om. T* || (t) nulli] velle *a.c. mg. M, T* || (u) creaturae] esse *a.c. mg. M, T* ; rei *S* || (v) se] te *MST* || (w) vel – eius] *om. S* || (x) poterit] potest *MST* || (y) hoc] *om. V* || (z) nunc non sit] non sit nunc *MT*

1. Lc 1 : 37.

[15] **(8)** Praeterea, nihil negandum est[a] a divino posse ex quo non possunt[b] inferri contradictoria simul fore vera, utpote quod esse et non-esse simul conveniant eidem ; sed ex hoc quod nunc aliquid totaliter non est et immediate post totum simul est, vel econverso quod modo totum sit et immediate post totaliter et simul non sit, sed destruatur vel non conservetur, nec ipsa nec aliquid eius[c], non sequitur quod aliquid simul sit[d] et non sit, sed solum quod esse alicuius totale immediate succedat suo non-esse vel econverso ; igitur hoc non est negandum[e] a[f] divino posse. Hoc et similia argui possunt, sed haec sufficiant[g].

*<Responsio propria ad rationes contra primam conclusionem>*

[16] Sed istis non obstantibus, absque aliqua assertione teneo illud quod prius, quod[h] idem est (apud me et multos alios) fieri instantanee seu in instanti, ad debitum intellectum, quod[i] simul fieri sic quod non per partem ante partem – non enim sunt secundum veritatem instantia mensurae tales quales quidam imaginantur, sicut supra tertium declarabo[1] ; sed impossibile est quod instans immediate succedat instanti vel mutatum esse unum in eodem motu continuetur[j] alteri vel unum indivisibile alteri situetur[k] immediate[l] ab eodem distincto – immo[m] hoc includit repugnantiam, ut satis patebit in materia de non-compositione divisibilis[n] ex indivisibilibus[2] ; igitur impossibile est quod aliquid immediate post instans in quo non est nec aliquid quod potest esse pars eius simul fiat[o] vel econverso.

[17] Praeterea, hoc dato, duo angeli essent factibiles immediate unus post alium, et non simul mensura, et hoc impossibile, tum quia pari ratione dicerem de mille ; tum quia creatio angeli non habentis[p] partes[q] est instantanea[r] solum, vel si habet partes[s], pono quod non divisibiliter et particulariter, licet[t] uterque[u] simul[v] producatur, et ita instans instanti immediatum. Probatio primae[w] consequentiae : quia Deus potest[x] in instanti praesenti producere angelum unum, si prius hoc voluit[y]. Ponatur igitur quod | sic faciat et quod tunc non[z] sit unus alius angelus[a] **S 38rb**
producibilis. Si igitur ille alius angelus possit simul produci immediate post ultimum instans sui non-esse, ita poterit fieri de tertio angelo non[b] nunc existente producibili post secundum ; igitur[c].

(a) negandum est] *tr. S* || (b) possunt] possit *V* || (c) quod modo – eius] *om. MT* ; *mg. infra S* ; *mg. sin. V* || (d) simul sit] sit sic *MT* ; sit *S* || (e) non – negandum] negandum non est *V* || (f) a] *om. M* || (g) sufficiant] sufficiat *V* || (h) quod] quia *MST* || (i) quod] et *MST* || (j) continuetur] continue *MT* ; continetur *a.c. S* ; continuo *V* (et continui *P*) || (k) situetur] situatur *MT* ; situaliter *V* || (l) immediate] *om. MT* || (m) immo] numero *S* || (n) divisibilis] indivisibili *MT* ; continui *S* || (o) fiat] stat *a.c. s.l. M*, stat *T* || (p) habentis] *a.c M* ; habet *p.c. M* ; habitus *a.c. mg. V* || (q) partes] partis *a.c. M*, *T* || (r) est instantanea] sed instantia *p.c. M* || (s) partes] solum *add. MST* || (t) licet] *om. S* ; sed vel *V* (+*P*) || (u) uterque] utraque *S* || (v) simul] *om. V* || (w) primae] *om. MST* || (x) potest] posset *T* || (y) voluit] voluerit *MT* || (z) non] *om. S* || (a) angelus] *om. S* || (b) non] *om. MST* || (c) igitur] etc. *add. T* ; (et *M*) quod ista (ita *S*) est concedenda deus si vellet potest non esse vel peccare **c** *add. mg. infra MS* (*M* 31vb)

1. Adam Wodeham, *Ordinatio Oxoniensis in Sententias*, III, d. 14, q. 10-11.

2. Adam Wodeham, *Tractatus de indivisibilibus*, q. 1, a. 1 et 3, ed. R. Wood, Dordrecht 1988, passim.

[18→8] Ad primum igitur in contrarium dicendum quod Deus etiam immediate post hoc instans posset si vellet seipsum[d] adnihilare, sicut[e] posset si vellet peccare T 27rb et | huiusmodi. Sed hoc est quia condicionalis propositae[f] antecedens significat impossibile, ex quo inferri potest impossibile. Sed si[g] sine[h] illo antecedente impossibili sumatur absolute quod posset Deus immediate post praesens instans[i], in quo supponatur[j] quod mundus sit[k], mundum simul adnihilare, dicendum quod hoc non est factibile, sed repugnantiam includens, quia infert quod aliquid quod[l] fieret simul vel[m] simul destrueretur, et per consequens instantanee, non[n] fieret nec destrueretur simul nec instantanee, cum instans instanti immediate succedere[o] non possit. Nec tamen ex hoc sequitur[p] quin Deus sit ita potens ad destruendum mundum simul[q] sicut fuit ad simul creandum[r] – immo est aeque potens simul facere hoc sicut illud[s]. Sed tamen si velit mundum simul adnihilare[t], hoc non erit immediate post ultimum instans sui esse – immo tunc non haberet ultimum sui esse[u] – sicut eo ipso quod crearet mundum simul non fuisset ultimum instans non-esse primi.

[19→9] Ad secundum assumptum[v], nego, nisi angelus sit particulariter destructibilis, tunc enim posset esse[w] praecise per instans. Sed tunc non simul sed particulariter destrueretur vel cessaret conservari, sicut est generale etiam in omnibus quae[x] solum fiunt successive et successive[y] solum destruuntur[z]. Sed hoc semper exclusi per hoc quod addidi « simul ».

[20→10] Ad tertium assumptum, bene verum est quod Deus[a] posset nolle praecise etc. Verum est etiam quod illo casu posito quod sol in illo instanti non illuminaret medium[b]. Sed posito toto illo casu quod sic praecise per instans sol non illuminaret medium[c], non est simul cum hoc factibile[d] quod sol immediate post simul illuminet medium[e], sed quod particulariter et successive bene contingit. Et cum[f] dicit quod nulla est causa quod[g] foret successio tunc[h], dicendum quod immo, Deus ipse esset in causa eo quod nollet tunc simul et subito producere lumen a sole causabile. Nam si vellet simul et subito lumen[i] producere[j] sine omni medio post hoc instans[k], ipse vellet ipsum[l] producere in hoc instanti[m], cum non sit huic instanti aliquod instans[n] immediatum, nec esse possit[o] in quo subito aut[p]

(d) seipsum] semet ipsum *MST* || (e) sicut] et *S* ; etiam *add. V* || (f) et – propositae] sed haec est consequentia condicionalis cuius propositio *S* || (g) si] *mg. M* ; *s.l. S* || (h) sine] in *T* || (i) praesens instans] hoc instans praesens *MT* || (j) supponatur] praesupponatur *T* || (k) sit] a deo adnihilabilis *add. MT* || (l) quod] *s.l. TV* || (m) fieret – vel] simul fieret vel quod *S* || (n) non] nec *S* || (o) succedere] immediate *add. M* ; immediato *add. T* || (p) sequitur] quod *add. sed del. M, add. T* || (q) simul] *s.l. M* ; *om. ST* || (r) creandum] causandum *M* || (s) immo – illud] *mg. MV* (*partim illeg. M*) ; *om. ST* || (t) simul adnihilare] *tr. MT* || (u) immo – esse] *mg. (hom.) M* (esse sui *M*) ; *om. hom. ST* || (v) assumptum] argumentum *MT* ; *p.c. S* || (w) esse] *om. MT* ; *mg. S* || (x) quae] simul *add. MT* || (y) successive] s^c^ce^v^ *V* || (z) destruuntur] destruantur *T* || (a) deus] *om. MST* || (b) medium] *mg. M* ; *om. ST* || (c) sed – medium] *mg. (hom.) V* || (d) factibile] scibile *V* || (e) simul – medium] illuminet medium simul *MT* || (f) cum] tamen *S* || (g) quod] quare *MST* || (h) tunc] etc. *MST* || (i) lumen] tale *add. MST* || (j) producere] *a.c. S* ; conproducere *p.c. S* || (k) sine – instans] in (modo *M*) hoc instanti cum non sit hoc instans *MT, a.c. mg. S* || (l) ipsum] tantum *MT* || (m) instanti] *om. MT* || (n) huic – instans] hoc (hic *M*) instans aliquod instanti *MT* ; *mg. V* || (o) possit] posset *MST, a.c. V* || (p) aut] vel *T*

simul produci | valeret[q]. Oppositum autem huius illati positum est, quia[r] positum est[s] quod Deus praecise per hoc instans soli nolit[t] cooperari. M 32rb

[21→20] Dices forte quod, sicut potest per instans praecise nolle cooperari soli ad lumen causandum, ita potest praecise per instans nolle simul producere[u] tale lumen, sic videlicet intelligendo[v] quod totum aliquod lumen a sole producibile secundum se et quamlibet sui partem per totum diem sit nisi praecise per unicum | instans, quo posito sequitur quod immediate post illud instans[w] simul producetur. V 52r

[22→21] Dicendum quod hoc non est possibile. Nec haec duo sunt similia, quia primum est possibile in similibus apud naturam, secundum vero infert quod[x] in continuo sunt indivisibilia immediata extra se invicem, quod est impossibile[y].

[23→11] Ad quartum, totum argumentum et quod infert[z] debet concedi, quod videlicet immediate post totum[a] medium sine successione in causatione luminis illuminaretur, sed non primo immediate post[b], immo primo[c] in instanti adnihilationis obstaculi interpositi, quia in illo instanti nullum esset obstaculum impediens luminis causationem.

[24→12] Ad quintum, dicendum quod discursus non valet, quia non bene sumitur « sub ». Deberet enim accipi « sub » aliquod individuum mensurae[d], et hoc non fit, sed accipitur « sub » hoc adverbialis determinatio « immediate », et fit fallacia figurae dictionis commutando rem in modum.

[25→13] Ad sextum, dicendum quod verum est quod assumitur et etiam[e] quod concluditur, scilicet quod Deus potest immediate post hoc instans simul aliquam rem producere, sed non primo immediate post hoc instans, immo tunc simul eam[f] produceret in hoc instanti.

[26→25] Contra : Deus potest immediate post hoc instans rem in hoc instanti[g] creatam totam simul primo conservare, nam in hoc instanti non conservat et sine medio conservabit ; sed conservare, per te, | est producere ; igitur immediate post potest primo producere totam[h]. S 38va

[27→26] Negandus est discursus propter fallaciam consequentis, sicut non sequitur : « Nunc primo sum albus, igitur nunc primo sum coloratus », nec sequitur : « Immediate post hoc instans primo moveberis »[i]. Si tamen sic, dici posset[j] vere. Forsitan enim non est hoc dandum. Sed illo modo intelligendo quo aliqui concederent non sequitur : « Immediate post primo moveberis, igitur immediate post hoc instans primo eris », quia arguitur in omnibus ab inferiori[k] ad superius utrobique praeposita negatione, sicut patet per exponentes, in quibus[l] non sequitur : « Nunc non moveris[m] ; sed sine medio moveberis ; igitur nunc non es, sed sine medio eris ».

(q) valeret] valent *M* || (r) positum – quia] *om. MST* ; *mg. V* || (s) est] scilicet *add. MST* ; sed *add. sed del. V* || (t) nolit] nolet *M* || (u) producere] comproducere *M* || (v) sic – intelligendo] sicut patet *MT* || (w) quo posito – instans] *om. hom. MST* || (x) quod] apud naturam *add. MT* || (y) quod – impossibile] *om. MST* || (z) et – infert] quod infertur *MST* || (a) totum] instans *add. MT* || (b) primo – post] immediate post instans *S* || (c) primo] *om. MST* || (d) mensurae] in secundo *T* || (e) etiam] *om. S* || (f) simul eam] *tr. V* || (g) in – instanti] *om. MST* ; *s.l. V* || (h) totam] tamen *M* ; dico *T* ; illam *add. V* || (i) moveberis] movebitur *MST* || (j) dici posset] *tr. V* || (k) in – inferiori] ab omnibus istis inferioribus *MST* || (l) quibus] quo *MST* || (m) moveris] moveberis *MST*

[28→14] Ad septimum dicendum per idem[n]. Tota enim ista syllogistica deductio vera[o] est et verum concludit. Sed quod additur, « etiam dato quod nunc non sit »[p], oporteret probari et non sine argumento apponi eo quod illud appositum falsum est[q] nisi instans instanti immediate[r] posset succedere.

[29→15] Ad octavum, quod est[s] quaedam reductio septimi[t], maior concedenda est, sed[u] minor neganda est, quia[v] eo ipso[w] quod simul et non per partem ante partem[x] capit suum esse seu producitur, sequitur quod instantanee et indivisibiliter producitur et ita in instanti[y], ex significato vocabuli, et tamen per positum datur ultimum instans sui non-esse. Cum igitur[z] non possit instans instanti immediate succedere, sequitur quod non producitur primo instantanee, et sic sequitur quod primo producitur instantanee et quod non primo[a] producitur instantanee, et sic patet quod[b] sequitur utrumque contradictoriorum.

## Secunda conclusio[c]

[30] Ex iam praedicta[d] condicionali conclusione sequitur alia, videlicet quod si angelus in hoc instanti non causat dilectionem[e], et tamen immediate post hoc instans causabit dilectionem, talis dilectio causabitur successive et non subito.

## Tertia conclusio[f]

[31] Tertio sequitur quod, cum partes[g] condicionalis huius quae est secunda conclusio sint possibiles, quod consequens categoricum est possibile. Sit igitur haec tertia conclusio[h] : quod dilectio aliqua est causabilis successive.

[32] Hanc probo aliter, quia omnis forma intensibilis et remissibilis est successive causabilis, saltem a Deo ; sed dilectio est talis forma[i] ; igitur etc. Minor patet, quia quilibet experitur quod aliquando idem[j] obiectum diligit[k] intensius et aliquando remissius. Similiter, caritas habitualis potest intendi ; igitur pari ratione potest[l] et actualis.

[33] Praeterea, in quacumque specie formae accidentalis potest inveniri forma simplex simplicitate opposita extensitati perfectior et minus perfecta, talis forma habet latitudinem graduum, et per consequens est saltem[m] a Deo successive
T 27va producibilis ; | sed sic est de dilectione eiusdem speciei, nam potest esse quod Linus et Petrus in eadem specie dilectionis fruitivae inaequaliter praemientur ; igitur.

(n) per idem] *om. MST* || (o) vera] bona *MST* ; *s.l. V* || (p) sit] sic *V* || (q) falsum est] *tr. S* || (r) immediate] immediato *MT* || (s) est] quasi *add. MST* || (t) septimi] ubi *S* || (u) sed] et *V* || (v) quia] *om. V* || (w) eo ipso] *tr. M* || (x) ante partem] *om. per hom. MST* || (y) et – instanti] *om. MST* ; *mg. V* || (z) cum igitur] *tr. V* || (a) primo] *om. MST* ; *s.l. V* || (b) || (b) quod] quia *M* || (c) secunda conclusio] *mg. MSTV* ; secunda conclusio quod si voluntas in hoc instanti non causat dilectionem et (*om. S*) immediate post hoc debeat causare illa causabitur successive **d** *mg. infra MS* || (d) iam praedicta] illa praedicta *M* ; illa probata *V* || (e) non – dilectionem] non esset *a.c. mg. MV, T* ; primo esset *S* || (f) tertia conclusio] *mg. MSTV* ; tertia conclusio quod dilectio potest creari (causari *M*) successive **e** *add. mg. infra MS* || (g) cum partes] tamen praecise *MT* ; cum praecise *a.c. V* ; haec* premissae *p.c. mg. V* || (h) tertia conclusio] *tr. MT* || (i) intensibilis – etc.] *mg. (hom.) M* || (j) idem] illud *V* || (k) diligit] diliget *S* || (l) potest] *om. V* || (m) est saltem] *om. M*

## QUARTA CONCLUSIO[n]

[34] Iuxta hanc[o] tertiam conclusionem pono quartam, quod dilectio est ab angelo vel ab anima causabilis successive.

[35] Hanc probo, quia angelus vel[p] anima non causat dilectionem nisi mediante[q] cognitione obiecti diligibilis[r] tamquam concausa cum ipsa voluntate, ex quaestione septima huius primae distinctionis[s] [1]; perfectior autem causa perfectius potest[t] agere; sed cognitio angelica vel[u] animae intendi potest; igitur et[v] effectus eius, scilicet dilectio[w]. Assumptum de cognitione[x] ex hoc patet quia obiectum potest perfectius et imperfectius[y], proportionabilius et minus proportionabiliter approximari potentiae cognitivae angeli, et per consequens magis[z] et minus perfecte immutare potentiam.

[36] Praeterea, non contingit dare maximam distantiam a qua obiectum aliquod potest immutare potentiam angeli cognitivam, tum quia remotius posset immutare ad cognitionem imperfectiorem; tum quia aliter esset dare ultimum instans rei permanentis in esse, ita quod nec ipsa nec aliquid eius remaneret post, et tunc instans[a] instanti immediatum. Consequentia patet, quia per motum localem inchoandum[b] ab illa distantia maxima[c] qua poneretur immutare potentiam posset magis[d] amoveri a potentia illa, et per consequens instans inchoationis motus esset ultimum instans[e] immutationis potentiae cognitivae[f]. Patet igitur assumptum quod non contingit dare distantiam maximam a qua obiectum possit immutare potentiam cognitivam angeli[g]. Igitur, cum tantum possit distare a tali potentia quod movere eam non possit per se a tali distantia[h], sequitur quod oportebit[i] esse distantiam aliquam minimam a qua non possit movere potentiam ceteris paribus, et per consequens in omni[j] | distantia propinquiori poterit. Et si hoc, igitur poterit **M 32va** dari ultimum instans[k] in quo non immutabit potentiam. Sed hoc esse non | poterit **V 52v** nisi immediate post illud instans successive causaret cognitionem in potentia secundum successivam approximationem obiecti versus | potentiam, et non simul, **S 38vb** sicut nec simul fit propinquius. Igitur aliqua cognitio potest successive causari immediate post instans in quo nec ipsa nec aliquid eius erat. Igitur et[l] volitio, quia amor respectu obiecti naturaliter convenientis et placibilis[m] mere naturaliter causatur, si obiectum eius apprehendatur apprehensione tantum simplici sine

(n) quarta conclusio] *mg. MSTV* ; quarta quod hoc potest facere anima vel angelus **f** *add. mg. infra MS* || (o) hanc] *om. T* || (p) vel] et *S* || (q) mediante] *mg. MSV* ; *om. T* || (r) diligibilis] *s.l. M* ; *p.c. S* ; *om. T* || (s) quaestione – distinctionis] quaestione septima primae distinctionis huius *a.c. S* ; praecedenti proxima quaestione *p.c. mg. S* || huius primae] *tr. V* || (t) perfectius potest] *tr. MT* || (u) vel] et *S* || (v) et] *om. MST* ; *s.l. V* || (w) dilectio] quod cognitio et visio fiunt successive et quod non est dare maximam distantiam per quam obiectum possit immutare potentiam sed bene minimam in qua non **g** *add. mg. infra MS* || (x) cognitione] dilectione *MT* || (y) et imperfectius] *om. MT* ; *mg. S* || (z) magis] maius *MST* || (a) instans] sicut *M* || (b) inchoandum] inchoantem *S* || (c) distantia maxima] iuxta *M* ; maxima *V* || (d) magis] maius *S* || (e) instans] *om. M* || (f) cognitivae] sensitivae *MST* || (g) angeli] *om. MST* ; *s.l. V* || (h) a – distantia] *om. MST* ; *mg. V* || (i) oportebit] patebit *M* || (j) omni] esse *M* || (k) instans] *om. V* || (l) et] *om. S* ; etc. *a.c. V* || (m) convenientis – placibilis] cognitі (et *add. M*) *MST*

1. ADAM WODEHAM, *Ordinatio Oxoniensis*, I, d. 1, q. 7, a. 1, concl. 2.

omni deliberatione seu compositione et divisione. Posita enim causa mere naturali et sufficienti et non existente impedimento, ponitur effectus in passo disposito, et hoc simul vel successive proportionabiliter et correspondenter productioni successivae[n].

[37] Praeterea, visio corporalis potest causari et etiam corrumpi sive cessare esse[o] successive, igitur et cognitio angelica. Assumptum patet, quia quando aliquod visibile in distantia summe[p] proportionali applicatur[q] visui, causat in ipso visionem perfectissimam quam potest. Volo igitur quod per motum localem magis distent[r], utpote quod plus removeatur obiectum a visu, ceteris paribus. Quaero igitur, quando visibile sic recedit a visu, an aliquid[s] praecedentis visionis deperdatur. Et habetur intentum, quia[t] pari ratione aliquando[u] per accessum obiecti versus potentiam intendetur[v] visio. Si non, sed semper remanet eadem visio aeque perfecta sine alicuius partis deperditione, sequitur quod semper rem aliquam in omni distantia qua videret eam aeque perfecte videret, quod est contra experientiam. Et consequentia patet, quia visionem informare visum est visum videre, igitur etc.

[38] Praeterea, sit[w] aliquod corpus continue motum iuxta aliquod corpus perforatum interpositum visui et tali visibili moto[x]. Tunc in tali visu humano reciperetur continue alia et alia visio secundum totum vel secundum partem, quia continue offeretur sibi alia et alia[y] pars obiecti. Si secundum totum alia[z], igitur erit dare ultimum rei permanentis in esse, quae tamen simul et non particulariter desineret esse, contra prius[1] declarata, eo quod tunc[a] esset instans instanti immediatum pro eo quod instantanee cessaret esse, quia simul; et non in instanti in quo est; igitur in alio. Et non in alio mediato, quia tunc maneret per tempus eadem visio, cum tamen nihil idem per tempus aliquod obiciatur directe visui sine obstaculo interposito, per casum. Consequens falsum, quia de parte qualibet inter quam et visum obstaculum interponitur per inde est[b] quoad causationem visionis ac[c] si non esset et posset poni et etiam continue destrui[d] per partes illas, sicut pertranseunt huiusmodi foramen[e]. Si tantum alia secundum partem, igitur visio illa habet partem et partem. Et non secundum extensionem, quia visio hominis non est[f] res extensa, sicut nec anima humana in qua recipitur. Igitur secundum intensionem, licet correspondentem partibilitati extensivae[g] obiecti alias modo alias declarato[h]. Igitur, sicut supra[i] [2], cum amor vel appetitio necessario sequens[j]

(n) successivae] *a.c. S* ; suae causae *p.c. mg. S* || (o) sive – esse] *mg. MV* ; *om. ST* || (p) summe] *om. MST* ; *mg. V* || (q) applicatur] approprinquatur *MT* || (r) distent] distet *MT* || (s) aliquid] aliquod *S* || (t) quia] et *MST* ; *s.l. V* || (u) aliquando] *post* potentiam *MT* || (v) intendetur] intenderetur *MST* || (w) sit] si *T* || (x) moto] mota *MT* || (y) alia – alia] aliqua et aliqua *M* (*def. T*) || (z) secundum totum vel – alia] *om. hom. T* || (a) tunc] *om. MST* || (b) per inde est] parum de est (deest *M* ; deesse *T*) *MST* ; vel per inde *s.l. S* || (c) ac] sic *MT* || (d) destrui] distrahi *MT* ; distrui *a.c. S* || (e) foramen] formam *M* ; quod visio non est res extensa **h** *add. mg. infra MS* || (f) est] haec *add. MST* || (g) extensivae] modo extensive *MT* ; per modum extensionis *S* || (h) modo – declarato] alias declaratae *MST* || (i) supra] *om. MT* ; *mg. S* || (j) necessario sequens] *tr. T*

1. *Supra*, 6-7.
2. *Supra*, 36.

modo praeexposito[k] simul fiant[l] cum factione cognitionis illius, sequitur quod partialiter tantum fieret[m] et destrueretur[n] etiam sicut ipsa visio.

[39] Praeterea, ponatur quod huiusmodi qualitas visibilis continue in sua specie intendatur vel remittatur, ceteris paribus. Hoc posito, ipsa etiam visio proportionabiliter intendetur[o] vel remittetur. Aliter enim sequitur vel quod videbitur ibi naturaliter, quod non est, si detur quod continue manet praecise eadem visio ; vel quod erit semper[p] continue alia et alia, et tunc vel continue in quolibet alio et alio instanti[q] totaliter alia[r] visio quam prius, et hoc improbatur sicut in argumento proximo praecedenti[1], vel solum alia particulariter, et tunc sequitur propositum sicut prius.

*<Contra conclusiones tertiam et quartam[s]>*

[40→31+34] Sed contra illas duas conclusiones ultimas[t] arguitur per aliquos tenentes[u] quod actus diligendi sit indivisibilis simpliciter carens partibus, quia aliter actus diligendi Deum esset imperfectior actu diligendi muscam. Consequens absurdum. Consequentia probatur, quia ex quo dilectio Dei habet partes et est per consequens in infinitum divisibilis in remissius et remissius, igitur in dilectione Dei[v] reperitur vel saltem in ipsa continetur aliqua pars ipsius quae est perfectior[w] actu diligendi muscam, et aliqua forte aequalis[x], et aliqua[y] forte minor ista et imperfectior[z]. Igitur, cum quaelibet pars dilectionis sit dilectio, sequitur propositum.

[41] **(2)** Sequitur etiam secundo, si dilectio Dei posset intendi et remitti, quod unus modicus foetor[a] actu diligendi Deum esset perfectior, simili deductione sicut prius.

[42] **(3)** Praeterea, simul et semel diligeret quis idem obiectum perfecte et imperfecte[b], quia toto actu perfecte et parte actus imperfecte[c]. Beata etiam Virgo et anima Christi[d] ita imperfecte diligerent[e] Deum sicut ego[f].

[43] **(4)** Praeterea, extensio potest fieri sine nova realitate[g], igitur et intensio. Et hoc confirmatur per Commentatorem, | IV[h] *Physicorum*[2], ubi vult quod aliquid **S 39ra**

(k) praeexposito] ipsam visionem *add. mg. S* || (l) fiant] sint *MT* || (m) tantum fieret] fiet tantum *MT* ; tantum fiet *S* || (n) destrueretur] destruetur *MST* || (o) intendetur] intenditur *MST* || (p) erit semper] fit *MST* || (q) instanti] est *add. S* || (r) totaliter alia] *tr. MT* || (s) quartam] arguitur quod visio sit indivisibilis et etiam dilectio, et per consequens quod fiant (fiat *M*) in instanti **j** *add. mg. MS* (*infra S*) ; contra 2 conclusiones *add. mg. T* ; contra istas duas conclusiones ultimas *add. mg. V* || (t) ultimas] *om. MST* || (u) tenentes] hoc pro conclusione *add. mg. S* || (v) dei] erit *add. S* || (w) perfectior *coni.*] imperfectior *MTV* ; fortior *S* || (x) et aliqua – aequalis] *om. MT* ; *mg. V* (*vide infra S*) || (y) forte – aliqua] *mg. S* ; forte *add. MST, a.c. V* || (z) ista – imperfectior] et imperfectior ipsa *MT* || (a) foetor] *a.c. M* ; fervor *p.c. s.l. M* || (b) diligeret – imperfecte] quis idem obiectum perfecte et imperfecte diligeret *MT* (*vide infra V*) || (c) et imperfecte – imperfecte] *mg. (hom.) V* || (d) et anima christi] *om. MT* || (e) diligerent] diligeret *MT* || (f) ego] eius *a.c. s.l. M* ; unus peccator *S* || (g) realitate] *p.c. M* (+*p.c. P*) ; re aliquando *TV* ; rei acquisitione || (h) iv] vii *MST*

---

1. *Supra*, 37.

2. AVERROES, *Commentum super libro Physicorum*, IV, comm. 84, transl. Michael Scotus, f. 97ra-b : Cologne : Digital Averroes Research Environment : https://dare.uni-koeln.de/app/fulltexts/FT13.

potest fieri calidius quam prius sine additione novae rei, sicut minus curvum potest fieri curvius[i] sine additione novae rei.

T 27vb [44] **(5)** Praeterea, anima Christi est perfectior | quam[j] anima Iudae, et sunt eiusdem speciei, et tamen neutra habet partes, igitur similiter poterit esse in proposito.

[45] **(6)** Praeterea, si habeant partes, accipio duas species in talibus actibus, et quaero an quodlibet individuum unius illarum specierum sit perfectius quolibet alterius vel non. Si sic, tunc sequitur quod quodlibet individuum speciei perfectioris[k] sit infinitum[l], quia tunc[m] habebit infinitas[n] partes quarum quaelibet valet infinita individua[o] speciei inferioris essentialia[p]. Si non, hoc[q] est contra Philosophum dicentem quod « species sunt sicut numeri »[1].

[46] **(7)** Praeterea, si sic, ponatur tunc[r] quod aliquis[s] actus intendatur per additionem unius gradus suae speciei, et post per medietatem unius gradus, et consequenter in infinitum per partes proportionales sic procedendo. Si[t] sic fieri valeat, aeque rationabiliter poterit poni simile[u] de speciebus quod[v] cuilibet V 53r augmentationi sic factae | corresponderet unum individuum unius speciei quod M 32vb esset praecise tantae perfectionis | sicut illud individuum sic augmentatum, et per consequens infra quascumque duas species possent[w] esse species infinitae.

[47] **(8)** Praeterea, ex hoc solo quod partes alicuius continui plus distant quam ante, ceteris paribus, illud quantum est maius[x] quam ante, igitur pari ratione ex hoc solo quod eodem actu possum[y] una vice perfectius cognoscere obiectum aliquod quam alias, poterit actus ille dici cognitio perfectior quam ante sine aliqua partium additione.

[48] **(9)** Praeterea, tunc intensio[z] respectu Sortis posset augeri per intensionem respectu Platonis, quia sunt eiusdem speciei et in eodem subiecto.

[49] Alia etiam multa ad hoc adducuntur quae apud me colorem[a] non habent.

### <*Responsio ad rationes contra tertiam et quartam conclusiones*[b]>

[50→40] Sed his non obstantibus, teneo illud[c] quod prius. Et nego primum assumptum in contrarium, quia dicendum est quod omnis actus dilectionis creatae[d] est divisibilis et habet partes. Et cum probatur quod non, quia tunc

(i) curvius] magis curvum *MT* || (j) quam] *om. S* || (k) perfectioris] imperfectioris *MT*, *a.c. S* || (l) infinitum] in infinitum perfectius *S* || (m) tunc] tamen *MT* || (n) habebit infinitas] *tr. T* || (o) infinita individua] *tr. T* || (p) inferioris essentialia] imperfectioris aequalia *MST* || (q) hoc] *om. MT* ; *s.l. V* || (r) tunc] sequitur *add. S* || (s) aliquis] quilibet *MT*, *a.c. mg. S* || (t) si] *om. M* || (u) poni simile] *tr. V* || (v) quod] quia *MV* || (w) possent] possunt *MST* || (x) maius] magnus *MT* || (y) possum] posset *MST* || (z) intensio] intellectus *MT* || (a) colorem] calorem *M* || (b) conclusiones] conceditur quod actus diligendi muscam aliquo actu diligendi deum potest esse perfectior **k** et quomodo comparativus gradus confundit terminum sequentem *add. mg. infra S* || (c) illud] id *T* || (d) creatae] datae *S*

1. E.g., Thomas Aquinas, *Summa theologiae*, I II[ae], q. 50, a. 2, ad 1 : « [...] species rerum sunt sicut numeri, qui differunt per additionem et subtractionem unitatis, ut dicitur in VIII *Metaphysicae* » ; Iohannes Duns Scotus, *In octo libros Physicorum Aristotelis*, IV, q. 18 : « [...] de qua habetur IV *Metaphysicae* quod species sunt sicut numeri » ; cf. Aristoteles, *Metaphysica*, VIII, c. 3 : 1043b35-1044a10.

actus diligendi Deum etc., potest dupliciter dici ad rem et praeter[e] hoc aliter[f] ad hominem. Primo modo, sicut prius[g] habitum est[1], quod aliquis actus dilectionis respectu[h] Dei est imperfectior hoc[i] actu respectu[j] alterius etc.[k] bonitate intrinseca[l] secundum quantitatem perfectionis actus, licet secundum qualitatem posset dici perfectior ipso pro quanto natura actus diligendi Deum minus qualitative recedit a divina perfectione et similior est Deo quam actus diligendi aliud a Deo – similior, inquam, secundum qualitatem perfectionis intrinsecae, non secundum quantitatem, vel[m] quod[n] pro eodem habeo « similior »[o] qualitative, non quantitative.

[51] Aliter potest dici, illo tamen ultimo praesupposito, quod consequentia ultima[p] nihil[q] valet, quia comparativus gradus proprie sumptus facit ablativum casum[r] sequentem stare confuse et distributive. Confundit enim obliquum[s] sequentem, sicut facit « quam » vel sicut[t] negatio[u], per quorum alterum haberet exponi. Aliter[v] enim vere posset dici quod canis modicus esset fortior leone isto[w] statim morituro[x] qui perdidit quasi omnes vires suas, et tamen hoc non conceditur[y]. Et propter hoc non deberet concedi quod actus diligendi Deum sit imperfectior actu diligendi muscam nisi esset imperfectior[z] hoc actu diligendi muscam[a], et illo actu, et sic de singulis[b], ita quod nullus actus diligendi muscam nec aliqua pars talis actus[c] esset ita imperfectus[d] sicut actus diligendi Deum datus, de quo fiebat sermo. Implicat igitur argumentum fallaciam consequentis.

[52] Ad hominem iterum[e] responderi[f] potest quod, si illa deductio arguitiva daretur, aeque esset contra arguentes, quia ipsi concedunt quod, et oportet[g], quod scilicet[h] perfectius et imperfectius[i] cognoscitur idem obiectum[j] diversis temporibus ab eadem potentia. Si[k] diversis actibus quando obiectum aliter et aliter approximatur potentiae, contra hoc[l] procedunt argumenta pro quarta conclusione facta. Si eodem actu, sicut isti concedunt, igitur omnino idem actus potest esse cognitio nunc perfectior, nunc[m] minus perfecta continue et successive. Igitur licet non dent quod actus diligendi Deum sit entitas[n] imperfectior hoc[o] actu diligendi muscam, oportet tamen quod dent quod actus diligendi Deum sic poterit esse[p] imperfectior[q] cognitio. Vel secundum alium modum loquendi, poterit esse entitas qua[r] imperfectius potentia cognoscat Deum quam | alio dato **S 39rb**

(e) praeter] praeterea *M* || (f) aliter] *om. MT* || (g) prius] *om. T* || (h) dilectionis respectu] *tr. MT* ; dilectionis *S* || (i) hoc] *om. MST* ; *s.l. V* || (j) respectu] dilectionis *add. MT* ; *om. S* || (k) etc.] cum *s.l. M* ; *p.c. S* ; *om. T* ; etiam *add. MT* || (l) intrinseca] increata *S* || (m) vel] et *S* || (n) quod] *om. MST* || (o) similior] simile *MT* ; *p.c. SV* || (p) ultima] illa *V* || (q) nihil] non *MT* || (r) casum] gradum *T* || (s) obliquum] oblius *M* ; oblitum *ST* || (t) sicut] *om. M* ; vel *add. V* || (u) nego] vel negatio *V* || (v) aliter] aut *MT* || (w) fortior – isto] perfectior leone cum (tamen *S*) fortior sit illo leone *MST* || (x) morituro] moritris *M* || (y) conceditur] concedam *S* || (z) imperfectior] perfectior *a.c. V* (*def. MST*) || (a) nisi – muscam] *om. hom. MST* || (b) singulis] similibus *T* || (c) actus] *om. MST* || (d) imperfectus] perfectus *MST* ; actus *add. S* || (e) iterum] tamen *MT, a.c. S* ; etiam *p.c. S* || (f) responderi] redditur *V* || (g) et oportet] et valet *a.c. M* ; oportet *p.c. s.l. M* ; etiam valet *S* ; et patet *T* || (h) quod scilicet] scilicet quod *M* ; secundum quod *T* || (i) perfectius – imperfectius] *tr. MT* || (j) idem obiectum] *tr. MT* || (k) si] sive *MT* || (l) contra hoc] *mg. M* ; *om. TV* || (m) nunc – nunc] modo perfectior modo *S* || (n) entitas] *om. M* || (o) hoc] *om. MST* || (p) poterit esse] sit *T* (*def. M*) || (q) actu diligenti – imperfectior] *om. hom. M* || (r) qua] quo *V*

1. *Supra*, 40.

actu cognoscat muscam, vel quod actus ille possit[s] simul esse et tamen[t] non esse cognitio, quorum utrumque[u] falsum et alias improbandum et similiter superius improbatum[v]. Et praeter hoc primum istorum illatorum ita apud vulgus reputaretur absurdum sicut illud ad quod ipsi per suam iam[w] dictam responsionem adducunt[x].

[53→41] Ad secundum dicendum est per omnia sicut ad primum. Ratio igitur illa non est magnae virtutis nisi quia ponitur in terminis magnae abhominationis. Mirabile tamen est quod intelligentes nituntur in talibus deducere ad inconvenientia vulgi tantum[y] qualia notum est sciolis quod plurima[z] eorum sunt certissimae et catholicae veritatis[a]. Quid[b] enim faciendum[c] est si[d] talis glorietur[e] respondentem deducere ad hoc inconveniens[f] ut[g] sit Deus in culo asini vel in stercore canis? Numquid[h] per hoc vitando negare debet articulum fidei de divina immensitate ex qua notum est sanctis omnibus Deum verum[i] esse in omnibus locis? Hoc autem ad verecundiam tantum[j] dixerim talium qui[k] pro defectu argumenti efficacis recurrunt ad suffragium sive[l] testimonium laicorum. Praeterea, dato quod esset indivisibilis, idem poterit inferri per intensionem foetoris[m] etc., sicut patet advertenti.

[54→42] Ad tertium dicendum[n] quod illud[o] nititur[p] ubique[q] improbare intensionem et remissionem[r] in formis ita directe sicut in actibus voluntatis. Unde nota quod licet detur[s] quod infertur, tamen non habetur quin anima Christi vel Beatae Virginis perfectius diligat Deum quam ego. Tamen si ly « in » aequivaleat[t] negationi[u], neganda est consequentia facta.

[55→43] Ad quartum respondebitur in materia de augmento formarum[1]. Quaere[v], quia consequentia est neganda.

[56→44] Ad quintum etiam patebit ibidem[2] quod praemissae[w] repugnant si intelligatur prima de perfectione[x] substantiali.

[57→45] Ad sextum etiam dicendum quod non. Et ad Philosophum qualiter intelligat exponetur[y] ibi[3].

[58→46] Ad septimum forte quod infert est verum ad mentem inferentis[z],
**T 28ra** licet non de virtute sermonis, quia | « infinite » de virtute sermonis sumitur ibi categorematice. Concedendum enim est[a] forte quod non tot quin plures possint[b]

(s) possit] posset *MST* || (t) tamen] *om. M* || (u) utrumque] est *add. s.l. M* || (v) superius improbatum] *tr. MST* || (w) per – iam] iam per suam *MT* || (x) adducunt] quomodo irridet illos qui ducunt ad inconvenientiam vulgi I *add. mg. infra S* || (y) tantum] *om. M* || (z) quod plurima] quid plurime *T* || (a) veritatis] veritates *a.c. M*; veritates *TV* || (b) quid] quod *MT* || (c) faciendum] gloriandum *MST* || (d) est si] sit *MT* || (e) glorietur] glorie et *M* || (f) respondentem – inconveniens] *om. MT*; respondentem deducere *S* || (g) ut] et *V* || (h) numquid] inquam *add. MT*; inquit *add. S* || (i) deum verum] *tr. T* || (j) ad – tantum] tantum ad verecundiam *MT* || (k) qui] quod *S* || (l) sive] seu *MT* || (m) foetoris] foetorum *MST* || (n) dicendum] *om. MTV*; *mg. S* || (o) illud] *om. MT*; *s.l. S* || (p) nititur] videtur *MT* || (q) ubique] verbum *MT*, *p.c. mg. S*; verbis *a.c. S* || (r) et remissionem] *om. S* || (s) detur] daretur *MT* || (t) aequivaleat] aequivalet *V* || (u) negationi] negationem *M* || (v) quaere] quare *S* || (w) praemissae] praecise *MT* || (x) perfectione] perfectioritate *S*, *p.c. mg. V*; formalitate *a.c. V* || (y) exponetur] exponam *MT* || (z) inferentis] sumptum *add. V* || (a) enim est] *tr. V* || (b) possint] possunt *V*

---

1. Adam Wodeham, *Ordinatio Oxoniensis*, I, d. 17, q. 5 (*V* 159r).
2. Adam Wodeham, *Ordinatio Oxoniensis*, I, d. 17, q. 5 (*V* 161v-162r).
3. Adam Wodeham, *Ordinatio Oxoniensis*, I, d. 17, q. 5, sed non invenimus.

esse species intermediae, sed ex hoc non sequitur quod inter quascumque sint species infinitae et non tot quin plures.

[59→47] Ad octavum, consequentia est neganda, et causa patebit[c] in eadem materia[1].

[60→48] Ad nonum, non habeo pro inconvenienti quin ex illis duabus intentionibus resultet una | composita[d]. Si tamen simul per distinctas[e] intentiones M 33ra eiusdem speciei intelligatur uterque[f], tamen ex hoc[g] non sequitur quod Sortes perfectius intelligitur[h] quam si sola pars illa[i] esset qua Sortes intelligitur.

## QUINTA CONCLUSIO[j]

[61] Quinta conclusio est directe ad quaesitum : quod voluntas potest simul ac subito causare volitionem meritoriam.

[62] Et hoc sufficienter suadetur[k] per hoc quod[l] ubi nec est formalis nec virtualis repugnantia vel contrarietas[m] in passivo causa sufficienter approximata subito agit. Quid enim esset causa successionis ? Sic est | in proposito etc. V 53v

[63] **(2)** Item, intellectus subito producit actum aliquem vel producere posset quantum est ex parte sui, igitur et voluntas. Antecedens probatur, quia saltem primo actui intellectus nihil est contrarium in intellectu, quoniam[n] non habitus, nec passio, nec aliquid simile[o], vel saltem non oportet quod sit, igitur[p] non oportet quod ibi sit[q] resistentia aliqua intrinseca, nec oportet quod extrinseca ; igitur subito aget. Consequentia patet per processum Philosophi et Commentatoris, IV *Physicorum*, capitulo de vacuo, commento 71[2].

[64] **(3)** Et praeterea per rationem, quia si nulla[r] existente resistentia, nec intra[s] nec extra, non[t] posset agere subito, sed necessario oporteret quod in tempore, igitur eodem modo aliquod[u] agens naturale, puta lumen vel calor, in receptivo in quo nulla adesset[v] resistentia, ageret[w] in[x] tempore necessario, igitur. Tamen quia[y] quando agens habens resistentiam producit in certo tempore[z], agens in duplo fortius agit[a] in duplo minori tempore productive, et sic semper proportionabiliter, secundum contrarium opinantes propositae conclusionis[b], sequitur quod habens resistentiam et non habens agerent[c] aequales effectus in aequalibus temporibus, etiam forsitan ceteris paribus ; consequens falsum, ergo etc.[d]

(c) patebit] dabitur *S* || (d) composita] componere *M* || (e) distinctas] *om. T* || (f) uterque] utrumque *MST* || (g) ex hoc] *om. V* || (h) intelligatur] intelligitur *S* || (i) pars illa] illa *a.c. V* ; *tr. p.c. s.l. V* || (j) quinta conclusio] *mg. MSTV* ; quinta conclusio quod voluntas potest subito producere actum suum **m** *add. mg. infra MS* (*M* 32vb) || (k) suadetur] suadere *V* || (l) quod] quia *T* || (m) vel contrarietas] *om. V* || (n) quoniam] quin *M, a.c. S* ; quia *T* || (o) simile] scibile *M* || (p) non – igitur] *mg. M* ; *om. ST* || (q) ibi sit] *tr. MST* || (r) si nulla] si media nulla *a.c. s.l. M* ; *p.c. S* ; si intra nulla *T* || (s) nec intra] in intelligendo *add. mg. M, ST, a.c. V* ; *om. p.c. V* || (t) non] *s.l. MV* || (u) aliquod] ad *V* || (v) adesset] esset *TV* || (w) ageret] esset *a.c. M, a.c. mg. S, T* ; agent *p.c. s.l. M* || (x) in] non *add. S* || (y) quia] om. *TV* || (z) certo tempore] *tr. MST* || (a) in – agit] *mg. V* || (b) conclusionis] *p.c. s.l. M* ; conclusiones *a.c. V* || (c) agerent] ageret *M* || (d) consequens – etc.] *mg. MV* ; *om. ST*

1. ADAM WODEHAM, *Ordinatio Oxoniensis*, I, d. 17, q. 5, sed non invenimus.
2. AVERROES, *Commentum super libro Physicorum*, IV, comm. 71, transl. Michael Scotus, f. 90rb-92va.

[65] **(4)** Praeterea, ex eodem medio potest argui in tali forma quod voluntas possit subito causare actum suum[e] quando omnia requisita concurrunt et nullum impedimentum adest, quia successio in causatione non requiritur nisi vel
S 39va propter indispositionem passi[f] | per[g] contrarietatem formalem vel virtualem cum limitatione seu[h] finitate activi principii ; vel[i] secundo propter insufficientiam agentis continue existentis in augeri in casu ubi non esset primum impedimentum ; vel tertio propter continuam approximationem activi ad passum[j], vel econverso ubi nimis erant prius ab invicem remota ad perfectum effectum causandum ; vel quarto in casu[k] ubi esset impedimentum propter successivam amotionem impedimenti vel propter aliquid aliud aequipollens. Sed haec omnia, ut videtur, tolli possunt in causatione meritoriae dilectionis a voluntate ; igitur etc.[l]

[66] **(5)** Praeterea, ad idem[m] potest argui sic per Commentatorem, III[n] *De anima*, commento 28[1], et textus concordat : intellectio et sensatio est actio perfecta et fit in instanti, nec praecedit illam actio aliqua diminuta[o]. Igitur eadem ratione voluntas poterit subito causare actum suum, cum voluntas ita sit prompte activa respectu volitionis[p] sicut intellectus respectu intellectionis, nec maior obstet[q] resistentia de volitione subito causanda quam de intellectione.

### <*Opinio FitzRalph*[r]>

[67→66] Nec valet dicere, ut videtur, sicut dicit[s] Firauf[t] [2], quod hoc dicit Philosophus et Commentator quia[u] licet sensatio vel[v] intellectio vel volitio successive producantur et intendantur, tamen dicuntur perfici in instanti, quia Philosophus et Commentator in productione tali[w] negant talem successivam generationem quae perficiatur in termino huius actionis, dicentes quod illam causationem[x] non praecedit aliqua[y] actio diminuta.

[68→67] Contra[z], illo modo aequaliter dicere haberent de omni forma[a] per alterationem acquisita[b]. Constat enim quod in instanti quolibet est talis forma perfectior forma praehabita.

(e) causare – suum] actum suum causare (*s.l.*) *M* ; actum suum *T* || (f) passi] et *add. M* ; vel *add. S* || (g) per] propter *S* || (h) seu] vel *MT* || (i) vel] et *MST* || (j) ad passum] et passivi *MST*, *a.c. V* || (k) ubi – casu] vel quarto *MST* || (l) etc.] de illa auctoritate philosophi et commentatoris quod intellectio sit in instanti **n** *add. mg. infra MS* (*M* 32vb) || (m) idem] illud *V* || (n) iii] vii *M* || (o) diminuta] distincta *MT* || (p) volitionis] dilectionis *a.c. M* ; dilectionis *T* || (q) obstet] obstat *T* || (r) fitzralph] sir'f *mg. S* ; opinio hibernicus *mg. T* ; hyber *mg. V* || (s) dicit] dicitur *V* || (t) firauf] stranf' *S* ; fire[a] *V* || (u) quia] quod *S* || (v) vel] et *MST* || (w) tali] *s.l. et i.l. M* || (x) causationem] actionem *a.c. T* || (y) aliqua] *inter l. M* ; *om. ST* || (z) contra] praeterea *MT* || (a) omni forma] *tr. V* || (b) acquisita] quia *add. S* ; quod *add. sed del. V*

---

1. Averroes, *Commentarium magnum in Aristotelis De anima libros*, III, comm. 28, transl. Michael Scotus, ed. F. S. Crawford (Corpus Commentariorum Averrois in Aristotelem 6.1), Cambridge, MA, 1953, p. 467.48-57.

2. Riccardus FitzRalph, *Lectura in Sententias*, I, q. 10, a. 2, Paris, Bibliothèque nationale de France, lat. 15853, f. 66rb-va.

[69→68] Sed hic dat[c] duplicem evasionem[1], unam quod non dicuntur perfectae in suis speciebus donec pertingant ad certam quantitatem ad quam in primo[d] instanti pertingunt[e]. Secundam[f] quod non dicuntur perfectae quando « coniunguntur cum motu vel transmutatione aliqua corporis vel animae, sed magis perficiuntur per quietem animae ab[g] omnimoda transmutatione, sicut[h] patet per Philosophum et Commentatorem, VII *Physicorum*, parte 10[2], econtrario cuilibet verae alterationi quae non dicitur esse perfecta[i] in sua specie in aliquo instanti in quo subiectum eius quiescit, quia tunc ipsa alteratio non est. Et hoc », ut dicit ille, « est ratio Philosophi, X *Ethicorum*, capitulo 4[3], ad declarandum quod delectatio[j] non est vera[k] generatio nec verus motus, sicut nec visio[l], quia delectatio[m] est perfecta in instanti, sicut et visio. Simili etiam modo, ut dicit[n], loquitur Philosophus et Commentator, VII *Physicorum*, commento 10[4], probantes[o] quod in virtutibus moralibus non est motus, quia non sunt virtutes nisi[p] perfectiones et consistunt in indivisibili, quia esse[q] perfectum virtute consistit[r] in quiete et in indivisibili et[s] ad illum gradum indivisibilitatis[t] attingunt[u], id est[v] in instanti. Hoc igitur modo loquitur Commentator et Philosophus[w] cum dicunt ubi prius quod intentio est actio perfecta et fit[x] in non-tempore nec eam praecedit actio diminuta[y], et eodem modo volitio[z]. Hoc est quod sunt perfectae in suis speciebus in instanti. Nec tunc requirunt actionem successivam immediate[a] praecedentem, sed sunt in perfecta quiete animae et corporis, et tunc maxime sunt perfectae ». Haec iste[b].

### *<Contra opinionem FitzRalph[c]>*

[70→69] Sed pro certo hic est color[d] quaesitus sine[e] re. Primo, quia aliud est qualitatem aliquam esse in sua absoluta specie in genere qualitatis et aliud[f] eam esse[g] in specie virtutis relativa vel[h] scientiae vel huiusmodi, sicut aliud est quantitatem aliquam esse in[i] absoluta specie quantitatis vel naturae et

(c) dat] dant *S* ; ponit *V* || (d) in primo] *tr. V* (*def. S*) || (e) unam – pertingunt] *mg. (hom.) M* ; *om. hom. S* || (f) secundam] unam *MS* ; aliam *V* || (g) ab] ad *T* || (h) omnimoda – sicut] omni motu transmutatione sed *V* || (i) quae – perfecta] *mg. V* || (j) delectatio] delectio *MST* || (k) vera] instantia *a.c. M* ; instantanea *T* || (l) visio] vino *M* || (m) delectatio] delectio *S* || (n) dicit] etiam *add. MST* || (o) probantes] probando *MT* || (p) non – nisi] non sunt virtute ante *a.c. M* ; virtutes sunt *p.c. mg. M* ; virtutes sunt *V* || (q) esse] omne *MST, a.c. V* || (r) virtute consistit] virtutum consistunt *V* || (s) in – et] *om. V* || et] *s.l. M* || (t) indivisibilitatis] indivisibiliter *MT* || (u) attingunt] attinguntur *T* || (v) primo] primo *S* ; *om. T* || (w) commentator et philosophus] *tr. V* || (x) fit] sit *MT* ; *p.c. V* || (y) nec – diminuta] etc. *MST, a.c. mg. V* || (z) volitio] est *add. MT, a.c. V* ; volitiones *S* || (a) immediate] in mediate *S* || (b) haec iste] *om. MST* ; *mg. V* || (c) fitzralph] contra sir'f *add. mg. S* ; contra opinionem *add. mg. T* ; contra *add. mg. V* || (d) color] calor *M* || (e) sine] illo *add. s.l. M* || (f) aliud] ad *a.c. mg. M, a.c. s.l. V* || (g) esse] *om. S* || (h) vel] et *M* || (i) in] sua *add. MT*

1. RICCARDUS FITZRALPH, *Lectura in Sententias*, I, q. 10, a. 2, Paris 15853, f. 66rb-va.

2. AVERROES, *Commentum super libro Physicorum*, VII, comm. 18, transl. Michael Scotus, f. 175ra.

3. ARISTOTELES, *Ethica Nicomachea*, X, c. 4 : 1174b10, recensio pura, ed. R.-A. Gauthier (AL XXVI. 1-3), Turnhout 1973, p. 570.3-9.

4. AVERROES, *Commentum super libro Physicorum*, VII, comm. 18, transl. Michael Scotus, f. 175ra-b.

aliud[j] eam esse in specie figurae vel[k] aequalitatis et[l] huiusmodi[m]. Exemplum :
facto circino cuius pes mobilis[n] sit argenteus et fixus undecumque, licet[o] si
M 33rb circinetur circulus[p] in tabula receptiva | argenteae lineae a puncto inceptionis[q]
statim causet[r] arcum[s] vel lineam[t] successive per partem post partem continue, et[u]
in instanti quolibet imperfectae circinationis[v] verum sit dicere « Linea ac[w] arcus
causatus est » quoad absolutam speciem quantitatis, in solo tamen illo[x] instanti
quo pertinget[y] pes circini[z] motus ad punctum a quo[a] incepit est circulus causatus,
nam nulla praehabita arcuatio[b] circulus est.

T 28rb [71] Similiter in proposito de re absoluta[c] secundum se | et in ordine ad
aliud. Igitur non est idem formam aliquam[d] indivisibiliter fieri secundum esse[e]
absolutum naturae suae et secundum esse relativum quo vere possit dici tale
vel[f] tale relative vel connotative[g]. Sed fieri virtuosum[h] non est praecise fieri[i]
S 39vb sub forma talis | speciei absolutae, sed sub forma et[j] tali[k] gradu, cum virtus
consistat in medio et sine[l] rebellitione passionis inclinativae ad excessum, propter
quod incontinens, licet bene eligat, tamen sua electio non vocatur a Philosopho
« virtus » sicut electio[m] temperati.

[72] Similiter est de virtute[n] sicut de sanitate vel pulchritudine quoad hoc
ex VII *Physicorum*[1]. Unde sicut illud idem quod, aliis sublatis[o] esset sanitas vel
purchritudo, non est sanitas[p] si simul concurrat alius superfluus humor tollens
debitam proportionem humorum, nec est pulchritudo concurrente alio deformante
V 54r vel proportionem ad pulchritudinem requisitam | turbante, ita illa eadem res quae
esset electio virtuosa, cessante passione per sedationem perfectam[q], iam non est
virtuosa si stet deordinata passio adhuc sedanda, secundum modum loquendi
Philosophi. Fieri vero intelligens vel volens est[r] fieri aliquale secundum naturam
absolutam illius qualitatis quae est intellectio vel volitio in quocumque gradu
fuerit parvo vel magno, sicut et fieri album est albedinem habere secundum
absolutam naturam[s] albedinis, absque aliqua determinatione ad gradum albedinis
hunc vel illum[t]. Igitur factio[u] intellectionis vel volitionis in eo quod intellectio
est vel volitio non plus fit[v] indivisibiliter[w], nisi fiat instantanee, quam albedo vel

(j) aliud] ad *a.c. s.l. MV* || (k) vel] et *S*, *a.c. s.l. V* || (l) et] vel *MT* || (m) huiusmodi] quod non est idem aliquid fieri secundum esse absolutum et secundum esse respectivum o et quomodo illud idem quod est sanitas sit aegritudo quibusdam additis *add. mg. infra MS* || (n) facto – mobilis] facto est ne cuius res mobilius *a.c. mg. V* || (o) licet] *om. S* || (p) circulus] angelus *a.c. i.l. M* ; angelus *T* || (q) inceptionis] receptionis *a.c. M*, receptionis *T* || (r) causet] esset *ST* || (s) arcum] arcus *a.c. s.l. M*, *ST* ; *p.c. V* || (t) lineam] linea *ST* || (u) et] *om. MST* || (v) circinationis] *p.c. mg. M* ; circulationis licet *S* || (w) ac] aut *S* || (x) illo] *s.l. M* ; *om. T* || (y) pertinget] pertingit *MST*, *a.c. V* || (z) circini] termini *a.c. S* ; *p.c. V* || (a) a quo] unde *S* ; *p.c. V* || (b) praehabita arcuatio] *tr. MT* || (c) absoluta] absolute *V* || (d) aliquam] quam *T* || (e) esse] eum *a.c. S* ; *p.c. V* || (f) vel] et *M* || (g) relative – connotative] vel te vel connotativa *a.c. mg. V* || (h) virtuosum] virtuosus *V* || (i) praecise fieri] *tr. MT* || (j) et] in *a.c. V* ; tali in *p.c. mg. V* || (k) tali] de *M* ; *om. T* || (l) medio et sine] *om. M* || (m) electio] *om. MST* ; *mg. V* || (n) virtute] virtuoso *MS* ; veritate *T* || (o) sublatis] ablatis *V* || (p) vel – sanitas] *mg. V* || (q) perfectam] per *M* || (r) est] et *MT* || (s) absolutam naturam] *tr. T* || (t) absque – illum] *om. MST* ; *mg. V* || (u) igitur factio] licet *MT* || (v) fit] sit *T* || (w) indivisibiliter] indivisibile *M*

1. ARISTOTELES, *Physica*, VII, c. 3 : 246a30-b25, ed. Bossier et Brams (AL VII. 1.2), p. 266.1-11.

quaevis[x] alia forma quae per alterationem acquiritur successive, licet in casu aliqua[y] cognitio successive[z] causata fiat indivisibiliter scientia, id est, vera notitia, et alia volitio vel electio particulariter facta subito fiat virtus.

[73] Praeterea, licet, tenendo viam illam quae ponit eandem rem continue manentem in potentia intellectiva secundum naturam absolutae qualitatis nunc esse intellectionem et[a] nunc non esse intellectionem[b], diceretur rationabiliter aliquid fieri intellectionem subito, licet illa natura non[c] produceretur in instanti, quam non legi istum tenere in casu quo illa qualitas est ab intellectu, tamen secundum viam veram, quae hoc habet pro impossibili[d], nullum habet colorem, cum tunc non sit dare naturam illius speciei in intellectu ita parvi gradus in entitate quin ipsa intellectum informante[e] intellectus ille[f] sit intelligens. Igitur supradicta evasio[g] nulla est, non plus quam valeret[h] in simili de albedine solummodo[i] particulariter acquisita.

[74] Similiter, licet turbatio corporis vel etiam animae per passionem aliquam possit forsitan impedire ne anima recipiat intellectionem vel volitionem perfectam in aliquo casu[j], nulla tamen turbatio vel[k] transitio seu[l] inquietatio desperata[m] potest tollere vel impedire quin, si intellectio huiusmodi[n] vel volitio, id est, illae qualitates, illam[o] informent animam[p], ipsa intelligat et velit secundum perfectionem intrinsecam intellectionis informantis, quamvis forte sua intellectio vel volitio non debeat felicitas vel virtus dici[q] nisi talis extranea perturbatio[r] tranquilletur.

[75] Praeterea, ille per hanc responsionem non salvat[s] istam negativam, nec praecedit eam actio alia diminuta, quam Commentator addit postquam dixerat quod intellectio fit in instanti, quia si intellectio secundum rem fiat divisibiliter, licet primo in indivisibili pertingat ad gradum quo potest dici intellectio, tamen illud fieri praecedit actio[t] diminuta, sicut patet de se. Si autem ista natura sub gradu quo, si[u] esset sine perturbatione corporis vel[v] animae, esset intellectio[w] iam non sit intellectio propter istam perturbationem[x] annexam, igitur istam oportet amoveri[y] et[z] sedari. Et ita instans illud in quo ipsa primo erit[a] intellectio praecedit illa actio diminuta sive successiva qua[b] amovebitur seu sedabitur illa[c] impeditiva perturbatio, et hoc immediate ante[d] et necessario, contra illud quod ipse dicit. Nec aliam tangit evasionem praeter istas. Igitur responsio eius non sufficit.

(x) quaevis] quavis *V* || (y) casu aliqua] hoc instanti (*om. S*) statu *MST* || (z) licet – successive] *iter. 3x sed del. 2x V* || (a) et] *om. V* (*def. T*) || (b) et – intellectionem] *om. hom. T* || (c) non] *om. V* || (d) pro impossibili] per impossibile *V* || (e) informante] informent *S* ; et *add. ST* || (f) ille] illa *MST, a.c. V* || (g) evasio] evacuatio *M* ; *p.c. V* || (h) valeret] valent *M* ; valeat *T* || (i) solummodo] simili modo *V* || (j) perfectam – aliquo] aliquam in casu aliquo perfectam *MT* || (k) vel] et *S* || (l) seu] vel *MT* || (m) desperata] disparata *V* || (n) huiusmodi] visio *M* || (o) illam] iam *V* || (p) animam] *om. M* || (q) dici] *s.l. ante* felicitas *V* || (r) perturbatio] turbatio *MT* || (s) salvat] salvabit *MT* || (t) actio] actus *M* || (u) si] *om. MST* ; *s.l. V* || (v) vel] et *S* || (w) intellectio] et *add. S* || (x) perturbationem] turbationem *S* || (y) amoveri] ammoveri *ST* || (z) et] *om. MTV* || (a) erit] et *M* || (b) qua] quam *V* || (c) illa] scilicet *add. S* || (d) ante] *om. MT* ; *mg. S*

[76] Praeterea[1], Commentator, III *De anima*, commento 28[2], et Commentator super[e] X *Ethicorum*, capitulo 4[f][3], dicunt[g] quod visio corporalis fit subito, igitur et volitio potest subito causari a voluntate, per medium praecedentis[4] argumenti.

[77] Praeterea[5], delectatio[h] fit subito, per Philosophum, X *Ethicorum*, capitulo 4[6], ubi[i] declarat[j] quod ipsa est actio perfecta et fit in indivisibili et non in tempore[k].

[78] Praeterea[7], Christus meruit in primo[l] instanti suae conceptionis summo merito suo, secundum Magistrum 18 distinctione tertii[m][8], et allegat pro se[n] **S 40ra** beatum Gregorium super Ezechielem, homelia 6[9], ubi | dicit quod « non habuit omnino Christus, iuxta animae meritum[o], quo potuisset proficere » ; sed Christus non meruit subito in primo instanti esse illius animae sine volitione causata ab anima illa ; igitur.

[79→78] Respondetur[10], et[p] verum est, quod Magister non dicit quod summe sibi meruit in primo instanti sui esse illa anima, sed a sua conceptione et ab initio suae conceptionis. Habuit igitur summum[q] meritum, secundum eos[r], a principio sui esse, non in principio[s]. Verba vero[t] Magistri[11] sunt haec : « Melior ipsius anima fieri non potuit quam ab initio suae conceptionis extitit, quia in meritis[u] **M 33va** proficere non potuit ». | Haec ille.

[80→79] Sed haec responsio nequaquam sufficit, quia illud meritum aut subito et simul fiebat aut successive et[v] per partem ante partem in infinitum. Si primo modo, tunc vel meruit in primo instanti, quod est intentum ; vel in instanti immediato illi, et hoc contra Philosophum et contra[w] veritatem ; aut stetisset per tempus sine merito, quia apud te idem est subito et simul[x] fieri quod[y] fieri in instanti. Si successive, tunc profecisset[z] in merito, contra dictas auctoritates.

(e) commentator super] *om. MST* ; *s.l. V* || (f) capitulo 4] capitulo *M* ; *tr. V* || (g) dicunt] dicitur *V* || (h) delectatio] delectio *STV* || (i) ubi] ubi enim *a.c. V* ; ibi enim *p.c. V* || (j) declarat] determinat *MT* || (k) tempore] an christus merebatur in primo instanti sui esse **p** *add. mg. infra MS* || (l) primo] in *add. M* || (m) tertii] dist. 18 cap. 2 *add. mg. T* || (n) se] eo *V* || (o) animae meritum] *tr. MST* || (p) et] quod *MST, a.c. V* || (q) summum] *om. T* || (r) eos] ipsos *S* ; istos *V* || (s) sui – principio] *mg. V* || (t) vero] autem *MT* || (u) in meritis] meritum *MT* ; secundum meritum *S* ; meritis *a.c. s.l. V* || (v) et] vel *MT* || (w) contra] *om. MT* || (x) subito et simul] *tr. V* || (y) quod] quia *a.c. M, T* ; et *S* || (z) profecisset] perfecisset *V*

---

1. Riccardus FitzRalph, *Lectura in Sententias*, I, q. 10, a. 2, Paris 15853, f. 64vb.
2. Averroes, *Commentarium magnum in Aristotelis De anima libros*, III, comm. 28, ed. Crawford, p. 467.48-57.
3. Michael Ephesius, *In Ethica Nicomachea*, X, c. 3, ed. H. Paul et F. Mercken (Corpus Latinum Commentariorum in Aristotelem Graecorum VI. 3), Turnhout 1991, p. 359-360, 365-366.
4. *Supra*, 75.
5. Riccardus FitzRalph, *Lectura in Sententias*, I, q. 10, a. 2, Paris 15853, f. 64vb.
6. Aristoteles, *Ethica*, X, c. 4 : 1174b10, ed. Gauthier (AL XXVI. 1-3), p. 570.3-9.
7. Riccardus FitzRalph, *Lectura in Sententias*, I, q. 10, a. 2, Paris 15853, f. 67ra.
8. Petrus Lombardus, *Sententiae*, III, d. 18, c. 2, in *Sententiae in IV libris distinctae*, ed. I. Brady, 2 vols. (Spicilegium Bonaventurianum IV-V), Grottaferrata 1971-1981, vol. 2, p. 113.1-17.
9. Gregorius Magnus, *In Ezech.*, I, hom. 6, n. 8, ed. A. Adriaen (CCSL 142), Turnhout 1971, p. 71 ; apud Petrum Lombardum, *Sententiae*, III, d. 18, c. 2, ed. Brady, vol. 2, p. 113.10-11.
10. Riccardus FitzRalph, *Lectura in Sententias*, I, q. 10, a. 2, Paris 15853, f. 64vb-65ra.
11. Petrus Lombardus, *Sententiae*, III, d. 18, c. 2, ed. Brady, vol. 2, p. 113.8-10.

[81] Praeterea, si immediate post primum instans produxit totum simul[a] actum suum meritorium[b], quare non potuisset anima illa in primo instanti vel saltem in aliquo instanti causasse talem actum qui secundum hoc non requirit successive[c] et[d] particulariter produci quando fit a voluntate ?

[82→81] Dices[e 1] forte aliter quod illud meritum animae Christi causabatur a Deo[f].

[83→82] Contra : non erat tunc in potestate illius animae nec ab ea dependebat sicut ab efficiente, igitur non erat[g] meritum illius[h] animae.

[84→83] Respondet[i 2] quod non sequitur : « Ille actus non dependebat ab anima Christi effective, igitur non erat[j] meritum Christi », quia hoc non obstante fiebat a[k] Christo in anima sua, et ideo fuit meritum Christi.

[85→84] Contra hoc : | saltem habetur tunc sicut prius quod anima Christi non **T 28va**
meruit. Contra auctoritatem Gregorii – quod[l] etiam non videtur[m] concedendum – sequitur etiam quod Christus non[n] tunc meruit secundum naturam humanam. Secundum autem naturam[o] divinam[p] non credo esse dicendum quod meruit etc.[q]

[86] Item, aliter : possibili[r] posito in esse[s] quod aliquis in aliquo instanti subito primo videret Deum clare, ipse non tunc per naturam suam amaret ipsum, nec[t] tunc[u] per consequens[v] delectaretur de sic viso. Consequens falsum, quia tunc respectu | dilectionis naturalis habentur omnes causae, igitur per consequens **V 54v**
et <respectu> delectationis[w], secundum Augustinum, libro[x] primo *De doctrina Christiana*, capitulo 38[y 3], ubi dicit quod « cum adest quod diligitur, delectationem secum gerere necesse est ». Et Commentator, XII *Metaphysicae*, commento 39[4], dicit quod voluptas sequitur apprehensionem sicut umbra corpus ; sed umbra sequitur corpus[z] pro eodem instanti ; igitur etc.

### <*Contra dictum FitzRalph*[a]>

[87→86] Nec sufficit dicere, sicut dicit Firauf[b 5], scilicet quod Augustinus intelligit quod cum adest quod actu secundo diligitur, tunc secum gerit delectationem. Sed dato quod quis videret[c] Deum clare in primo instanti sui esse[d],

(a) simul] *om. MST* ; *mg. V* || (b) suum meritorium] *tr. V* || (c) successive] successionem *S* || (d) et] *i.l. M* ; *mg. S* ; *om. T* || (e) dices] et dices *a.c. M, ST* || (f) causabatur – deo] a deo *a.c. s.l. M* ; a deo (a deo] de novo *a.c. mg.*) causabatur *S* ; donatur a deo *T* || (g) erat] *p.c. MS* ; dat *T* || (h) illius] *om. T* || (i) respondet] respondetur *V* || (j) erat] dat *M* ; *p.c. S* ; *om. T* || (k) a] in *T* || (l) quod] et *V* || (m) etiam – videtur] videtur etiam non *S* || (n) non] nec *V* || (o) autem naturam] *tr. V* || (p) divinam] humanam *M* || (q) etc.] de delectatione an fiat in instanti **q** *add. mg. infa MS* || (r) possibili] possibile *a.c. M, T* || (s) in esse] *om. MV* || (t) nec] *p.c. s.l. M* ; et *S* || (u) tunc] *om. V* || (v) consequens] non *add. S* || (w) delectationis] delectiones *S* ; delectionis *V* || (x) libro] hoc *V* || (y) 38] 28 *T* || (z) sed – corpus] *om. hom. a.c. V* ; sequitur *add. post* sicut umbra *p.c. V* || (a) fitzralph] contra sir'f *add. mg. S* ; ex hybernici *add. mg. T* ; hiber *add. mg. V* || (b) firauf] sirauf' *M* ; firauf' *S* ; franc'*T* ; fire *p.c. V* || (c) videret] viderit *V* || (d) sui esse] *tr. V*

---

1. RICCARDUS FITZRALPH, *Lectura in Sententias*, I, q. 10, a. 2, Paris 15853, f. 67ra-b.
2. RICCARDUS FITZRALPH, *Lectura in Sententias*, I, q. 10, a. 2, Paris 15853, f. 67rb.
3. AUGUSTINUS, *De doctrina Christiana*, I, c. 33, n. 37, ed. I. Martin (CCSL 32), Turnhout 1962, p. 27.21-22.
4. AVERROES, *Commentum super libros Metaphysicorum*, XII, comm. 39, ed. Iuntina II, 1562, f. 322vaG.
5. RICCARDUS FITZRALPH, *Lectura in Sententias*, I, q. 10, a. 2, Paris 15853, f. 67rb.

adhuc non posset Deum actu secundo[e] diligere in illo instanti, et ideo nec tunc sequitur delectatio.

[88→87] Sed illud non videtur sufficere, quia per istum nulla est causa quare non sequitur[f] delectatio[g] in primo instanti nisi quia tunc non diligitur actu secundo. Igitur si Deus crearet tunc actualem dilectionem, naturaliter sequeretur tunc delectatio[h]. Sed[i] non minus est voluntas, habitis[j] omnibus ad hoc requisitis, potens causare dilectionem[k] subito quam delectationem[l], et hoc maxime secundum illum, qui tenet alibi[1] quod videns Deum non potest non diligere Deum et quod fruitio illa necessario sequitur claram[m] visionem sicut umbra corpus non impediente Deo, igitur[n] etc.[o]

[89] Praeterea[2], aliquis potest subito peccare, igitur et[p] subito mereri. Antecedens probatur, quia si non sit primum instans quo quis praeexistens in caritate peccat, igitur[q] erit[r] ultimum[s] caritatis, quia pro nulla mensura destruitur eius prima caritas in qua non sit peccator[t]. Sed consequens est falsum, quia secundum Philosophum et Commentatorem, VIII *Physicorum*[3], in his quae simul destruuntur non est dare instans ultimum sui esse, sed primum productionis in
**S 40rb** his quae simul producuntur. Et tamen, ut acceptum est, | si non est dare primum instans[u] malae volitionis sequentis caritatem, oportebit dare ultimum caritatis[v].

[90→89] Ad illud[4] respondetur quod Philosophus et Commentator loquuntur de rebus quae naturaliter corrumpuntur[w], sed caritas non potest naturaliter corrumpi, sed a Deo solo, sicut nec generatur nisi a Deo nec augetur[x]. Ideo non est inconveniens, dicit Firauf[y], quod habeat ultimum instans sui esse.

[91→90] Contra : si est dare ultimum instans[z] caritatis et immediate sequitur[a] mortale peccatum[b], nulla pars caritatis illius[c] manet post illud instans, igitur simul destruitur, licet a solo Deo. Et si simul destruitur, igitur[d] in instanti. Et non in instanti[e] in quo est, nec in instanti mediato[f], quia tunc starent[g] simul per tempus illud medium in eodem subiecto caritas et peccatum mortale. Igitur in instanti immediato, et[h] ita instans instanti immediatum[i].

(e) deum – secundo] actu secundo deum *MT* || (f) sed illud – delectatio] *mg. (hom.) S* || (g) delectatio] delectio *S* || (h) delectatio] delectatio *mg. M* ; delectio *SV* || (i) sed] tunc *a.c. mg. M, ST* || (j) habitis] communiter *MST* || (k) dilectionem] delectationem *M* ; delectionem *T* ; et hoc *add. MT* || (l) delectationem] delectionem *TV* || (m) sequitur claram] *tr. V* || (n) igitur] *om. S* || (o) etc.] an sit dare ultimum instans caritatis **r** *add. mg. infra MS* || (p) et] *om. MT* || (q) igitur] illud *add. S* || (r) erit] est *MST* || (s) ultimum] instans *add. S* || (t) quia pro – peccator] *iter. M* || (u) dare – instans] primum instans dare *V* || (v) caritatis] opinio hybernici *add. mg. T* || (w) corrumpuntur] corrumpetur *M* || (x) augetur] et *add. V* || (y) firauf] sirauf' *MS* ; fransis *T* ; fire *p.c. V* || (z) instans] *om. MST* ; *mg. V* || (a) sequitur] scitur *M* || (b) mortale peccatum] *tr. MT* || (c) caritatis illius] *tr. S* || (d) igitur] non *add. S* || (e) et – instanti] *om. hom. MST* || (f) mediato] mediate *M* || (g) starent] staret *MT* || (h) et] *om. V* || (i) instans – immediatum] in instanti immediato *MT*

---

1. Riccardus FitzRalph, *Lectura in Sententias*, I, q. 1, a. 4, Paris 15853, f. 9vb.
2. Riccardus FitzRalph, *Lectura in Sententias*, I, q. 10, a. 2, Paris 15853, f. 68ra.
3. Averroes, *Commentum super libro Physicorum*, VIII, comm. 69, transl. Michael Scotus, f. 225vb-227ra.
4. Riccardus FitzRalph, *Lectura in Sententias*, I, q. 10, a. 2, Paris 15853, f. 68ra.

[92→91] Sed hic diceretur[j], sicut dicitur communiter, quod caritatem destrui etiam non per partem ante partem non est nisi quod Deus, qui in hoc instanti in quo ponitur ultimo[k] esse, conservat eam et non ultra, ita quod sensus est : immediate post[l] tota simul[m] destruitur, id est[n], immediate post nulla eius pars conservatur vel[o] conservabitur, et ideo immediate post nulla pars eius erit[p].

[93→92] Contra : non est possibilius apud Deum facere quod, postquam aliquid est in aliquo instanti, immediate[q] post[r] simul et non per partem ante partem desinat esse, sive[s] immediate post simul[t] totaliter non sit, quam econverso[u] quod aliquid[v] in aliquo instanti non sit nec aliquid eius et[w] immediate post totaliter et simul capiat esse[x]; sed secundum est simpliciter impossibile et repugnantiam includens[y], et per consequens non factibile etiam a Deo ; igitur et[z] primum. Minorem probo, quia secundum veritatem instans, ut saepe praeacceptum[a] est, non est indivisibilis mensura, sicut solet imaginari ; sed fieri in instanti est simul fieri seu non per[b] partem ante partem ; | igitur rem fieri sic simul est eam **M 33vb**
in instanti fieri et non successive sive in tempore[c] fieri, distinguendo nunc fieri contra conservari ; igitur si est dare ultimum instans in quo[d] res aliqua non est, non est[e] possibile quod immediate post illud instans[f] fiat illa res tota simul, quia tunc esset instans instanti immediatum etc.[g]

(j) diceretur] dicetur *MT* || (k) ultimo] *iter. M* || (l) post] *om. V* || (m) tota simul] totaliter *MT* || (n) id est] et *MT* || (o) conservatur vel] *om. S* || (p) pars – erit] est pars eius *M* ; pars erit eius *a.c. S* ; eius pars erit *T* || (q) immediate] immediata *M* ; immediato *ST* || (r) post] prius *MT* || (s) sive] quod *add. S* || (t) simul] *om. MST* ; *s.l. V* || (u) econverso] econtra *S* || (v) aliquid] aliquis *MT* || (w) et] etiam *MT* || (x) esse] et sit sicut patet de se *add. V* || (y) includens] inducens *S* || (z) et] nec *M* || (a) praeacceptum] prius actum *MT* ; *mg. S* ; praeactum *add. S* || (b) per] *om. MST* || (c) et non – fieri] *om. hom. MST* ; *mg. V* || (d) quo] est *add. S* || (e) non est] *om. MT* ; *mg. S* ; *s.l. post* aliqua *V* || (f) post – instans] post *MST* ; *mg. V* || (g) etc.] igitur *V*

## SECUNDUS ARTICULUS[a]

[1] Secundus articulus est arguere contra istam ultimam conclusionem et solvere[b].

### <RATIONES PRO MAGNA PARTE FITZRALPH CONTRA QUINTAM CONCLUSIONEM>

[2] Arguitur[c] primo[1] quod voluntas non possit subito causare actum meritoriae dilectionis, quia eadem ratione posset subito peccare, et hoc in primo instanti sui esse. Consequentia probatur, quia si habeat in illo instanti cognitionem boni et mali infusam a Deo, quae cognitio requiritur et sufficit ad volendum bene vel male[d] et libertatem arbitrii, aeque libere poterit[e] in illo instanti velle bene et male[f] sicut in alio : quid enim obstaret plus in illo quam in alio ? Sed falsitas consequentis probatur, quia illud peccatum esset vitium voluntatis[g], igitur noceret voluntati[h] ; igitur adimeret aliquod bonum a voluntate sive corrumperet[i] ; igitur illud bonum vel ademptum[j] praefuit in voluntate, et per consequens voluntas in qua praefuit illud bonum praefuit, et per consequens instans in quo primo peccat non est primum instans sui esse.

[3] Iste[k] modus arguendi[2] habetur ab Augustino, XII[l] *De civitate Dei*, capitulo 6[3], ubi probat quod mala voluntas, id est, mala[m] volitio, non potest esse coaeva voluntati in qua est, quare et notitia[n].

(a) secundus articulus] *mg. MSV* ; *om. T* || (b) solvere] arguitur per multas rationes quod actus voluntatis non possit in instanti fieri **s** *add. mg. infra MS* (*M* 33va ; *S* 40va) ; hyber *add. mg. V* || (c) arguitur] igitur *add. MT* || (d) male] velle *add. sed del. M, add. ST* || (e) poterit] *om. S* (*mg. M* ; *def. T*) || (f) et libertatem – male] *mg. MS* ; *om. hom. T* || (g) voluntatis] voluntati *MT* || (h) igitur – voluntati] *mg. M* ; igitur vitiaret voluntatem *S* ; igitur *T* || (i) sive corrumperet] seu corrumpet *V* || (j) ademptum] adeptum *M* ; ademptis *S* || (k) iste] idem *MT* || (l) xii] xxii *ST* || (m) voluntas – mala] voluntas *a.c. T* ; *om. p.c. T* || (n) et notitia] et no[2] *MT* ; etc. *S*

1. RICCARDUS FITZRALPH, *Lectura in Sententias*, I, q. 10, a. 2, Paris 15853, f. 59ra.
2. RICCARDUS FITZRALPH, *Lectura in Sententias*, I, q. 10, a. 2, Paris 15853, f. 59ra.
3. AUGUSTINUS, *De civitate Dei*, XII, c. 6, ed. B. Dombart et A. Kalb (CCSL 48), Turnhout 1955, p. 360.14-41.

[4] **(2)** Praeterea[1], Augustinus, XI *De civitate*, capitulo 15[2], reprobat opinionem dicentium quod angelus malus peccavit in primo instanti sui esse, propter illud[o] Iohannis in canonica[p], capitulo 3[3] : « *Ab initio Diabolus peccat*, non intelligunt »[q], inquit, « si natura talis est, nullo modo[r] esse peccatum ». Ubi, ut videtur, intendit[s] argumentum illud : Si peccasset in instanti primo sui esse, quod tunc naturale fuisset ei peccare, et per consequens non peccasset[t]. Et vult ibi[u] quod illa auctoritas debet aliter exponi[v], sic scilicet : Diabolus ab initio peccat, id est, peccatum Diaboli initium erat peccati.

[5] **(3)** Praeterea[4], in principio capituli 17[5] exponit illam auctoritatem Iob quae videtur esse contra se, scilicet : « Hoc est initium figmenti eius, id est, Diabolus, propter naturam », inquit[w], « non propter malitiam. Hoc dictum esse recte intelligimus, quia[x] sine dubio ubi esset[y] vitium malitiae, natura non[z] vitiata praecessisset ». Igitur natura[a] et vitium non possunt esse coaeva.

**S 40va** [6] **(4)** Praeterea[6], si voluntas | aliqua peccaret in primo instanti sui esse, tunc non posset illud peccatum vitare, et per consequens non peccaret, quia nullus
**V 55r** peccat in eo quod vitare non potest, secundum Augustinum, III[b] *De* | *libero*
**T 28vb** *arbitrio*, capitulo 28[c][7], ubi dicit sic : | « Hoc brevissimum[d] tene : quaecumque ista causa est voluntatis, id est, volitionis, si non ei potest resisti, sine peccato ei ceditur; si autem potest[e], non ei cedatur[f] et non peccabitur[g]. An forte fallit incautum[h]? Igitur caveat[i] ne fallatur. An tanta fallacia est ut caveri omnino non possit? Si ita est, nulla[j] peccata sunt. Quis[k] enim peccat in[l] eo quod nullo modo caveri potes[m]? Peccatur autem, caveri igitur[n] potest ». Similia etiam[o] et multotiens dicit Augustinus in libello *De duabus animabus*[8]. Prima consequentia patet, quia ante illud instans non potuit peccatum vitare, quia ante[p] non fuit. Nec

(o) illud] quod *add. V* || (p) canonica] sua *add. MT* || (q) intelligunt] intelligit *MT* || (r) modo] potest *add. MST* || (s) intendit] quod *add. MT* || (t) in – peccasset] *mg. M* ; *mg. infra S* ; *om. hom. T* || (u) ibi] scilicet *MT* || (v) et – exponi] *mg. V* ; et actu secundo diligitur tunc secum gerit delectionem causat debet aliter *a.c. V* || (w) inquit] inquam *S* || (x) quia] quoniam *MST, a.c. V* || (y) esset] erit *V* (est *ed.*) || (z) natura non] et ita non *a.c. mg. M, T* ; et ita natura *S* || (a) igitur natura] gratia enim *a.c. S* ; haec ille igitur natura *p.c. mg. S* || (b) iii] libro *add. MT* || (c) 28] 128 *T* || (d) brevissimum] verissimum *M* ; brevissimi *ST* || (e) potest] *mg. MS* ; *om. T* || (f) si – cedatur] *mg. (hom.) V* || potest – cedatur] ei non ordinatur *a.c. mg. M* ; potest (*mg.*) non ei cedinatur (*a.c.*) *S* ; non ei non ceditur *T* || (g) peccabitur] peccabit *MT* || (h) incautum] ibi canunt *M* ; in tantum *T* || (i) igitur caveat] *tr. MST* || (j) nulla] omnino *add. MT* || (k) quis] non *S* || (l) peccat in] peccat *MT* ; peccatur *S* || (m) omnino – potest] *iter. a.c. M* ; *iter. T* || (n) caveri igitur] *tr. MT* || (o) etiam] autem *MT* ; igitur *S* || (p) ante] *om. T* ; *p.c. V*

1. Riccardus FitzRalph, *Lectura in Sententias*, I, q. 10, a. 2, Paris 15853, f. 59ra.
2. Augustinus, *De civitate Dei*, XI, c. 15, ed. Dombart et Kalb (CCSL 48), p. 335.1-3.
3. 1 Io. 3 : 8.
4. Riccardus FitzRalph, *Lectura in Sententias*, I, q. 10, a. 2, Paris 15853, f. 59ra-b.
5. Augustinus, *De civitate Dei*, XI, c. 17, ed. Dombart et Kalb (CCSL 48), p. 336.1-4.
6. Riccardus FitzRalph, *Lectura in Sententias*, I, q. 10, a. 2, Paris 15853, f. 59rb.
7. Augustinus, *De libero arbitrio*, III, c. 18, n. 50, ed. W. M. Green (CCSL 29), Turnhout 1970, p. 304.6-11.
8. Augustinus, *De duabus animabus contra Manichaeos*, c. 10 (PL 42), coll. 103-105.

post, quia « hoc solo privatur Deus » etc.[1] Nec in illo instanti, quia[q] « omne quod est, quando est » etc.[2]

[7] **(5)** Praeterea[3], si sic, tunc aliquis[r] posset mereri in primo instanti sui esse. Consequens falsum, quia nullus potest mereri[s] nisi quando potest iustitiam amittere ; sed meritum habitum in primo instanti sive iustitiam non potest tunc amittere, quia[t] « omne[u] quod est » etc. Nec prius, quia prius[v] non fuit. Igitur tunc non meretur. Ita enim arguit Anselmus, *De casu Diaboli*, in principio 5 capituli[4], probans ibi bonos angelos potuisse peccare antequam mali caderent, quia, inquit, « si non potuerunt[w] peccare, non possibilitate sed necessitate servaverunt iustitiam. Quare non magis meruerunt gratiam quia steterunt aliis cadentibus quam quia servaverunt rationalitatem[x] quam perdere nequiverunt ».

[8] **(6)** Praeterea[5], si sic, tunc aliquis invitus et necessario peccaret, posito casu possibili, quia posito quod Deus creet in hoc instanti unum[y] angelum, dando sibi perfectam[z] cognitionem, et libertatem arbitrii, et praeceptum[a] quod eliciat actum diligendi Deum quo[b] citius[c] poterit, et quod[d] Deus nolit cooperari voluntati[e] in hoc instanti, et ita praecise per instans suspendat[f] voluntatem ab agendo[g], hoc facto, cum[h] inter hoc instans et quodlibet aliud sequens est[i] tempus medium, iste angelus toto illo tempore medio inter hoc instans et primum instans quo actum eliciet omittet[j], contra praeceptum, actum elicere, et ita vellet-nollet in tali[k] casu peccaret, si actus dilectionis causabitur in instanti. Nam si non exspectabit[l] per[m] tempus, sed immediate post eliciet actum, cum actus voluntatis sit indivisibilis, et ideo subito tantum et[n] simul producibilis, et etiam non nisi[o] subito et simul produceretur[p], sequeretur[q] quod agens in passo disposito et agens in passo indisposito in aequali mensura ceteris paribus producerent effectus suos, quod videtur absurdum ; vel[r] sequitur quod instans[s] instanti erit[t] immediatum, quod est impossibile.

(q) quia] quod *T* || (r) aliquis] etiam *add. s.l. V* || (s) in – mereri] *mg. (hom.) V* || (t) quia] quod *V* || (u) omne] *s.l. M* ; *om. ST* || (v) prius] primum *S* || (w) potuerunt] poterunt *V* || (x) rationalitatem] naturam rationalem *MST* || (y) unum] unde *M* || (z) perfectam] *p.c. mg. M* ; per suam *T* || (a) praeceptum] sit *add. MT* || (b) quo] quam *S* || (c) citius] actus *a.c. s.l. M* ; actius *T* || (d) quod] *om. MST* ; *s.l. V* || (e) voluntati] *mg. post* instanti *M* ; *om. ST* || (f) per – suspendat] despendat *a.c. mg. V* || (g) agendo] agere *MST* || (h) cum] *om. S* || (i) est] *om. M* || (j) omittet] omittat *MT* || (k) tali] om. *T* || (l) exspectabit] peccabit *a.c. s.l. M, a.c. s.l. et mg. S, T* || (m) per] post *a.c. M, T* || (n) et] non *add. T* ; *a.c. V* ; ac *p.c. s.l. V* || (o) non nisi] nisi *S, a.c. s.l. V* ; non *T* (*def. M* ; si non *p.c. P*) || (p) producibilis – simul] *om. hom. M* || (q) sequeretur] sequitur *T* || (r) vel] *om. V* || (s) instans] in *add. sed exp. SV* || (t) erit] erat *a.c. M* ; sit *p.c. mg. M, ST* ; *p.c. V*

1. Aristoteles, *Ethica*, VI, c. 1 : 1139b10, ed. Gauthier (AL XXVI. 1-3), p. 480.5-6.
2. Aristoteles, *De interpretatione*, c. 9 : 19a7-9, *Les Auctoritates Aristotelis. Un florilège médiéval. Étude historique et édition critique*, ed. J. Hamesse, Louvain-Paris 1974, p. 306.
3. Riccardus FitzRalph, *Lectura in Sententias*, I, q. 10, a. 2, Paris 15853, f. 59rb.
4. Anselmus Cantuariensis, *De casu diaboli*, c. 5, ed. F. S. Schmitt (Opera Omnia 1), Edinburgh 1946, p. 242.28-243.3.
5. Riccardus FitzRalph, *Lectura in Sententias*, I, q. 10, a. 2, Paris 15853, f. 59rb-va.

[9] **(7)** Praeterea[1], si sic, sequeretur quod duo merita essent aequalia quorum unum omnibus aliis paribus existentibus ex[u] parte utriusque merentis[v] fieret[w] in tempore et aliud in instanti, quod falsum est, quia nihil prodesset[x] continuare
**M 34ra** meritum. Consequentia patet[y] : ponatur quod duo mereantur, | unus tantum per instans et alius per unam horam, cum omnibus condicionibus aliis[z] similibus ex parte utriusque, et cum aequali conatu et[a] aequali caritate et intensione actuum et huiusmodi. Tunc meritum factum[b] in hora est maius[c]; et non in infinitum, quia quicquid aliquod finitum excedit in infinitum est infinitum[d]; igitur finite. Sit igitur quod duplo, gratia exempli. Sit tunc[e] tertius[f] qui ceteris paribus mereatur tantum per dimidium unius horae. Tunc eius[g] meritum erit subduplum ad meritum secundi merentis per horam, et per consequens aequale merito primo instantaneo. Et quod meritum tertii sit subduplum ad meritum secundi probatur, quia meritum secundi[h] pro prima medietate horae est[i] aequale merito tertii, et pari ratione meritum ipsius secundi pro secunda medietate horae est[j] similiter[k] aequale[l] merito tertii[m], igitur et[n] meritum secundi in tota hora erit duplum. Et voco « aequalia » merita quibus debentur aequalia praemia. Et quod meritum[o] secundi pro prima medietate horae sit aequale merito totali tertii probatur, quia si ille secundus habuisset aliquam interruptionem inter istas medietates horae in qua meretur, tunc manifestum foret quod meritum eius in utraque medietate esset aequale totali merito tertii;
**S 40vb** sed[p] nunc suum meritum | est tantum quantum foret si esset interruptum, ceteris omnibus paribus; igitur.

[10] **(8)** Item[2], tunc merito instantaneo[q] deberetur praemium aeternum et peccato mortali instantaneo poena aeterna, igitur posito casu possibili alicuius peccata vel peccatum non posset Deus sufficienter punire nec ex alia parte alicuius merita instantanea praemiare. Consequentia probatur, quia quaelibet voluntas est naturae finitae[r], et per consequens contingit assignare poenam maximam quam potest recipere, vel saltem aliquam[s] ita magnam quod non poterit eam recipere, et sit illa[t] *a*. Inter *a* et poenam debitam peccato instantaneo[u] mortali est aliqua proportio, cum neutra sit infinita. Sit igitur quod dupla[v], gratia exempli. Sed in tempore quocumque quantumcumque parvo potest angelus non solum decies sed centies peccare ita graviter sicut fecit in uno instanti. Igitur in finito[w] tempore potest mereri *a* poenam et etiam maiorem. Et non potest maiorem recipere, igitur

(u) ex] de *S* || (v) merentis] nitis *a.c. s.l. M* ; merentes *a.c. V* || (w) fieret] esset *MST* || (x) prodesset] tunc *add. MST* || (y) patet] quia *add. MST* || (z) aliis] requisitis *add. MT* || (a) et] cum *add. MT* ; in *add. S* || (b) factum] suum *T* || (c) maius] magis *S* || (d) quicquid – infinitum] nullum finitum aliud finitum excedit in infinitum *a.c. mg. M, ST* || (e) sit tunc] *tr. MST* || (f) tertius] alius *MT* || (g) eius] *p.c. M* ; erit *T* || (h) probatur – secundi] *mg. V* || (i) est] similiter *add. sed del. V* (*add. P*) || (j) aequale – est] *om. hom. MST* || (k) similiter] simpliciter *MST* || (l) aequale] aequalis *MT* || (m) et – tertii] *mg. (hom.) V* || (n) et] *om. V* || (o) meritum] praemium *S* || (p) sed] sicut *MT* ; sicut *a.c. i.l. S* || (q) instantaneo] *p.c. s.l. M* ; *p.c. V* || (r) finitae] *s.l. MT* || (s) aliquam] *om. MT* || (t) illa] *om. MST* || (u) instantaneo] *om. MST* ; *s.l. V* || (v) quod dupla] dupla *a.c. S* ; decupla *p.c. mg. S* || (w) finito] quo *V* (aliquo *P*)

1. Riccardus FitzRalph, *Lectura in Sententias*, I, q. 10, a. 2, Paris 15853, f. 59va-b.
2. Riccardus FitzRalph, *Lectura in Sententias*, I, q. 10, a. 2, Paris 15853, f. 59vb-60ra.

propositum. Et quod angelus ille possit[x] plus quam decies peccare[y] in tempore dando quantumcumque[z] parvo peccato aequali peccato instantaneo patet, quia in quocumque tempore quantumcumque parvo posset ipse, stante eadem cognitione sufficienti, dimittere[a] malam volitionem qua sic peccaret et eam resumere plus quam decies, immo quotienscumque voluerit habens liberam voluntatem et nondum confirmatus, quia nullam[b] difficultatem patitur in volendo.

[11] **(9)** Praeterea[1], si sic, tunc continuans meritum instantanee causatum, utpote unam bonam volitionem cum aliis condicionibus, per tempus[c] meretur praemium infinitum intensive, et cum tale[d] tunc capere non possit, non posset a Deo sufficienter praemiari. Consequentia probatur, quia sicut pro primo instanti intrinseco[e] illius temporis debitur[f] isti merenti aliquod praemium[g] praecise, ita[h] pro quolibet instanti posteriori illius temporis; aut igitur pro quolibet sequenti praemium aequale vel maius et maius[i] semper vel semper minus et minus[j]. Et[k] tunc pro omnibus simul[l] aequalia praemia[m] infinita vel finita[n] maiora aliquo[o] determinatae quantitatis[p] praemio dando vel assignabili, sicut in[q] communi argumento[r] probari[s] solet, quia vel ibit[t] processus ad perfectiora merita in instantibus posterioribus, et tunc capietur unum meritum instantaneum praecedens
| quo quodlibet[u] infinitorum[v] sequentium erit maius[w]; si ad imperfectius, tunc **T 29ra**
capietur unum de sequentibus meritis, et tunc quodlibet praecedentium erit[x] illo perfectius; aut procedit[y] aequaliter et uniformiter, et tunc merita[z] instantanea erunt aequalia, et per consequens talis meretur unum infinitum praemium, si componant
unum, sicut possunt, cum sint[a] eiusdem speciei[b] – possibile est[c] saltem, | vel si **V 55v**
non, aequivalenter saltem, et neutro modo posset praemio sibi debito praemiari.

[12→11] Respondetur[2] quod tantum[d] primo instanti correspondet meritum praecisum et nullo posteriori.

[13→12] Sed contra[3] : ex hoc sequitur[e], posito casu possibili, quod inaequaliter merentes debeant aequaliter praemiari, nam posito quod Sortes continue mereatur in aliquo tempore, quod sit *a*, et in primo eius instanti et[f] in ultimo similiter et non ultra, et Plato uniformiter in omnibus per tempus *a*, ita tamen quod non mereatur in ultimo instanti ipsius *a*, quod sit *c*, hoc posito, tunc sic : vel praemia illorum

(x) possit] posset *MST* || (y) peccare] et *add. MT*, *add. a.c. S* || (z) quantumcumque] quodcumque *a.c. s.l. S* ; quocumque *V* || (a) dimittere] amittere *S* || (b) nullam] nulla *T* || (c) per tempus] paribus *MT* || (d) tale] tali *V* || (e) intrinseco] extrinseco *V* || (f) debitur] debetur *MST* || (g) aliquod praemium] aliquod primum *a.c. V* ; *tr. p.c. mg. V* || (h) ita] quod *add. MT*, *add. sed del. S* || (i) maius – maius] magis et magis *S* ; minus et maius *T* || (j) et minus] *om. T* || (k) et] si primis duobus modis *add. S* || (l) simul] vel *S* || (m) aequalia praemia] *tr. V* || (n) infinita – finita] *tr. M* ; infinita vel infinita *S* ; finita vel finita *T* || (o) aliquo] *a.c. M* ; alicuius *p.c. mg. M* || (p) determinatae quantitatis] *tr. T* || (q) in] *om. V* || (r) communi argumento] argumento priori *MT* || (s) probari] *om. T* || (t) vel ibit] ut ibi *MT* ; vel ibi fit *S* || (u) quodlibet] quolibet *M* || (v) infinitorum] inferiorum *MT* ; inferiorum *a.c. mg. V* || (w) maius] magis *S* || (x) erit] est *MST* || (y) procedit] ut *add. V* || (z) merita] omnia *add. mg. S* || (a) sicut – sint] possunt cum *mg. M* ; *ST* || (b) speciei] sicut *add. MST* || (c) possibile est] *tr. S* || (d) tantum] in *S* || (e) sequitur] *a.c. S* ; sequeretur *p.c. S* || (f) et] etiam *MT*

1. Riccardus FitzRalph, *Lectura in Sententias*, I, q. 10, a. 2, Paris 15853, f. 60ra.
2. Riccardus FitzRalph, *Lectura in Sententias*, I, q. 10, a. 2, Paris 15853, f. 60ra.
3. Riccardus FitzRalph, *Lectura in Sententias*, I, q. 10, a. 2, Paris 15853, f. 60ra-b.

sunt aequalia, et sequitur probandum, quod inaequaliter merentes[g] praemiabuntur aequaliter[h], quia Sortes meruit quandocumque[i] Plato meruit uniformiter cum eo et etiam in *c* quando[j] Plato non meruit. Si[k] praemia eorum[l] sunt inaequalia, et per consequens praemium Sortis[m] maius[n], hoc non erit[o] nisi per illud praecise quod correspondet *c*[p] instanti, et ita sequitur quod pro aliquo instanti posteriori debetur meritum praecisum, et pari ratione pro quolibet, igitur[q].

[14] **(10)** Praeterea[1], si sic, tunc voluntas posset libere subito volitionem producere sine aliqua motione immediate praecedente, cuius illa causatio vel **M 34rb** volitio sit | terminus, et tunc transmutatio subita foret[r] per se, scilicet absque[s] hoc quod esset finis alterius transmutationis[t] successivae, contra Commentatorem, VI *Physicorum*, commento 32[2], ubi habet[u] hoc pro impossibili.

[15] **(11)** Item[3], tunc secundum legem communem posset quis gravius iuste puniri pro peccatis venialibus finitis secundum numerum quam pro maximo mortali peccato facto[v] in eodem tempore vel maiori, quia[w] pro veniali unius instantis debetur aliqua poena; et illa non exceditur[x] infinite *a* poena debita pro **S 41ra** mortali maximo; igitur totiens poterit secundum | multitudinem finitam peccare venialiter aeque graviter praecise sicut ante, et[y] sequetur propositum[z].

[16] **(12)** Praeterea[4], pro merito instantaneo debetur augmentum certum[a] caritatis, igitur cum illius augmentum[b] sit aliqua certa proportio ad caritatem Christi, sequitur quod in tempore quantumcumque parvo posset quis acquirere sibi[c] tantam caritatem quantam habet Christus. Consequens falsum. Probatio consequentiae, quia in quocumque tempore potest totiens subito sic velle vel in se meritorie uniformiter causare huiusmodi volitionem[d] quotiens illud augmentum continetur in caritate Christi, et sequitur conclusio inferenda.

[17] **(13)** Praeterea[5], tunc obesset continuare actum suum meritorium, quia constat quod[e] pro illo debetur sibi praemium certum secundum quantitatem, et pro merito instantaneo debetur sibi etiam praemium determinatae quantitatis, licet minus. Sit igitur gratia exempli minus in decuplo. Cum igitur decem actus subitos, immo centum, posset ipse tales elicere dum continuat illum actum[f] unum, et tunc maius[g] praemium acquireret[h], ut argutum est, igitur continuatio actus illius[i] in tali casu potest sibi obesse.

(g) merentes] *om. M* || (h) aequaliter] inaequaliter *MT* || (i) quandocumque] quandoque *M* || (j) c quando] ca quam *M* || (k) si] sed *a.c. S* || (l) eorum] illorum *T* || (m) sortis] est *add. MST* || (n) maius] magis *S* || (o) erit] est *MT* || (p) c] ca *M* || (q) igitur] etc. *add. S* || (r) foret] fieret *V* || (s) scilicet absque] *tr. MT* || (t) transmutationis] praecise *add. V* || (u) habet] habetur *S* || (v) facto] facti *S* || (w) quia] *iter. T* || (x) exceditur] excedetur *MST* || (y) et *P*] quod *MSTV* || (z) propositum] *om. MST* || (a) certum] augmentum *om. MST* || (b) augmentum] augmenti *MST* || (c) sibi] *s.l. M*; scilicet *MT*; *om. S* || (d) huiusmodi volitionem] *tr. MT* || (e) quod] quo *T* || (f) illum actum] *tr. MT* || (g) maius] magis *S* || (h) acquireret] acquiret *V* || (i) actus illius] nullius actus *V*

---

1. RICCARDUS FITZRALPH, *Lectura in Sententias*, I, q. 10, a. 2, Paris 15853, f. 60va.
2. AVERROES, *Commentum super libro Physicorum*, VI, comm. 32, transl. Michael Scotus, f. 148rb.
3. RICCARDUS FITZRALPH, *Lectura in Sententias*, I, q. 10, a. 2, Paris 15853, f. 60rb.
4. RICCARDUS FITZRALPH, *Lectura in Sententias*, I, q. 10, a. 2, Paris 15853, f. 60va.
5. RICCARDUS FITZRALPH, *Lectura in Sententias*, I, q. 10, a. 2, Paris 15853, f. 60va.

[18] **(14)** Item[1], sequitur tunc quod aliquis habens summum meritum sibi possibile circa aliquod obiectum, ex hoc quod staret continue in eodem actu[j] dilectionis respectu illius per unam horam, plus in[k] eadem hora in decuplo posset mereri habendo diversos actus interscalariter, circa illud[l] obiectum unum actum[m] et circa aliud obiectum alium actum. Et ita nullus deberet rationabiliter eligere[n] continuare actum[o] meritorium respectu unius obiecti per tempus in quo[p] posset amare multa successive vel duo alternatim frequenter[q]. Sed consequens est falsum, ut videtur[r], quia in hoc praecise laudatur felicitas[s] a Philosopho, X *Ethicorum*, capitulo 8[2], quia est maxime continua.

[19] **(15)** Praeterea[3], tunc si aliquis peccaret venialiter continuando actum suum uniformiter per aliquod tempus in cuius fine moreretur, sequitur[t] quod pro quolibet instanti illius temporis deberetur sibi aliqua poena in purgatorio, et ita pro omnibus simul deberentur sibi poenae infinitae[u], et per consequens semper foret in purgatorio, et pari ratione, posito quod suum peccatum sit mortale, sequitur quod pro illo tempore debebitur sibi[v] poena aeterna infinita intensive. Et hoc falsum, quia tunc Deus non posset eum punire sufficienter.

[20] Hae sunt rationes sumptae ex Firauf[w] pro magna parte.

[21] **(16)** Praeterea[4], quod non sit dare primum instans in quo voluntas vult, licet sit dare primum instans in quo volitio haec vel illa sit, probat Firauf[x] in positione sua sic : quia si sit primum instans in quo voluntas velit[y], igitur hoc erit[z] de volitione ab ipsa potentia volitiva libere producta vel de illa quae necessario sequitur ad aliquam apprehensionem, qua[a] scilicet habita[b] voluntas non libere sed naturaliter producit volitionem. Non de libere producta, quia omnis mutatio subita est finis successivae mutationis[c], per Commentatorem, VI *Physicorum*, commento 32[5]; sed cum voluntas libere producit suam volitionem, sua prima volitio, si aliqua sit talis, non est tunc[d] finis alicuius mutationis sic praecedentis immediate; igitur etc. Nec de volitione naturaliter producta, si apprehendatur actualiter beatitudo[e] vel aliquid aliud tale placibile conveniens, quia[f] non est aliquod primum instans in quo intellectus cogitat de tali volito vel tale volitum[g] – sit illud *a* – igitur nec est aliquod instans primum[h] illius volitionis naturaliter et

(j) actu] gradu *MST* ; *s.l. V* || (k) in] *om. V* || (l) illud] idem *MST* || (m) unum actum] quam habendo unum actum circa unum obiectum *MT* || (n) eligere] elicere et *MT* || (o) actum] opus *S* || (p) quo] p *add. S* || (q) alternatim frequenter] *tr. MST* || (r) ut videtur] peccaret venialiter *T* || (s) praecise – felicitas] felicitas *MT* ; felicitas commendatur *S* || (t) sequitur] *om. V* || (u) poenae infinitae] poenae *a.c. V* ; *tr. p.c. mg. V* || (v) debebitur sibi] debebitur *a.c. V* ; *tr. p.c. mg. V* || (w) firauf] sirauf' *M* ; franf' *ST* ; ffirauf *V* || (x) firauf] sirauf' *M* ; fi ranf' *S* ; franf' *T* ; ffiraf' *V* || (y) velit] vellet *MST* ; *p.c. V* || (z) erit] vel *add. S* || (a) qua] quia *M* ; *p.c. V* || (b) scilicet habita] habita qua *a.c. V* ; *tr. p.c. s.l. V* || (c) mutationis] *om. MTV* ; et *add. MST* || (d) tunc] omnino *S* ; *s.l. T* || (e) beatitudo] veritudo *T* || (f) quia] quod *MT*, *a.c. V* || (g) vel – volitum] *om. MT* ; *mg. SV* || (h) instans primum] *om. MT*, *a.c. S* ; *tr. p.c. s.l. S*

---

1. Riccardus FitzRalph, *Lectura in Sententias*, I, q. 10, a. 2, Paris 15853, f. 60va.
2. Aristoteles, *Ethica*, X, c. 8 : 1177a20, ed. Gauthier (AL XXVI. 1-3), p. 576.20-21.
3. Riccardus FitzRalph, *Lectura in Sententias*, I, q. 10, a. 2, Paris 15853, f. 60rb.
4. Riccardus FitzRalph, *Lectura in Sententias*, I, q. 10, a. 2, Paris 15853, f. 65vb.
5. Averroes, *Commentum super libro Physicorum*, VI, comm. 32, transl. Michael Scotus, f. 148rb.

necessario sequentis[i] illam cognitionem. Assumptum probatur, quia illa[j] cogitatio nova vel libere causaretur, et tunc, sicut praeargutum est de volitione libere causanda, ipsa non fieret subito, per auctoritatem Commentatoris, eo quod non esset finis mutationis successivae ; aut secundo, illa cogitatio actualis generaretur naturaliter ab aliqua specie imaginativa, et tunc vel est aliqua species debilissima et minima ipsius *a* in virtute imaginativa quae potest agere in[k] intellectum vel est aliqua talis maxima quae non potest agere in intellectum[l]. Sed prima pars est falsa, quia si non, sit illa minima quae potest agere in intellectum[m] *b* ; si igitur *b* potest agere in[n] intellectum[o], igitur potest causare speciem seu cogitationem intentionis **T 29rb** certae[p] in intellectu, quae vocetur | *c* ; et per consequens aliqua species debilior imaginativa potest agere aliquam speciem *c* debiliorem in intellectu. Sic[q] est enim[r] in aliis actionibus naturalibus quod si aliqua virtus potest movere aliquid aliqua **S 41rb** **V 56r** velocitate, virtus | minor | potest movere idem[s] motum tardius. Quod probatur ex hoc quod idem[t] motum potest moveri tardius a virtute debiliori, et ita sequitur quod non sit aliqua minima virtus quae potest idem[u] movere. Igitur similiter erit de passione intellectus a specie in memoria, quod scilicet non est aliqua minima sive debilissima species in imaginativa quae potest agere in intellectum. Relinquitur igitur quod sit aliqua species maxima sive intensissima in imaginativa de obiecto *a* quae non[v] potest agere[w] in intellectum, et quaelibet intensior potest[x] agere[y] in intellectum.

[22] Hoc declarato, probat[1] iste quod non est aliquod primum instans in quo **M 34va** species in imaginativa agit | in[z] intellectum, et per consequens nec cogitationis in intellectu quae[a] *a* specie in[b] imaginativa causetur. Quia[c] si aliquod sit tale instans, sit illud gratia exempli instans praesens ; tunc sic : species in imaginativa agit nunc in intellectum[d] ; et certum est quod agit[e] naturaliter et non libere ; igitur nunc primo est ista[f] species satis fortis intensionis ad agendum, quia si prius fuisset satis fortis[g], prius egisset. Igitur si nunc primo agit, sequitur quod est[h] aliqua[i] species minima in imaginativa quae potest agere in intellectum, cuius oppositum est prius probatum. Igitur praesens instans[j] non est primum instans in quo[k] species imaginative agit in[l] intellectum, et per consequens non est aliquod primum instans in quo intellectus cogitat quando sua cogitatio fit[m] naturaliter a specie imaginative.

(i) sequentis] sequens *M* || (j) probatur – illa] probo quia *MST* || (k) in] om. *T* || (l) vel – intellectum] vel maxima quae non poterit *S* ; *om. hom. T* (*def. M*) || (m) vel – intellectum] *om. hom. M* || (n) in] *om. V* || (o) intellectum] b *add. MT* || (p) certae] *om. MST* ; *mg. V* || (q) sic] sicut *T* || (r) enim] *om. MST* || (s) idem] illud *V* || (t) idem] illud *V* || (u) idem] illud *V* || (v) non] *s.l. T (prima vice)* || (w) agere] *om. MS* || (x) potest] poterit *V* || (y) relinquitur – agere] relinquitur igitur quod sit aliqua species maxima sive intensissima in imaginativa quae non (*s.l.*) potest agere in intellectum [+[va]relinquitur autem species maxima intensissima in imaginativa de obiecto a quae non potest in intellectum et quaelibet intensior potest agere[cat]] *T* || (z) in] *om. T* || (a) quae] *om. V* || (b) in] *om. S* ; *s.l. V* || (c) quia] quod *ST* || (d) intellectum] intellectu *S* (*def. M*) || (e) nunc – agit] *om. hom. M* || (f) est ista] *tr. S* || (g) intensionis – fortis] *om. hom. M* ; quia si prius fuisset satis fortis *mg. S* || fortis] ad agendum *T* || (h) est] *om. V* || (i) aliqua] aliqualiter *a.c. T* || (j) praesens instans] praesens *M* ; *mg. S* ; prius *T* || (k) non – quo] est *M* ; est in quo *(sed del.) T* || (l) in] *om. V* || (m) fit] fuerit *M* ; fuit *a.c. S, T* ; sit *V*

---

1. Riccardus FitzRalph, *Lectura in Sententias*, I, q. 10, a. 2, Paris 15853, f. 65vb-66ra.

[23] Igitur[n] habetur totum intentum principaliter. Et propter illum argumentum[o] et alia praecedentia tenet iste conclusionem ad quam vadunt, praecipue quia tunc angelus posset[p] peccare in primo instanti sui esse, quod, ut dicit ille[1], reputat Augustinus includere contradictionem, ut patet per argumenta varia XI *De civitate*[2], et per argumenta[q] Anselmi[3] et Magistri, libro II, distinctione 3[4] : tum quia tunc posset unus homo tantum peccare quod Deus non posset ipsum sufficienter punire, et ita Deus vellet-nollet dimitteret aliquod peccatum impunitum, ex 8[r] principali[5]. Tum quia[s] meritum instantaneum et temporale ceteris omnibus paribus essent aequalia, sicut evidenter – inquit – demonstratum est in 7 principali[6]. Tum quia tunc aliquis peccaret necessario mortaliter, ex 6 argumento[7]. Tum quia tunc quilibet continuans[t] meritum vel demeritum mortale per tempus uniformiter deberet habere praemium vel poenam intensive infinitam[u], ex argumento 15[8], et semper esse in purgatorio pro peccato uno veniali continuato per tempus, ex eodem 15 argumento[9]. Tum etiam[v] propter auctoritatem Commentatoris, VI *Physicorum*[w], commento 32[x] [10], ut supra 10 et 16 argumentis[11].

### <RESPONSIO AD RATIONES 1-5 FITZRALPH CONTRA QUINTAM CONCLUSIONEM>

[24] Istis non obstantibus, teneo quod prius[y].

[25→2] Ad primum argumentum in oppositum, concedendum est quod voluntas aliqua, si sibi infunderentur cognitiones naturaliter praesuppositae peccato, posset peccare in primo instanti sui esse, et quod[z] illud peccatum tunc vitiaret voluntatem[a].

[26] Et cum[b] dicitur quod tunc adimeret illud vitium voluntatis[c] bonum aliquod, dicendum quod Augustinus ibi contra istos arguit[d] qui dicerent quod

(n) igitur] hic *M, p.c. S* ; igitur *a.c. S* ; *s.l. T* || (o) illud argumentum] illa argumenta *MST, a.c. V* || (p) posset] potuisset *V* || (q) argumenta] argumentum *M* || (r) 8] 0[a] *S* || (s) tum quia] *tr. a.c. S* ; tunc quia *T* || (t) continuans] continuens *T* || (u) infinitam] infinita *V* || (v) etiam] quia *MST, a.c. V* || (w) vi physicorum] *om. V* || (x) 32] 22 *M* || (y) istis – prius] *om. MST* || (z) quod] *om. S* || (a) voluntatem] quomodo exponitur illa auctoritas augustini peccatum semper adimit aliquod bonum **t** *add. mg. infra S* || (b) cum] quod *T* || (c) adimeret – voluntatis] illud vitium voluntatis adimeret *MT* || (d) contra – arguit] arguit contra istos *MT*

1. RICCARDUS FITZRALPH, *Lectura in Sententias*, I, q. 10, a. 2, Paris 15853, f. 66ra-b.
2. AUGUSTINUS, *De civitate Dei*, XI, c. 15, ed. Dombart et Kalb (CCSL 48), p. 335-336 ; c. 17, p. 336-337.
3. ANSELMUS CANTUARIENSIS, *De casu diaboli*, c. 5, ed. Schmitt, p. 242.28-243.3.
4. PETRUS LOMBARDUS, *Sententiae*, II, d. 3, c. 4, ed. Brady, vol. 1, p. 343.15-344.2.
5. *Supra*, 10.
6. *Supra*, 9.
7. *Supra*, 8.
8. *Supra*, 19.
9. *Supra*, 19.
10. AVERROES, *Commentum super libro Physicorum*, VI, comm. 32, transl. Michael Scotus, f. 148rb.
11. *Supra*, 14 et 21.

malam voluntatem, id est, malam volitionem, « nulla res fecerit », sed « semper fuerit »[e], quia mala voluntas, ut ait, « in aliqua[f] natura fuit. Si enim in nulla fuit[g], omnino non fuit. Si autem in aliqua, vitiabat[h] eam et corrumpebat. Eratque[i] illi[j] noxia ac per hoc bono privabat. Porro si nocuit, bonum auferendo vel minuendo utique nocuit[k]. Non igitur esse potuit sempiterna voluntas mala in ea re in qua bonum naturale praecesserat, quod mala voluntas nocendo[l] posset[m] adimere ». Haec ille.

[27] Dicendum est igitur quod argumentum Augustini[n] non concludit nisi supponendo voluntatem angelicam creatam fuisse sub bono aliquo naturali vel gratuito vel post ante peccatum tale recepisse, cui naturaliter vel de lege statuta Dei repugnaret peccatum eo modo vel simili quo tenetur peccatum mortale repugnare[o] gratiae, et certe cum hoc supposito nullo modo staret quod talis[p] natura in primo instanti sui esse peccaret. Et ideo signanter dicit Augustinus quod « esse non potuit sempiterna mala voluntas in ea re in qua bonum naturale praecesserat ». Dato enim quod praecise praecesserit natura bona substantialis sine omni bono accidentali cui repugnet peccatum, quam naturam[q] creavit Deus, non esset[r] necesse quod actus peccandi causatus a[s] tali natura in seipsa bonum
S 41va aliquod adimat. Quando autem[t] infuerit vel tunc insit, licet bene excludere | possit bonum quod inesse deberet[u] tamquam repugnans naturaliter vel de lege Dei statuta tali bono, et hoc pro mensura pro qua ponitur actus ille[v] peccati, sed[w] tunc non proprie corrumpit nec adimit tale bonum, quia quod nec est nec umquam fuit non corrumpitur[x], sed bene tunc excluditur[y] vel impeditur causari vel obstatur[z] ne sit.

[28] Breviter igitur dicendum ad formam quod non oportet quod peccatum nec omissionis nec commissionis[a] semper privet bonum aliquod quod infuit, sed quod potius[b] inesse deberet. Et ideo non requiritur aliqua praecessio nisi forte naturae inter naturam quae[c] peccare potest et peccatum, positis supernaturaliter cognitionibus requisitis, cuius oppositum imaginatur argumentum, nisi modo praeexposito exponatur.

[29] Aliter etiam potest dici quod Augustinus[d] tantum intendit ibi probare quod mala volitio non est naturalis voluntati sic quod naturaliter eam consequatur, sicut calor ignem vel huiusmodi[e], quia cum[f] mala volitio adimat bonum – non quidem substantiale, sed[g] accidentale – quod posset inesse vel quod infuit, cui et[h] repugnat, quia aliter illud non adimeret, sequitur quod mala volitio non sit
V 56v naturalis | voluntati non plus quam bonum quod[i] adimit, sed quod ipsa praecedat utrumque, saltem natura, et per consequens ipsa non est coaeva vel coaeterna

(e) fuerit] fuit *MST* || (f) in aliqua] mala *T* || (g) fuit] vitium *add. MST* || (h) vitiabat] vitiabit *MST* || (i) eratque] erat *MT* ; erat enim *S* ; *p.c. V* || (j) illi] eius *M* ; illius *ST*, *a.c. V* || (k) bonum – nocuit] *om. hom. S* || (l) nocendo] nolendo *a.c. i.l. M*, *ST* || (m) posset] poterat *p.c. M*, *S* ; poterit *T* || (n) quod – augustini] ad argumentum quod *MT* || (o) repugnare] divinae *add. MT* || (p) cum – talis] *mg. M* ; *om. T* || (q) naturam] natura *V* || (r) esset] est *V* || (s) a] in *MST*, *a.c. V* || (t) quando autem] quod ante *MST* || (u) deberet] debet *T* || (v) actus ille] *tr. S* || (w) sed] da* *add. s.l. a.m. M* || (x) corrumpitur] corrumpit *MST* || (y) excluditur] concluditur *S* || (z) obstatur] ostatur *T* || (a) omissionis – commissionis] *tr. MST* || (b) quod potius] *tr. MST* || (c) quae] qua *MT* ; qui *S* || (d) augustinus] alius *a.c. mg. M*, *T* || (e) vel huiusmodi] *om. MST* ; *s.l. V* || (f) cum] tamen *MS* || (g) sed] vel *a.c. mg M*, *ST* || (h) et] *om. MST* || (i) quod] *om. V*

voluntati quasi sibi naturalis, cuius oppositum dicunt Manichaei ponentes hanc malitiam esse sibi comproductam a malo principio, secundum Augustinum, *De duabus animabus*[1], et saepe alibi[2].

[30] Item, etiam tertio modo omne peccatum commissionis adimit de bono, id est, de pronitate ad bonum, quia statim actus malus positus relinquit habitum vel dispositionem ad actum consimilem, et[j] forte etiam una omissio reddit proniorem ad aliquas consimiliter omittendum. Et si relinquitur | habitus vel dispositio ad **T 29va** simile[k] | malum, igitur non solum erit ad malum pronior[l] quam prius, sed etiam **M 34vb** nec[m] poterit ceteris paribus in actum ita intensum sicut prius potuisset, quia sicut habitus bonus facit ad actus intensionem[n], ita malus videtur impedire intensionem actus consimilis boni, et haec habituatio potest per consequens « boni ademptio » nominari.

[31→4] Ad secundum, bene verum est quod Augustinus ibi reprobat opinionem tenentium angelum peccasse in primo instanti sui esse, sed non ponentium angelum potuisse peccare[o] in primo instanti sui esse. Longe autem aliud est loqui de facto et loqui de possibili. Quod autem sequitur, « non intelligunt, si natura talis est » etc., non dicitur contra ponentes angelum potuisse peccasse in primo instanti sui esse, nec etiam contra ponentes eos peccasse in primo instanti sui esse[p], licet eorum[q] opinionem reprobet[r], sed contra Manichaeos ponentes angelos malos malas habere naturas a malo principio, sicut bonos bonas a bono principio[s]. Nam si sic, natura peccaret et[t] non peccaret, et ita simul peccaret et non peccaret. Et haec est intentio eius[u], quod probatur[v] ex capitulo 14 immediate praecedenti ubi, cum improbasset ponentes angelos a primo instanti sui esse peccasse, nihilominus[w] consequenter excusat eos ab haeresibus[x] dicens[y][3] : « Huic sententiae quisquis adquiescit, non cum[z] illis haereticis[a] sapit, id est, Manichaeis. Et si quae aliae[b] pestes[c] ita[d] sentiunt[e], quod suam quandam propriam[f] tamquam ex adverso quodam principio Diabolus habeat naturam mali ». Et contra illos Manichaeos pro se trahentes illud Iohannis[4] : *Ab initio Diabolus peccat* et similia, capitulo 15 dicit quod assumpsit argumentum[5] : « Non intelligunt »[g] etc. Non autem, ut dictum est[h], contra ponentes eum ab initio potuisse peccare, nam secundum principium eiusdem[i] Augustini contra Arium, nulla repugnantia est effectum esse coaevum

(j) et] vel *S* || (k) simile] similem *T* || (l) pronior] promptior *S* || (m) nec etiam] *tr.* *V* || (n) actus intensionem] actum intensiorem *MT* || (o) in – peccare] *mg. (hom.)* *V* || (p) nec – esse] *mg. (hom.)* *T* || (q) eorum] illorum *V* || (r) opinionem reprobet] opinio reprobetur *S* ; *p.c.* *V* || (s) bono principio] *tr.* *S* || (t) et] *om.* *V* || (u) est – eius] eius intentio *V* || (v) probatur] probat *S* || (w) nihilominus] tamen *add.* *MST* || (x) haeresibus] haeresi *V* || (y) dicens] *om.* *MT* ; *mg.* *S* || (z) cum] est *V* || (a) haereticis] haeresibus *MST* || (b) aliae] *om.* *M* ; *mg.* *S* || (c) pestes] postes *M* || (d) ita] *om.* *MT* || (e) sentiunt] sentient *MS* || (f) propriam] semperam *M* ; *p.c.* *S* || (g) intelligunt] intelligant *MT* ; intelligebant *S* || (h) est] et *add.* *MT* || (i) principium eiusdem] principia eius *V*

1. AUGUSTINUS, *De duabus animabus contra Manichaeos*, c. 12 (PL 42), coll. 105-108.
2. AUGUSTINUS, *Confessiones*, *De moribus ecclesiae catholicae et de moribus Manichaeorum*, *De Genesi contra Manichaeos*, *Contra Adimantum*, *Contra epistolam Manichaei quam vocant fundamenti*, *Contra Faustum*, *Contra Felicem*, et *Contra Iulianum*.
3. AUGUSTINUS, *De civitate Dei*, XI, c. 13, ed. Dombart et Kalb (CCSL 48), p. 334.48-52.
4. 1 Io. 3 : 8.
5. AUGUSTINUS, *De civitate Dei*, XI, c. 15, ed. Dombart et Kalb (CCSL 48), p. 335.1-3.

suae causae[j]. Nec maior repugnantia apparet circa hoc si alia requisita concurrant de voluntate et suo effectu quam alibi, ut[k] ipse hic concedit, de pede scilicet et[l] vestigio eius et de igne et splendore eius. Igitur breviter[m] Augustinus non intendit illam consequentiam : « Si peccavit[n] in primo instanti[o], igitur natura », sed sumit contra Manichaeos dictum eorum quod natura peccavit, et ex illo infert oppositum
**S 41vb** quod tunc non peccavit. Verum est | etiam quod nulla natura[p] potest peccare in primo instanti sui esse relicta in omnibus naturae suae et communi Dei influentia[q], quia peccatum requirit deliberationem vel tempus in quo possit deliberari, sed hoc in instanti fieri non potest per naturam voluntatis creatae[r].

[32→5] Ad tertium dicendum quod optime dicit Augustinus. Deus enim non est per se loquendo auctor mali seu malitiae[s], sed naturae, et ideo oportet naturam praeesse a qua malitia posset[t] esse. Sed hanc praecessionem[u] non oportet esse temporis vel mensurae, sed solum causalitatis et[v] naturae, sicut nec alibi, secundum eum, ut dictum est prius.

[33→32] Contra, dicit : « natura non vitiata praecessisset »[w].

[34→33] Dicendum quod intelligit « non vitiatam »[x] ex hoc quod natura est, et hoc sibi sufficit contra Manichaeos dicentes contrarium.

[35→6] Ad quartum satis dictum est quaestione 6 huius distinctionis[1].

[36→7] Ad quintum, concedendum est[y] quod posset mereri in primo instanti, sicut et peccare, si omnes cognitiones necessariae, quarum naturalis causatio[z] requirit tempus, essent sibi a Deo infusae.

[37] Et cum probatur quod nullus potest mereri nisi quando iustitiam potest[a] amittere, dicendum quod, si per iustitiam intelligatur aliquod positivum informans naturam intellectualem, illud assumptum est falsum. Si sola innocentia naturalis, quae nihil positivum addit super naturalem bonitatem substantialem[b], verum est, quia eo ipso quod quis peccaret, iam non esset innocens, posito peccato, iam[c], licet simul duratione, prius tamen natura, potuerit[d] innocentiam conservare vel habere. Et ideo sicut potest in primo instanti peccare, ita potest iustitiam secundo modo dictam in primo instanti amittere, id est, facere ne sit tunc innocens.

[38] Verum est tamen quod[e] ulterius assumit argumentum, quod iustitiam positivam, id est, bonum actum quem tunc causaret, non posset tunc amittere, quia ex hoc sequeretur quod simul haberet eam et non haberet, si possibile illud inesse poneretur. Unde propositio accepta innitens auctoritati Anselmi, quae veritatem habet bene intellecta de lege communi, licet instantiam habuerit[f] in Christo et

(j) suae causae] suae *a.c. V* ; *tr. p.c. s.l. V* || (k) ut] *a.c. V* ; ubi *p.c. V* || (l) et] de *add. MST* || (m) igitur breviter] *tr. MT* || (n) peccavit] peccat *MST, a.c. V* || (o) instanti] *mg. MS* || (p) natura] *a.c. V* ; creatura* *p.c. V* || (q) communi – influentia] tantum dei influentiae *MST* || (r) creatae] quod nullus potest peccare in primo instanti sui esse v *add. mg. infra MS* || (s) seu malitiae] *om. MST* || (t) posset] possit *S* || (u) praecessionem] processionem *a.c. S, V* || (v) et] vel *MT* || (w) natura – praecessisset] naturam non vitiatam praecessisse *S* || praecessisset] praecessissent *V* || (x) vitiata] vitiatam *S* || (y) est] *om. MT* ; *s.l. S* || (z) naturalis causatio] quaelibet naturalis cognitio *MST* (naturalis creatio *P*) || (a) iustitiam potest] *tr. MST* || (b) substantialem] *iter. M* || (c) posito – iam] *om. MST* ; *mg. V* || (d) potuerit] potuit *MST, a.c. mg. V* || (e) tamen quod] quod cum *S* ; *tr. T* || (f) habuerit] habuit *MT*

1. Adam Wodeham, *Ordinatio Oxoniensis*, I, d. 1, q. 6 (*V* 46v-47r).

Beata Virgine ex privilegio, debet intelligi ad hoc quod universaliter[g] vera sit de iustitia hac vel[h] illa disiunctim. Nam de iustitia positiva accidentali superaddita per informationem non[i] esset processus suus bonus nisi supponatur, sicut etiam[j] secundum veritatem Anselmus supponit, angelos bonos fuisse prius[k] et talem iustitiam aliquam habuisse prius[l] quam angeli mali bonis concreati ceciderunt. Et hoc supposito, ille processus nihil faceret[m] contra dicta.

### <RESPONSIO AD RATIONEM SEXTAM FITZRALPH CONTRA QUINTAM CONCLUSIONEM>

[39→8] Ad sextum, dicendum quod illud quod facit Firauf[n] hic[o] non est contra me, qui[p] pono actum talem posse fieri divisibiliter per partem ante partem. Sed tunc mutetur casus, quia[q] praecipiatur ei quod totum actum simul et non per partem ante partem[r] eliciat ita cito sicut potest; et tunc quid dicendum est patet ex[s] responsione ad tertiam obiectionem contra primam conclusionem [1]. Contradictionem enim implicat illo casu posito quod immediate post hoc[t] instans in quo voluntas suspenditur a causando actum suum simul et subito causet illum[u] successive, cum poterit bene, et[v] ideo non oportet quod exspectet per tempus | ad **M 35ra**
causandum, sicut ibi de subita causatione luminis a sole dictum est[w].

[40] Et cum in contrarium assumitur – non tamen[x] per Firauf[y] – quod actus voluntatis est indivisibilis, non est verum nisi loquendo[z] de indivisibilitate opposita extensivae magnitudini[a].

[41] Ad aliam improbationem[b] neganda est consequentia ubi[c] agentia naturalia relinquuntur[d] suis naturalibus activitatibus. Ubi autem miraculose suspenduntur vel in agendo adiuvantur | et reguntur, non esset consequens in casu inconveniens. **V 57r**
Et sic esset in casu isto, ut in illa responsione in simili dictum est.

[42] Propter aliud etiam est calumnia in hac secunda probatione[e] pro eo quod universaliter[f] ubi passum uniformiter indisponitur indispositione contraria effectui[g] producendi, in tali subito prius duratione amovetur[h] indispositio quam forma intenta inducatur ab activo creato naturaliter. Et[i] ita necessario[j] interveniet tempus antequam incipiet[k] introduci forma intenta, quia non[l] subito nec simul auferetur talis indispositio[m] gradualiter divisibilis[n], dato ultimo instanti totalis

(g) universaliter] *om. MT* || (h) vel] et *a.c. s.l. M* ; et *ST* || (i) non] *om. MST* ; *s.l. V* || (j) etiam] *om. S* ; et *V* (et *a.c. P*) || (k) fuisse prius] *tr. MST* || (l) prius] post *M* || (m) faceret] facit *MT* || (n) firauf] fronri *M* ; frnªst’ *S* ; frauf’ *T* ; ffirauf’ *V* || (o) hic] *post* me *MST* || (p) qui] quia *S* || (q) quia] quod (*mg.*) *MS* (*def. T*) || (r) sed – partem] *mg. (hom.) M* ; *mg. infra (hom.) S* ; *om. hom. T* || (s) ex] quod *MT* ; in *add. s.l. MT* || (t) hoc] *om. S* ; *p.c. T* || (u) illum] illis *MST*, *a.c. V* || (v) et] *om. MST* || (w) est] etc. *add. MT* || (x) assumitur non tamen] assumatur *S* || (y) firauf] frauf’ *MT* ; frnªf’ *S* ; ffirauf’ *V* || (z) loquendo] *s.l. M* ; *om. T* || (a) magnitudine] magnitudinis *MT* ; *p.c. mg. S* || (b) opposita – improbationem] *mg. V* || (c) ubi] nisi a.c. *s.l. M* ; nisi *ST* || (d) relinquuntur] relinquantur *MST* || (e) probatione] improbatione *MST* || (f) universaliter] videtur *MT*, *a.c. mg. S* || (g) effectui] effectum *M*, *a.c. STV* || (h) amovetur] amor *M* || (i) et] *om. MT* ; *mg. S* || (j) necessario] necesse *MT*, *a.c. V* ; necesse est *a.c. S* || (k) incipiet] incipiat *V* || (l) non] nec *MST* || (m) indispositio] sed *add. S* || (n) divisibilis] divisibiliter *MST*

1. *Supra*, q. 8, a. 1, 20→10.

indispositionis. Sed sic non oportet ubi[o] passum est sufficienter dispositum, ut patet de visu et visibili movendo[p] versus visum[q] quiescentem ab hoc instanti, in
T 29vb quo pono[r] quod sit in[s] minima distantia | a qua immutare visum non possit. Nam
S 42ra posito hoc[t] | immediate post visum immutabit.

[43] Et si quaeras an semper ubi passum[u] est indispositum oporteat tempus intervenire, dicendum quod non, quia posset contingere quod passum esset sic indispositum[v] difformiter quod continue ab uno extremo passi[w] secundum extensionem versus aliud esset[x] semper remissius et remissius[y] indispositum donec ex modo[z] continuae remissionis totaliter cesset[a] indisponi[b]. Illo autem casu posito[c], approximato activo sufficienti et sufficienter ex parte illa ubi cessat indispositio per remissionem, aestimo quod immediate post instans sufficientis[d] approximationis cessaret[e] alia[f] pars passi prius[g] indisposita[h] esse secundum se indisposita, vel magis in hoc instanti sic desineret indisponi et inciperet[i] perdere indispositionem et formam[j] novam recipere[k] et per partem ante partem in infinitum, cum non sit dare gradum remississimum[l] versus illam partem[m].

[44→43] Sed contra hanc responsionem potest argui ponendo casum parum[n] aliter, utpote quod in hoc instanti nolit Deus cooperari tali voluntati ad dilectionem eliciendam, sed praecipiat sibi quod ita cito sicut potest simul et non partibiliter[o] eliciat talem actum, et tunc stat in suo robore argumentum.

[45→44] Ad illud potest dupliciter dici[p], uno modo imaginando quod intellectus creatus posset distincte omni tempore assignabili quantumcumque parvo minus tempus[q] naturaliter distincte percipere, utpote dividendo tempus aliquod[r] futurum in eius primam et secundam medietatem[s]; de secunda non curet[t], sed primam sic dividat in suas medietates; et posteriorem abiciat[u], et[v] primam iterum dividat; et ita deinceps, et quamlibet semper particulam distincte cognoscat. Ita enim certum[w] est Deum distinctissime[x] cognoscere partes temporis finiti[y] futuri cuiusvis dandi proportionales[z] infinitas. Et si talis cognitio partium temporis esset creaturae possibilis sicut est[a] Deo – et aliqui etiam simile dicunt de angelo – secundum hoc dicendum esset consequenter sicut est de facto in hoc

(o) ubi] si *S* || (p) movendo] motus *M* ; moto *ST* ; *p.c. V* || (q) visum] finem *MT*, *a.c. mg. S* || (r) pono] posito *mg. M* ; *om. T* ; *mg. S* || (s) in] *om. MT* || (t) posito hoc] *tr. S* || (u) passum] possum *M* || (v) oporteat – indispositum] *om. hom. M* ; *mg. infra (hom.) S* || (w) passi] passivo *M* || (x) esset] esse *V* || (y) et remissius] *om. MT* ; *mg. SV* || (z) ex modo] extremum *MT* ; extensio *S* || (a) cesset] esset *M* || (b) indisponi] indisposito *MT* ; *p.c. S* ; in *add. MT*, *a.c. S* || (c) posito] *om. MTV* ; *mg. S* (posito *P*) || (d) sufficientis] sufficienter *MTV* (sufficientis *P*) || (e) cessaret] *a.c. S* ; restaret *p.c. S* || (f) alia] aliqua *ST* || (g) prius] pars illius *MT* || (h) indisposita] disponat *V* || (i) inciperet] *post* indispositionem *MST*, *a.c. V* || (j) formam] formaret *M* || (k) recipere] partem *add. M* || (l) remississimum] remissionis *M* ; *p.c. S* || (m) partem] an si angelus crearetur in hoc instanti posset simul et indivisibiliter producere actum diligendi deum ita cito sicut posset **x** *add. mg. infra MS* || (n) parum] partim *MST* || (o) partibiliter] partialiter *M* || (p) potest – dici] dici potest dupliciter *MT* ; potest dici dupliciter *S* || (q) tempus] *om. MST* ; *mg. V* || (r) aliquod] ad *MT* || (s) medietatem] et *add. V* || (t) curet] tenet *T* || (u) abiciat] aliciat *M* || (v) et] sed *T* || (w) certum] verum *S* || (x) distinctissime] distincte *S* || (y) finiti] *om. S* || (z) proportionales] proportiones *MT* ; per portiones *S* || (a) creaturae – est] possibilis creaturae sicut *MT*

casu dicendum de Deo, videlicet[b] quod tunc necessario[c] exspectabit per tempus, et tamen per nullum[d] tempus necessario exspectabit[e].

[46] Et cum supponitur quod praecipiatur tali, retenta illa[f] imaginatione quod ita cito post instans praesens eliciat actum simul sicut potest, dicendum quod illud positum tunc includit contradictionem sicut et quod[g] Deus[h] ita cito post hoc instans sicut potest causet aliquid simul. Signatur enim per propositionem hanc quod non posset citius post hoc instans causare simul aliquid, puta *a*, quam causabit[i] ipsum, quod repugnantiam includit, quia ex quo tempus intervenit[j] in medio instanti illius temporis, posset illud simul[k] causare[l]. Nullum est enim primum instans[m] possibile assignari[n] post hoc instans ante quod[o] non valeat ipsum simul causare.

[47→46] Contra[p] : huius propositionis « Deus potest ita cito post hoc instans causare *a* sicut potest *a* causare » subiectum includit praedicatum[q].

[48→47] Dicendum quod ipsa non est vera, non plus quam ista : « Tantum potest Deus[r] facere quantum potest facere ». Prima non, quia significat[s] quod ita cito posset simul causare quod non citius. Et secunda etiam falsa est, quia significat quod Deus potest aliquid ita magnum[t] facere quod non maius[u]. Et ad propositionem dicendum quod multae propositiones sunt impossibiles in quibus tamen subiectum includit praedicatum, verbi gratia : « Homo irrationalis est homo », et similes. Similiter[v] haec[w] : « Omnis homo est omne[x] animal », et haec[y] : « Omne album est omne[z] coloratum », ad communem intellectum loquentium subiectum includit praedicatum, id est, definitio subiecti haberet praedicatum partem sui, et tamen illae possunt esse falsae. Et praeterea propositio illa[a] est hypothetica, et plures, non una. Ibi enim magis est[b] consequentia quaedam, et[c] antecedens et[d] consequens habent[e] idem subiectum, et imaginatur falso argumentum quod antecedens sit subiectum et consequens praedicatum[f].

[49→48] Sed quid si dicatur[g] tunc : « Ibi antecedens | includit consequens, **M 35rb**
igitur consequentia bona » ?

[50→49] Dicendum quod non, sed potius econverso. Nam quantum[h] potest Deus facere, tantum[i] potest facere et non econtra, et quam cito potest post hoc instans aliquid instantanee producere, tam cito potest etc. et non econtra[j]. Si autem, sicut verum est, teneatur quod creatura non potest per naturam suam

(b) videlicet] oportet *S* || (c) necessario] actus *add. T* || (d) per nullum] parvum *M* ; per alium *T* || (e) per tempus – exspectabit] *mg. (hom.)* V || (f) illa] *om. MST* || (g) quod] *om. MT* ; *s.l. V* || (h) deus] existens *M* ; ens *T* ; *p.c. V* || (i) causabit] causaret *MS* || (j) intervenit] ita erit *M* || (k) illud simul] *tr. V* || (l) causare] causaret *M* || (m) primum instans] *tr. V* || (n) assignari] assignare *MST* || (o) ante quod] aut quod *M* ; antequam *V* || (p) contra] si dicatur *S* || (q) praedicatum] igitur vera *add. mg. S* || (r) potest deus] *tr. MST, a.c. V* || (s) significat] significatur *S* || (t) aliquid – magnum] ita magnum aliquid *MST* ; aliquid magnum ita *a.c. V* || (u) maius] magis *S* || (v) similiter] et *add. S* || (w) haec] hoc *M* || (x) omne] *om. V* || (y) et haec] et hoc *M* ; haec et haec *S* || (z) omne] *om. MTV* || (a) praeterea – illa] prima propositio (proposita *M*) *MT* || (b) ibi – est] et non magis differt M || (c) et] *om. T* || (d) antecedens et] minus *M* || (e) habent] habens *MS* ; *p.c. V* || (f) praedicatum] nota an deus possit aliquid facere ita cito sicut potest facere *add. mg. T* || (g) idem subiectum – dicatur] *om. M* || (h) quantum] coniunctim *MT, a.c. V* ; quantumcumque *S* || (i) tantum] quantum *MT* ; quam *a.c. V* ; *p.c. s.l. V* || (j) econtra] econverso *MST*

ceteris partibus tempus sic in infinitum dividere ut quamlibet particulam distincte apprehendat[k], tunc dicendum est quod saltem in fine[l] minimi temporis ab eo perceptibilis distincte vel maxime[m] non perceptibilis[n] ab eo[o] distincte ceteris paribus[p] tenetur habere actum sibi praeceptum[q] subito ab eo causabilem, si sibi praecipiatur simul elici[r].

S 42rb [51] Aliter a principio potest totum | argumentum fieri contra arguentem in modico mutato casu, sicut ipsemet[s] tangit in quodam alio argumento contra semet ipsum[1], quia creetur[t] unus angelus iuxta suam opinionem cum tempore, id est, non in instanti, sed immediate post instans, et hoc[u] cum sufficienti[v] cognitione et praecepto quod diligat Deum quam cito possit. Tunc quaero utrum ita cito[w] possit libere diligere Deum sicut est vel non. Si non[x], necessario exspectabit per[y] tempus, et per consequens toto illo tempore velit-nolit peccabit peccato omissionis, quod habet ille[z] pro inconvenienti. Si sic, contra : tunc talis[a] non libere haberet talem actum, quia libertas, secundum illum, est respectu futuri, sicut dicit Magister[2], et per consequens non posset meritorie implere quod sibi praecipitur[b] illo casu[c] posito. Et praeterea non magis videtur quod possit actum simul producere quam cito est illo casu posito quam si crearetur in instanti ceteris paribus.

[52→51] Ad illud[3] dicit[d] quod necessario stabit per tempus non volens aliquid – per quantum autem tempus, Deus novit ! – et quod praeceptum hoc esset irrationabile. Non sic[e] in casu argumenti sui.

[53→52] Contra : praeceptum non est nisi quod diligat ita cito sicut potest, igitur si necessitetur[f] stare per tempus non volens, ita quod non possit ita cito velle sicut creatur[g], igitur non volendo ita cito[h] sicut creatur non[i] faciet contra
V 57v praeceptum, et ita non peccabit[j] | ex hoc quod non ita cito volet. Et ita praeceptum non necessitat[k] eum ad sibi[l] impossibile, nec ad aliquid inobservabile, igitur non est irrationabile[m] plus quam in priori casu. Et praeterea[n], quid ibi[o] impediret ne posset statim velle, cum[p] est, secundum te, primo in tempore ?

T 30ra [54→53] Sed hic leviter dicetur quod immo, hic obligatur | ad sibi impossible et ibi non, quia licet necessario exspectabit per tempus nihil volens, tamen per

(k) apprehendat] et *add. MST* || (l) in fine] infinite *M* || (m) maxime] maximi *S* (*def. V*) || (n) distincte – perceptibilis] *om. hom. V* || (o) ab eo] *scr. sed. del. (post hom.) V* || (p) paribus] tunc *add. MST* || (q) sibi praeceptum] *tr. S* || (r) si – elici] sed sibi simul elici praecipiatur *M* ; si sibi non repugnet simul elici *S* ; si sibi elici praecipiatur *T* || elici] an si non esset primum instans esse angeli posset diligere deum etiam successive ita cito sicut posset y *add. mg. infra MS* || (s) ipsemet] ipsum *MST, a.c. V* || (t) creetur] detur *M* ; causetur *T* || (u) hoc] similiter *MST, a.c. s.l. V* || (v) sufficienti] insufficienti *M* || (w) possit – cito] potest quaero utrum ita cito *mg. V* || (x) non] ergo *add. S* || (y) per] *om. MST* ; *s.l. V* || (z) habet ille] *tr. S* || (a) tunc talis] *tr. V* || (b) sibi praecipitur] *tr. S* || (c) casu] *om. MST* || (d) dicit] potest dici *MT* ; dici potest *S* || (e) sic] autem *add. MT* || (f) necessitetur] necessitaretur *V* || (g) creatur] crearetur *MST, a.c. V* || (h) ita cito] *om. MT* ; *mg. S* || (i) non] nec *S* || (j) peccabit] ut *add. M* ; nec *add. T* ; contra praeceptum *add. mg. V* || (k) necessitat] necessitet *a.c. S* ; necessitaret *p.c. S* || (l) sibi] similiter *M* || (m) irrationabile] non *add. V* || (n) praeterea] propter *MT* || (o) ibi] *om. M* || (p) cum] quod *MT*

1. RICCARDUS FITZRALPH, *Lectura in Sententias*, I, q. 10, a. 2, Paris 15853, f. 67va.
2. PETRUS LOMBARDUS, *Sententiae*, II, d. 25, c. 1, ed. Brady, vol. 1, p. 461.13-19.
3. RICCARDUS FITZRALPH, *Lectura in Sententias*, I, q. 10, a. 2, Paris 15853, f. 67vb.

nullum tempus[q] necessario[r] exspectabit, quia nullum est tempus[s] ita parvum quin ante finem illius poterit velle, et ideo impossibile est quod ita cito velit sicut potest velle nisi vellet a principio illius temporis extrinsecus[t], id est, quam cito esset. Verbi gratia, si Deus movebit lapidem post primum instans, Deus non poterit ita brevi tempore[u] movere ipsum[v] sicut poterit; non sic in priori casu.

[55→54] Sed nec haec responsio clara est, quia si per nullum tempus necessario exspectabit[w], et tamen[x] necessario exspectabit per tempus, igitur quantumcumque cito incipiet, in infinitum citius incipere posset successive vel subito actum producere, quia plus quam duplo et quadruplo citius et sic in infinitum. Sed[y] hoc non videtur nisi[z] ita cito poterit incipere sicut esset[a] si primo erit in tempore, iuxta fantasiam illius.

[56] Praeterea, si necessario exspectabit[b] per tempus, licet per nullum tempus necessario, aut igitur ideo[c] necessario exspectabit quia actus non est ab eo simul factibilis, vel[d] quia tunc non est voluntas[e] receptiva eius, vel quia voluntas non ita cito agere potest[f] sicut ipsa est, vel quia non potest ita cito agere in se sicut ipsa est, vel quia ipsa[g] voluntas primo est in tempore, secundum positionem illam, vel propter aliquid aliud simile. Non primo modo, quia saltem a Deo posset voluntas produci sub[h] actu in ipsa receptibili. Et etiam quia saltem[i] non obstaret tunc aliquid quin possit partibiliter produci, ita[j] videlicet quod sicut non est dare primam partem[k] temporis, ita etiam non esset[l] dare actum remississimum[m] quem habuisset a se talis voluntas. Non enim hoc[n] apparet impossibilius fieri per tempus certum cum quo immediate post instans intrinsecum[o] illius crearetur[p] angelus quam si crearetur[q] in illo instanti intrinseco[r], sicut per exempla plura[s] posset ostendi, dato quod aliquid[t] posset simul fieri in tempore primo, ita quod non instantanee[u], igitur. Nec secundo modo, quia tunc[v] Deus non posset eam producere sub actu, quod notum est esse falsum. Nec[w] tertio modo, tum quia sol ita cito sicut crearetur iuxta[x] receptivum luminis absque impedimento quolibet extrinseco statim illuminaret. Quare igitur negaretur activitas sibi[y] correspondens respectu susceptivi summe dispositi ipsi voluntati coaeva ? Primum patet per Philosophum, II *De anima*[1], et[z]

(q) exspectabit – nullum tempus] *iter. M* || (r) necessario] *om. MT* ; *mg. S* || (s) nullum – tempus] per tempus (nihil volens *exp.*) est *M* ; (per *exp.*) nullum tempus est *S* ; per nullum tempus est *T* || (t) extrinsecus] extrinseco *a.c. S, V* || (u) brevi tempore] breviter *MT* || (v) ipsum] *ante* ita brevi *MST, a.c. V* || (w) per – exspectabit] exspectabit poterit successive vel subito actum producere *a.c. mg. V* || (x) tamen] tunc *MT* || (y) sed] *om. V* || (z) nisi] *om. M* || (a) esset] esse *V* || (b) exspectabit] *om. MST* || (c) ideo] *om. MST* ; *s.l. V* || (d) vel] *om. MT* ; *s.l. V* || (e) non – voluntas] voluntas non est *MT* || (f) agere potest] *tr. MT* || (g) ipsa] *om. T* || (h) sub] in *MT* ; *p.c. S* || (i) quia saltem] *om. MST* || (j) ita] id est *MST, a.c. V* || (k) partem] illius *add. MT* || (l) esset] est *M* || (m) remississimum] remissum *a.c. S* ; remissius *p.c. S* || (n) hoc] *om. MST* ; *s.l. V* || (o) intrinsecum] extrinsecum *V* || (p) crearetur] daretur *MS, p.c. T* || (q) angelus – crearetur] *mg. V* || crearetur] daretur *MST* || (r) intrinseco] extrinseco *V* || (s) plura] pura *M* || (t) aliquid] aliquis *S* ; aliquis aliquid *T* || (u) in – instantanee] *mg. V* || (v) tunc] *om. MT* ; *mg. S* || (w) nec] neque *S* || (x) crearetur iuxta] daretur medium *S* || (y) sibi] *om. T* || (z) et] *om. M*

1. ARISTOTELES, *De anima*, II, c. 7 : 418b20-26.

per Augustinum[a][1], quia ex quo est activum naturale, agit semper quantum tunc potest et ita cito sicut[b] potest. Tum etiam quia voluntas, statim cum esset intellectui alterius angeli praesentata, ibi ageret cognitionem sui, vel[c] agere posset
**M 35va** cognitionem sui, nam quid obstaret ? Nec quarto modo, quia statim potest[d] | agere in alium angelum, igitur pari ratione poterit in se. Nec quinto modo, quia[e] non
**S 42va** plus quam sol | necessario[f] exspectaret producere radium suum[g] in instanti – sive in primo[h] tempore, secundum illam imaginationem – produceretur a Deo. Quid[i] enim plus obstaret ex parte voluntatis quin statim agere valeat quam[j] ex parte solis ? Breviter nulla poterit causa assignari sufficiens quare non valeat statim velle[k] simul et subito vel[l] particulariter et successive, igitur etc.

[57] Praeterea, secundum illum, si angelus produceretur in instanti, tunc posset primo agere in tempore immediate sequenti simul producendo actum volendi vel successive, licet non in primo instanti sui esse, alias non esset praeceptum sexti argumenti sui rationabile, etiam secundum istum, nisi posset immediate post primum[m] instans agere. Sed si possit[n] primo[o] causari[p] immediate post illud instans, angelus nulla penitus activitate carebit in illo tempore respectu producendorum ab eo in tempore quam habuisset si in instanti illo[q] fuisset productus. Quare ergo[r] non ita poterit nunc agere in toto illo tempore sicut tunc[s] ? Igitur adhuc[t] secundum hoc praeceptum illud foret irrationabile.

[58] Praeterea, tu arguis per illud praeceptum tamquam rationabile, contra illos qui ponunt angelum posse peccare in primo instanti sui esse omittendo quod praecipitur diligi, dato quod praecise pro[u] illo instanti Deus sequestraret actum diligendi[v], quia tunc, dicis tu[w], peccabit velit-nolit si praecipiatur sibi[x] quod diligat quam cito[y] poterit, sed ita impossibile. Si tamen[z] impossibile[a] erit sibi, illo casu posito, ita cito facere sicut poterit, sicut in casu isto ubi dicis[b] praeceptum esse irrationabile, sicut satis patet[c] prius ex probatione primae conclusionis et multis prius declaratis[2], igitur non plus est praeceptum ibi[d] irrationabile quam hic, sive actus solum sit simul producibilis sive successive per partem ante partem.

[59] Praeterea, ostendetur in responsione argumenti principalis, quia non solum exspectabit necessario per tempus manentibus praecise eisdem dispositionibus aliis quibus prius, sed etiam quod per tempus hoc supposito in talibus necessario exspectabit ceteris omnibus paribus, igitur etc.

(a) augustinum] et *add. V* || (b) sicut] tunc *add. MST, add. sed exp. V* || (c) ageret – vel] *om. MST* ; *mg. V* || (d) cum – potest] *iter. M* || (e) quia] quod non *a.c. S* ; *om. V* || (f) necessario] *om. T* || (g) suum] sive *V* || (h) sive – primo] sine *MT* ; sive in *a.c. S* ; sive primo in *p.c. s.l. S* || (i) quid] quin *V* || (j) quam] quare *p.c. S* || (k) velle] et *add. V* || (l) vel] *om. V* || (m) primum] illud *MST* || (n) possit] posset *MST, a.c. V* || (o) primo] *a.c. S* ; prius *p.c. S* || (p) causari] dare *M* ; causare *a.c. S* ; creare *T* ; creare* *a.c. V* || (q) instanti illo] *tr. MT* || (r) ergo] *om. MST* || (s) sicut tunc] *om. T* || (t) adhuc] ad hoc *V* || (u) pro] ab *MST, a.c. V* || (v) diligendi] deum *add. MST* || (w) tu] *om. V* || (x) sibi] *om. MST* || (y) cito] cite *M* || (z) tamen] est *add. V* (*def. M*) || (a) si – impossibile] *om. hom. M* || (b) dicis] dicitur *MST* || (c) satis patet] *tr. V* || (d) ibi] *om. M* ; *del. V*

1. Augustinus, *De civitate Dei*, XII, c. 6, ed. Dombart et Kalb (CCSL 48), p. 360.14-41.
2. *Supra*, q. 8, a. 1, 5-29.

## <RESPONSIONES AD RATIONEM SEPTIMAM FITZRALPH CONTRA QUINTAM CONCLUSIONEM[e]>

### *<Responsio Rodington ad rationem septimam>*

[60→9] Ad septimum respondet Rodinton[f] quod si meritum unius horae detur esse duplum ad meritum instantis, quod bene potest – secundum istum – fieri, tunc non est dandum quod excedat in duplo meritum per dimidiam horam cum eisdem condicionibus, sed in aliqua[g] alia proportione, ut in sesquealtera[h], sexquequarta[i], vel huiusmodi[j], quia[k] non est tunc dandum[l] quod in secunda medietate illius horae tantumdem mereatur sicut in prima.

[61] Et cum probas quod sic, quia modo non minus meretur quam si actus esset interruptus in fine primae medietatis et iterato causatus ; sed tunc[m] tantum mereretur[n] in secunda medietate sicut in prima ; igitur et[o] modo, non enim[p] minus meretur[q] ex continuatione : dicendum, secundum istum, quod si ponatur huiusmodi interruptio, tunc vel non reinciperet[r] in secunda medietate horae[s] in principio vel[t] actus praecedens non fuisset continuatus per totam primam medietatem. Sed illud, ut arguit et bene, non solvit, quia ponatur unus alius qui incipiat in secunda medietate[u] actum meritorium cum[v] eisdem condicionibus : ille[w] tantum merebitur in secunda medietate sicut prior in prima, et tamen prior non merebitur minus in secunda medietate ex hoc quod continuat actum. | Igitur **V 58r** tantum meretur[x] ille primus[y] in secunda medietate sicut ille ultimus. « Dico igitur », inquit[z], « quod plus meretur[a] in secunda medietate quam in prima, sed illa merita non sunt totaliter distincta[b]. Unde[c] argumentum procedit ex falsa imaginatione quod in prima medietate | mereretur[d] certo merito et in secunda alio[e] **T 30rb** merito cuius nulla pars praecessit, quod est impossibile si continue mereatur eo quod non potest accipi distinctio talis inter meritum in prima medietate et meritum in secunda tamquam inter merita totaliter distincta[f], quod[g] tamen[h] imaginatur argumentum ». Haec ille.

(e) argumentum] responsio ad illam responsionem quae probat quod si meritum esse posset instantaneum meritum horae et meritum instantaneum ceteris paribus forent aequalia **z** *add. mg. infra MS* || (f) rodinton] idem *M* ; rod *p.c. S* ; rodinton *mg. S* ; rodyn° *T* ; rod' *V* ; rod *mg. V* || (g) aliqua] *om. S* || (h) sesquealtera] sexquaealtera *MT* ; sesquiuntia* *V* || (i) sexquequarta] sexquiquarta *M* ; sesquiquarta *V* || (j) ut – huiusmodi] et sexquialtera sexquiquartum *a.c. mg. V* (in *om. p.c. V*) || (k) quia] quae *M* || (l) tunc dandum] *tr. MST* || (m) sed tunc] *tr. V* (si tunc *P*) || (n) mereretur] meretur *MST, a.c. V* || (o) et] *om. V* (*om. P*) || (p) enim] *om. S* || (q) meretur] *s.l. M* ; *om. ST* || (r) reinciperet] reincipiet *MST, a.c. V* || (s) horae] actum meritorium *T* (*def. M*) || (t) vel] si *s.l. T* (*def. M*) || (u) horae – medietate] *om. hom. M* ; *mg. infra (hom.) S* || (v) cum] *om. T* || (w) ille] illa *M* ; *p.c. S* || (x) meretur] merebitur *MT* ; *p.c. V* || (y) primus] prius *M* ; tantum *T* || (z) inquit] inquam *S* || (a) in – meretur] *mg. supra (hom.) V* || (b) totaliter distincta] *tr. T* || (c) unde] *s.l. M* ; sed *MST* || (d) mereretur] meretur *MST* || (e) alio] aliquo *MT, a.c. SV* || (f) distincta] indistincta *MT, a.c. S* || (g) quod] quia *a.c. S* ; quia *T* || (h) tamen] tunc *MT*

*<Contra responsionem Rodington ad rationem septimam>*

[62→61] **(1)** Haec responsio, licet sit cauta, non tamen est vera, nec sufficiens, primo quia ille ponit se ad impediendum primam consequentiam et eius probationem, et tamen realiter concedit eam. Nam eo ipso quod dat meritum horae esse duplum ad meritum instantaneum, habet concedere quod meritum temporaliter continuatum[i], omnibus aliis condicionibus existentibus paribus, sit aequale merito instantaneo. Quia vel imaginatur meritum instantaneum subduplum ad meritum unius horae includi in merito illius horae duplo, et tunc statim patet
**S 42vb** propositum, | videlicet quod meritum correspondens toti residuo horae a primo instanti est aequale merito primi[j] instantis[k], quia duplum praecise continet[l] illud cuius est duplum et iterum tantumdem, et ita habetur intentum quod meritum continuatum per tempus est aequale merito instantaneo. Vel ipse imaginatur quod meritum horae duplum ad meritum instantaneum[m] non includit ipsum, sed[n] est distinctum meritum superadditum, ita quod resultans ex utroque iam esset triplum ad meritum instantaneum, et adhuc sequitur idem, quia ad illud meritum
**M 35vb** continuatum per tempus duplum ad meritum instantaneum | convenit invenire aliquod[o] meritum temporale, scilicet partem[p] eiusdem meriti[q] sic durantis, subduplum ad suum totum – hoc enim verum est in omnibus quantis[r] quod medietas est subdupla respectu totius – et adhuc habetur intentum quod meritum illud temporale subduplum merito horario[s] sit[t] aequale merito instantaneo, quod erat probandum.

[63] **(2)** Praeterea, sicut iam[u] acceptum est, meritum horarium duplum ad meritum instantis vel[v] includit ipsum, et tunc ut prius, vel non, et tunc male dicit negando meritum totius horae posse dari esse duplum ad meritum dimidiae horae sequentis ex continuatione temporali meriti dati instantanei[w], quia exclusis[x] omnibus extrinsecis – primo scilicet et ultimo – datae horae, cum omnia reliqua[y] supponantur[z] uniformia et aequalia praeter mensuram, nulla videtur ratio quare ad meritum dimidiae horae non debeat dari esse duplum meritum ex continuatione totius horae.

[64] **(3)** Praeterea, falsum est et totaliter irrationabile illud in quo finaliter stat illa responsio, videlicet[a] quod non possit accipi distinctio inter meritum primae partis horae et meritum secundae partis[b] tamquam inter totaliter[c] distincta, sicut imaginatur argumentum, quia[d] tu concedis[e] quod meritum totius horae est maius[f] merito habito in fine primae medietatis. Cum igitur meritum primae medietatis

(i) habet – continuatum] *om. MT* || temporaliter continuatum] temporaliter contiguum *a.c. V* ; *tr. p.c. mg. V* || (j) primi] primo *MST* || (k) instantis] instans *M* ; instanti *a.c. S* ; *p.c. T* || (l) continet] continente *M* || (m) instantaneum] vel ipse imaginatur quod meritum *add. a.c. M* ; quod meritum *add. p.c. M* || (n) sed] si *M* || (o) aliquod] ad *M*, *a.c. V* || (p) scilicet partem] in parte *MT* ; vel partem *S* || (q) eiusdem meriti] *iter. mg. V* || (r) quantis] praedicatis* *M*, quantitatis *ST*, *a.c. V* || (s) horario] horae *V* || (t) sit] sic *M* || (u) iam] *om. MST* || (v) instantis vel] instantaneum vel tunc *MST* || (w) instantanei] instanti *MT* || (x) exclusis] instantibus *add. S* || (y) omnia reliqua] *tr. MST* || (z) supponantur] omnia *add. MT* ; esse *add. S* || (a) videlicet] scilicet *MT* || (b) partis] horae *add. MT* || (c) inter totaliter] *tr. MST* || (d) quia] quod *M* || (e) concedis] concedo *M* ; concedi *T* || (f) maius] magis *S*

remaneat, nec corrumpatur in maioratione meriti ex secunda medietate, ut patet ex materia de augmento formarum – et ille, ut aestimo, in illo mecum concordat – sequitur quod meritum accrescens ex continuatione actus per secundam medietatem horae[g] totaliter distinguitur a merito habito in fine primae medietatis[h] illius[i] horae, sicut una pars meriti totius[j] horae a sua parte, licet non totaliter distinguatur a merito totius horae, cum sit pars eius. Omne enim quod est, quando aliud non est nec aliquid eius, si post existat illud aliud, remanente[k] primo, ab ipso[l] totaliter distinguitur ; sed sic est in proposito de merito habito in fine primae medietatis[m] horae[n] et[o] parte totalis meriti accrescente ex continuatione actus meritorii per secundam partem illius horae, quoniam[p] si tunc mortuus fuisset, nihil accrescentis meriti ex continuatione per[q] secundam medietatem horae habuisset[r] ; igitur etc.[s]

[65→64] Ad illud tertium[t] nulla dari potest – ut mihi videtur – vera evasio nisi dicendo forte quod ipse actus causatus et continuatus est utrobique meritum[u], et illud non[v] distinguitur[w] a se ipso.

[66→65] Sed hoc non[x] valet, nam[y] mutatis terminis dicendo sic : « Ille meretur ex hoc quod libere instantanee causat actum[z] et ex hoc etiam[a] quod continuat », vel igitur aequaliter ex utroque vel non. Si aequaliter, inconveniens primum. Si non, stat argumentum in[b] iteratis[c] terminis[d] per omnia simile facto in terminis prioribus. [*add. V mg. infra* : Similiter, non valet ista consequentia : « Iste actus causatus et continuatus utrobique est meritorius, nec sic distinguitur a seipso, igitur pars non distinguitur a parte » ; consequentia non valet, quia dato quod idem non distinguatur a seipso, tamen pars a parte distinguitur.]

[67→62-63] Ad prima[e] tamen[f] duo posset quis dicere quod non[g] est negandum quin[h] meritum temporale proveniens praecise[i] ex continuatione actus[j] meritorii per tempus sit aequale vel esse possit merito instantaneo. Et ideo concedendum est quod meritum horarium datum esse[k] duplum respectu meriti instantanei[l] includit ipsum et residuum proveniens praecise ex continuatione per horam est aequale merito instantaneo, sicut deducunt argumenta. Nec hoc intendit negare supradicta responsio, sed solum vult[m] vitare meritum causatum[n] per instans et continuatum per tempus posse esse aequale merito eidem[o] instantaneo per se sumpto. Nam ad hunc intellectum vadit argumentum principale, ut videtur, sicut apparet per illud quod apponitur de interruptione.

(g) horae] *om. MST* || (h) primae medietatis] *tr. MST* || (i) illius] *om. V* || (j) totius] totus *M* || (k) remanente primo] re* aliqua prima *T* (*def. M*) || (l) non totaliter – ipso] *om. hom. M* ; qualibet *a.c. mg. infra (hom.) S* || ab ipso] *post* totaliter *V* || (m) primae medietatis] medietatis illius primae *a.c. mg. V* (*def. MST*) || (n) de – horae] ut patet deducenti igitur *MST* || (o) et] *om. M* || (p) quoniam] quam *T* || (q) per] post *S* || (r) habuisset] fuisset *M* || (s) etc.] responsio alia responsio ad illud argumentum **aa** *add. mg. MS* (*infra S*) || (t) tertium] igitur *S* || (u) est – meritum] ex utroque merito *M* ; ex utroque est meritum *a.c. S* ; utrobique est meritum *p.c. s.l. S* || (v) non] *om. MT* ; *mg. S* ; ex utroque meritum est *T* ; *s.l. V* || (w) distinguitur] dicitur *S* ; *p.c. V* || (x) non] *om. MT* || (y) nam] *om. V* || (z) instantanee – actum] causat actum instantanee *MT* || (a) ex hoc etiam] *om. MST* ; *mg. V* || (b) in] *om. MST* ; *s.l. V* || (c) iteratis] mutatis *T* || (d) terminis] quod *add. MT* ; quia *add. S* || (e) prima] ista *S* || (f) tamen] *om. MST* || (g) non] *om. M* || (h) quin] quando *T* || (i) praecise] *om. MST* || (j) actus] *om. M* ; *i.l. T* || (k) esse] est *T* || (l) instantanei] quod *add. S* || (m) vult] *om. MST* ; *mg. V* || (n) causatum] tantum *M* || (o) eidem] eiusdem *MS* ; e[d]' *T*

[68→67] **(1)** Sed contra illud stat difficultas argumenti principalis, videlicet quod non proderit homini continuare per horam meritum suum, sed magis expediet sibi saepe interrumpere actum suum quam continuare eum sine interruptione[p]. Quia modo, ex dato, continuatio per totam horam non valet nisi instantaneam causationem actus in principio horae, secundum istam responsionem, et tamen si saepe interrumperetur[q] actus in illa hora et resumeretur in se vel in simili specie, ita quod vix per decimam partem horae in omnibus vicibus haberet actum huiusmodi meritorium, tantum meretur qualibet vice ex resumptione actus sicut nunc meretur
**S 43ra** in primo instanti horae[r] illius, quia per casum | cetera omnia sunt paria, igitur frequens interruptio actus multum prodest, et per consequens continuatio opposita obesset, quod videtur inconveniens, sicut supponit argumentum principale.

[69] **(2)** Praeterea, secundam illam responsionem nihil valet supradicta responsio cavillatoria quod posita interruptione vel non resumeretur[s] actus in principio secundae medietatis vel non continuaretur usque in finem primae medietatis[t]. Certe hoc verum est, sed nihil valet ad evadendum argumentum, quia[u] dato quod cesset actus a[v] fine primae medietatis horae usque ad medium secundae medietatis et[w] ulterius continuetur solum usque ad finem[x] illius[y]
**V 58v** secundae medietatis, adhuc | illa renovatio actus ita parum continuati, cum
**T 30va** cetera omnia supponantur esse paria, aequivaleret[z] vel excederet[a] | causationem primam instantaneam actus meritorii. Et per consequens continuatio sibi obesset <et> interruptio sibi proficeret, quia[b] totalis continuatio non pertingeret[c] nisi ad meritum aequale primo merito instantaneo, et modo ex interruptione unius quartae horae dictae[d] et recausatione[e] actus haberetur[f] tantumdem et per tantum plus
**M 36ra** quantum acrescit ex continuatione | trium quartarum horae; igitur[g].

[70] **(3)** Praeterea, sicut contingit[h] dare minimum sensibile a sensu vel maximum quod sentiri[i] non potest, ex libello Aristotelis *De sensu et sensato*[1], ita contingit dare minimum tempus[j] a nobis perceptibile[k] vel maximum quod[l] a nobis distincte percipi non potest, secundum exigentiam certarum[m] dispositionum praesentialiter[n] habitarum[o]. Ita etiam de motu, nam rotam horarum in horologio moveri sensibiliter[p] visu non[q] statim percipimus, licet coram[r] oculis realiter, quamvis lente, rotetur – sed nec solem in caelo, quamvis multum velociter moveatur. Cuius causa est, ut aestimo, quod est aliqua minima[s] magnitudo motu

(p) eum – interruptione] *om. MST* ; *mg. V* || (q) interrumperetur] interrumpere *S* (*def. MT*) || (r) secundum – horae] *om. hom. MT* ; *mg. infra S* || (s) resumeretur] reservetur *MT, a.c. S* || (t) medietatis] sed *add. MST* ; vel non *add. sed del. V* || (u) quia] quod *T* || (v) a] in *MST* || (w) certe – et] *mg. (hom.) V* || et] vel *MST* || (x) ad finem] finem *M* ; ad medium *S* ; in finem *T* ; *mg. V* || (y) illius] *om. V* || (z) aequivaleret] aequivalerent *M* ; aequivalent *T* || (a) excederet] excederent *MT* || (b) quia] quod *V* || (c) pertingeret] contingeret *MST* || (d) dictae] *om. V* || (e) recausatione] recausationem *M* ; recreationem *a.c. S, T* || (f) haberetur] *om. MT* || (g) igitur] etc. *add. MT* || (h) contingit] concedit *M* ; *p.c. V* || (i) sentiri] sentire *MT* || (j) tempus] sensum *M* ; sensus *a.c. mg. S* || (k) perceptibile] perceptibilem *MT, a.c. S* || (l) quod] quia *MST* || (m) certarum] distinctarum aliarum *MT, a.c. mg. S* || (n) praesentialiter] principaliter *MT* || (o) habitarum] habendarum *MT, a.c. S* ; *p.c. V* || (p) sensibiliter] *om. V* || (q) non] nam *T* || (r) coram] cora *S* || (s) aliqua minima] maxima minima *M*

1. Aristoteles, *De sensu et sensato*, c. 7 : 449a20-25.

pertranseunda a nobis distincte visu perceptibilis vel maxima[t] aliqua quae non potest a[u] nobis sic distincte percipi secundum exigentiam praesentium dispositionum illorum[v] quae ad talem perceptionem requiruntur[w].

[71] Ex hoc sequitur quod[x] si voluntas in hoc instanti imperet sibi dilectionem[y] alicuius obiecti pro illo nunc[z], non est in potestate voluntatis quod pro alio nunc perceptibiliter[a] et distincte per nolitionem[b] illius actus tollat ipsum donec lapsum fuerit tempus illud[c] minimum quod distincte percipere potest vel maximum quod percipere[d] non potest. Nam ex quo modo vult actum illum esse, volet eum esse, ex primo ostensis[e], [*V mg.* : scilicet quod si non vult, non potest immediate simul illum actum dimittere, quod sic instans esset instanti immediatum], et quamdiu volet eum esse[f], non habebit nolle per quod tollatur quo quasi imperet « Nunc non velis », et hoc non libere poterit[g] facere citra[h] lapsum talis temporis minimi quod[i] vel maximi quod non. Igitur, cum non possit tollere libere huiusmodi actum nisi per tale nolle imperativum vel alio simili, sequitur quod non est in potestate voluntatis quin habeat actum[j] quem nunc vult esse et quem nunc per hoc causat usque ad finem talis temporis.

[72] Et hoc iterum aliter probatur, quia potest agens liberum aliquando[k] agere libere secundum ultimum potentiae suae sicut naturale necessario et naturaliter ita agit. Nitatur[l] igitur ita cito sicut poterit secundum praesentes dispositiones actum quem nunc vult esse, ex praeostensis[m], dimittere. Et cum non possit immediate post dimittere, dabitur tempus aliquod intra quod non possit[n] actum dimittere ex se libere, cum non possit[o] distincte omne[p] instans advertere[q], et per consequens per illud tempus non addit novum meritum super suum meritum instantaneum. Haec ultima consequentia probatur, quia in nulla mensura meretur voluntas per aliquem actum novo merito pro qua non potest non habere actum talem, quia pro tali mensura non est actus sibi imputabilis non plus quam quod sit rationabilis, secundum[r] consequentiam Anselmi[1]; sed[s], ut visum est, si voluntas pro aliquo instanti libere causat actum aliquem, non est in eius libera potestate tollere ipsum, ceteris paribus, per tempus determinatum aliquod, et hoc si simul | tollet eum et **S 43rb** non[t] per partes, in quo casu nunc est sermo; et si per tantum tempus non[u] additur meritum, igitur meritum instantaneum est aequale eidem merito[v] per tempus illud continuato, quod erat probandum, quod et[w] concedo.

(t) vel maxima] et maxima *MST* ; *mg. V* || (u) a] *om. M* || (v) illorum] *om. MST* ; *s.l. V* || (w) requiruntur] requiritur *MT* || (x) quod] *om. S* || (y) dilectionem] delectationem *MT* || (z) nunc] tunc *S* || (a) perceptibiliter] perceptum *T* || (b) nolitionem] volitionem *MT, p.c. S* ; *a.c. S* || (c) tempus illud] *tr. M* || (d) percipere – percipere] perceptibiliter *a.c. mg. (hom.) V* || (e) primo ostensis] praemissis *MST* (*mg. T*) || (f) ex – esse] *mg. (hom.) T* || (g) libere poterit] *tr. MT* ; poterit *a.c. mg. S* || (h) citra] circa *MT, a.c. S* || (i) quod] *om. MST* || (j) nisi – actum] *iter. M* || (k) potest – aliquando] agens liberum potest ita cito aliquando *MST, a.c. mg. V* || (l) nitatur] totaliter *MT* || (m) ex praeostensis] *om. MST* ; *mg. V* || (n) possit] posset *MST* || (o) possit] posset *MST* || (p) distincte omne] distincte esse *M* ; esset distincte *a.c. V* ; *p.c. s.l. V* || (q) advertere] avertere *MT* ; avertere *a.c. S* || (r) secundum] sed *MT* || (s) sed] *om. MST* || (t) non] hoc *MT* || (u) non] *om. MST* || (v) eidem merito] *tr. MT* || (w) et] etiam *MT*

1. ANSELMUS CANTUARIENSIS, *De casu diaboli*, c. 5, ed. Schmitt, p. 242.28-243.3.

### *Responsio propria*[x] *<ad rationem septimam>*

[73→9] Et ita respondeo aliter ad argumentum principale quod consequens[y] illud ad quod deducitur est concedendum[z]. Bene tamen[a] volo quod si in medio illius temporis infunderet sibi Deus[b] notitiam deliberativam perfectam quod actus esset[c] tunc dimittendus, bene[d] posset, sed illa esset de specie[e] alia a priori.

[74→73] Sed dices : probatio praedicta[f] supponit quod si nunc volo actum aliquem esse, oportet habere unum nolle[g] oppositum huic velle ad hoc quod libere nollendo[h] tollam actum[i] illum. Sed hoc non videtur, quia nunc[j] possum velle nunc habere actum talem et per hoc ponere ipsum, si alia[k] requisita concurrant, et nunc nolle ipsum habere post illud nunc, et illud praesens[l] nolle sufficere videtur[m] ad hoc ut[n] non sit actus iste[o] post illud instans.

[75→74] Dicendum quod nec[p] tale nolle tollit actum, quia cum ipso stat velle ipsius actus, nec etiam velle aut nolle praesens creaturae[q] sufficit ad liberum effectum causandum in anima pro futuro ubi non causat eum in praesenti. Nec est respectu praesentis, sed respectu futuri solum. Et eodem modo per omnia respectu destructionis[r] effectus nunc existentis in anima. Igitur oportet habere aliud[s] nolle[t] repugnans actui tollendo, et tale haberi non poterit, ut visum est – libere[u], dico, citra[v] lapsum determinati temporis. Et propterea[w] voluntas in illo[x] casu vult sibi impossibilia, ut patet.

[76→75] **(1)** Sed adhuc[y] contra dictam responsionem potest argui aliter, primo quia velle causare actum et continuare ipsum est maioris meriti quam velle praecise causare actum sine hoc quod velit continuare actum sive[z] cum nolitione[a] continuationis, sive sit in eius potestate continuare actum sive non[b]. Igitur multo
**M 36rb** fortius libere causare et libere[c] continuare | actum talem[d] est maioris meriti quam praecise causare ipsum, et hoc non, si[e] meritum instantaneum et meritum illud[f] per tempus[g] aliquod continuatum sunt aequalia, ut[h] responsio concedit ; igitur male responsum est.

[77] **(2)** Item, qualiter tunc vitabitur[i] quin[j] interruptio actus quandoque expediat et continuatio minus prosit[k] ?

(x) responsio propria] *mg. STV* || (y) consequens] *mg. MS* ; *om. T* || (z) concedendum] argumentum *a.c. i.l. M, T* ; *p.c. S* || (a) bene tamen] detum *T* || (b) sibi deus] *tr. MST* || (c) esset] *om. MT* ; *s.l. S* || (d) bene] *s.l. T* || (e) de specie] dispositio *MST* || (f) praedicta] praedictam *M* || (g) nolle] velle *S* || (h) nollendo] *om. MST* ; *mg. V* || (i) actum] aguum *M* || (j) nunc] non *S* || (k) alia] aliqua *T* || (l) praesens] *prius MST* || (m) sufficere videtur] *tr. MT* || (n) ut] quod *V* || (o) iste] illius *MT* || (p) nec] non sit *MT, a.c. S* ; non quia nec *p.c. mg. S* || (q) creaturae] dare *MT* ; *p.c. S* || (r) destructionis] consecutionis *MT* ; desitionis *S* || (s) aliud] ad *M* || (t) velle] velle *a.c. s.l. T* || (u) libere] *a.c. S* ; hoc *p.c. S* || (v) citra] circa *MT, a.c. S* || (w) propterea] praeterea *MT* || (x) in illo] in primo *MT* ; *tr. p.c. S* || (y) adhuc] ad hoc *MST* || (z) sive] suum *MT* || (a) nolitione] volitione *a.c. S* (*def. MT*) || (b) cum – non] *om. hom. MT* || (c) libere] *om. MST* || (d) actum talem] signum *MT* ; actum suum *S* || (e) non si] *tr. a.c. V* ; si *p.c. V* || (f) illud] idem *MST* || (g) per tempus] post *a.c. V* || (h) ut] et *V* || (i) vitabitur] et *add. MT* ; vitabatur *V* || (j) quin] quando *T* || (k) prosit] nota multa continuatione meriti an magis mereatur qui continuat et quomodo est aliquod tempus, et homo non meretur plus si continuet per illud tempus eo quod est vel maximum quod non potest ab anima distincte percipi stantibus eisdem dispositionibus ab **aa** usque **bb** *add. mg. infra S*

[78→76] Ad primum istorum dicendum quod velle causare actum bonum et continuare ultra tempus infra quod libere posset ab actu desistere ceteris paribus est magis meritorium quam si non vellet sic continuare[l], et[m] eodem modo causare et continuare actum meritorium est magis meritorium[n] quam non sic[o] continuare[p]. Si tamen elective et deliberative[q] hoc faciat, tamen continuare praecise per tempus ante cuius complementum[r] non potest libere[s] ab actu huiusmodi desistere non est magis meritorium quam libere actum talem[t] ceteris paribus elicere. Non tamen nego[u] quin velle causare et continuare talem actum bonum[v] per tempus infra quod
non posset libere ab actu desistere sit magis meritorium quam praecise | velle V 59r
causare, cum sit volitio maioris boni vel[w] duplicis boni, scilicet causationis et continuationis actus, et alia[x] non est nisi volitio actus vel causationis actus, et
una earum[y] volitionum, scilicet causationis, non | necessario ponit volitionem T 30vb
continuationis[z]. Quia tamen exsecutio causationis non est in libera nostra potestate[a] ut fieri valeat sine exsecutione continuationis, ideo neganda est consequentia argumenti.

[79→77] Ad aliud, dicendum quod ceteris paribus interruptio numquam prodest ubi[b] continuatio bona est, nec nocet continuatio[c] nisi[d] frequens electio[e] actus prodesset ceteris paribus, quia in fine temporis minimi quod[f] vel maximini quod non[g], de quo supra, si[h] pro tunc distincte vult[i] actum illum esse ita quod poneret eum, dato quod non esset, tantum valet sibi sicut si noviter poneret illum, si libere hoc facit[j] et non a[k] casu. Et[l] libere hoc[m] potest in toto aliquo tempore totiens quot instantia distincte poterit[n] advertere[o] secundum praesentes[p] dispositiones habitas[q], et illa sunt in certo numero sicut et tempora qualia iam
descripsi. Quotiens igitur distinctis vi|cibus[r] in aliquo toto tempore libere posset et S 43va
distincte ab actu cessare et[s] tamen libere actum continuat, totiens[t] tantum meretur ceteris paribus sicut si[u] noviter eliceret[v] talem actum, et per consequens quotiens si actum interrumperet.

(l) vellet sic continuare] sic continuare vellet *MT* || (m) et] in *M* || (n) meritorium] *om. MT* || (o) non sic] si non sic *MT* ; non *S* || (p) continuare] vellet quia si non vellet non continuaret *add. T* || (q) deliberative] deliberate *S*, *p.c. V* (deliberative *P*) || (r) complementum] completum *MST* || (s) libere] libero *M* || (t) actum talem] *tr. MST* || (u) tamen nego] et minime* igitur *M* || (v) bonum] *om. MST* ; *i.l. V* || (w) vel] et *MST* || (x) alia] alii *MT* ; aliquando *S* || (y) earum] harum *MST* || (z) continuationis] continuationem videlicet *MT* || (a) nostra potestate] *tr. M* || (b) ubi] vel *M* ; *p.c. TV* || (c) nocet continuatio] nocent continua *M* || (d) nisi] ubi *MST* ; *p.c. V* || (e) electio] elictio *V* || (f) quod] sit *add. T* || (g) non] nunc *M* || (h) si] sed *M* || (i) distincte vult] vult *a.c. V* ; *tr. p.c. mg. V* || (j) facit] faciat *p.c. S* || (k) et non a] *om. M* ; et non *T* || (l) non a casu et] *mg. S* || (m) libere hoc] *tr. V* || (n) distincte poterit] *tr. MT* || (o) advertere] avertere *MT*, *a.c. S* || (p) praesentes] *om. MT* || (q) habitas] habitus *M* || (r) vicibus] volitionibus *MST* || (s) cessare et] cessaret *M* || (t) totiens] rationes *M* || (u) si] sibi *M* || (v) eliceret] ibi *add. T*

## <RESPONSIO AD RATIONES 8-16 FITZRALPH CONTRA QUINTAM CONCLUSIONEM>

[80→10] Ad octavum argumentum principale, primam consequentiam concedo. Secundam nego ; cuius consequentiae probatio, si[w] valeret[x], contra ipsum aeque et contra quemlibet hominem concluderet, ut tibi patet de se primo intuitu[y], si homo diutius viveret vel bene[z], virtuose, et ex caritate ageret[a] postquam[b] pertingeret ad gradum maximum praemii in anima receptibilem[c].

[81→80] Sed leviter responderi potest quod vita humana non sufficeret pro statu isto attingere[d] per merita ad talem gradum. In statu autem innocentiae, si homo non peccasset, cum[e] ad illum pervenisset, translatus[f] forte ad gloriam extitisset. Et[g] hoc dico de communi lege, licet aliter fuerit de anima Christi, quae ex privilegio statim, secundum Magistrum, libro III[1], summum habuit meritum[h]. Et dato quod quis[i] a Deo conservaretur donec ad gradum maximum sibi possibilem in certa specie pertingeret, sicut alias respondisti[j], Deus praemiaret istum[k] praemio alterius speciei ex tunc vel eiusdem speciei miraculose[l], sicut in corporibus istis potest miraculose in vase iam repleto adhuc tantumdem simul ponere, licet natura hoc non posset[2]. Quod autem supponit argumentum per medium ibi positum[m], quod in[n] omni tempore quantumcumque parvo posset ad tantum meritum pervenire, declaratum est falsum esse[o] in solutione proxima praecedenti[3].

[82→11] Ad nonum dicendum sicut ad octavum : neganda est enim[p] consequentia. Et ad probationem consequentiae, respondet[q] Rodinton[r] quod argumentum est contra Firauf[s] facientem[t] eo quod ponit in augmento formae[u] in quolibet instanti esse[v] aliam formam totalem quam prius. Aut igitur maiorem semper vel minorem vel aequalem. Si aequalem[w], et instantia[x] sunt ibi[y] infinita, igitur in finitate[z] haberetur[a] infinita perfectio[b]. Si maiorem semper[c] vel minorem,

(w) probatio si] si prius *a.c. M* ; *tr. p.c. mg. M* ; *tr. S, a.c. V* ; si *T* || (x) valeret] valet *add. T* || (y) tibi – intuitu] ibi patet de se (saepe *a.c. M, T*) primo intuenti *MT* ; ibi patet saepe primo in morte *a.c. mg. S* || (z) bene] et *add. s.l. S* || (a) ageret] agerit *S* || (b) postquam] quando *M* ; quandoque *T* ; quam *V* || (c) receptibilem] quod non potest aliquid in statu praesenti recipere tantam gratiam vel mereri tantam gloriam quantam potest et si hoc esset possibile adhuc posset postea mereri et daretur sibi una gloria melior alterius speciei vel eiusdem speciei miraculose **bb** *add. mg. infra MS* || (d) attingere] ut attingeret *MT* || (e) cum] tamen *MS* || (f) translatus] translato *a.c. M, T* || (g) et] sed *T* || (h) et – meritum] *scr. sed del. per vacat V* (*om. P*) || (i) quis] aliquis *M* || (j) respondisti] *a.c. S* ; respondi *p.c. S* || (k) istum] illum *S* ; eum *V* || (l) miraculose] vel *add. MT* ; unde *add. S* || (m) per – positum] *om. MST* ; *mg. V* || (n) in] *om. MST* ; *s.l. V* || (o) falsum esse] *tr. MT* || (p) enim] *om. MST* || (q) respondet] respondit *S* || (r) rodinton *coni.*] red'*M* ; rod'*STV* || (s) firauf] firauf' *M* ; firn[a]f' *S* ; frauf' *T* ; ffir[a]uf *V* || (t) facientem] *om. M* || (u) augmento formae] argumento fore *MT, a.c. mg. V* || (v) esse] *om. MST* ; *p.c. V* || (w) aequalem] aequale *T* || (x) et instantia] *om. M* || (y) sunt ibi] *tr. M* ; sunt *TV* || (z) in finitate] *om. S* || (a) haberetur] in fine *add. mg. S* ; habetur T || (b) perfectio] et ita esset infinitae perfectionis *S* || (c) semper] *om. MST*

---

1. PETRUS LOMBARDUS, *Sententiae*, III, d. 18, c. 2, ed. Brady, vol. 2, p. 113.1-17.

2. Cf. ADAM WODEHAM, *Ordinatio*, prologus, q. 1, a. 3, ed. O. Grassi, « Il problema della conoscenza di Dio nel commento alle *Sentenze* di Adam Wodeham (Prologo e q. 1) », *Medioevo*, 8 (1982), p. 43-136, p. 91-93.

3. *Supra*, 78.

arguatur sicut ipsi arguunt[1] : « Dico igitur », inquit, « quod in quolibet posteriori instanti plus meretur quam prius, sed non merito totaliter distincto ita quod nulla pars praecesserit. Unde argumentum procedit ac si continue causaretur alius et alius actus, cuius[d] nihil praecessit, et hoc non est verum ». Haec ille[e].

[83→82] Ista responsio est superius improbata tractando septimum[f] principale argumentum, ubi probatum est quod non in quolibet instanti meretur plus quam ante, sed[g] meretur praecise eodem merito prius[h] instantanee elicito usque ad finem temporis minimi quod[i] vel maximi quod non etc., in casu de quo nunc est sermo, ubi videlicet meretur praecise[j] eodem actu meritorio continuato eo quod per infinita alia instantia[k] non est in eius potestate non habere actum illum post instans causationis illius[l], si iam causavit illum.

[84] Similiter[m], reductio argumenti contra Firauf[n] non valet, ut videtur, quia[o] ille arguit sic : « Si pro primo | instanti extrinseco debetur merenti[p] aliquod **M 36va** meritum praecise, tunc pari ratione pro quolibet posteriori illius[q] temporis. Et sic sequitur ultra », ut sibi videtur, « aut igitur[r] maius[s] aut minus[t] aut aequale » etc. Constat quod illud argumentum[u] per locum a divisione factum supponit primam consequentiam esse bonam et consequens esse[v] verum, si antecedens sit etiam[w] verum, scilicet quod cuilibet instanti posteriori, sicut et primo, debetur praemium praecisum[x], sicut plane exprimit argumentum. Sed certe illud non ponit ipse in augmento formae, quia ibi exprimit cum Scoto quod nulla particula formae generatur simul[y] secundum se totam, sed successive[2]. Immo[z], ne incurrat inconveniens quod sibi ex hoc sequi videtur[a], negat talem formam posse[b] a creatura in intellectu fieri in instanti. Et ita nihil penitus fit in tali processu in aliquo instanti intrinseco temporis mensurantis successivam augmentationem formae, secundum eum et secundum veritatem. Igitur argumentum quoad hoc nihil[c] est contra ipsum, cum etiam ipse in hoc teneat veritatem.

[85] Praeterea[d], falsam imaginationem et contra intentionem arguentis sibi imponit. Non enim imaginatur quod continue causatur[e] sic alius et alius actus cuius nihil praecesserit, sed sufficeret argumento quod pro eodem actu praecise instantanee causato[f] per tempus | aliquod continuato deberetur[g] merenti pro **S 43vb**

(d) cuius] eius *M* ; tempus *T* || (e) ille] respondetur ad illud argumentum quod si pro primo instanti alicuius temporis debetur aliquod praemium eadem ratione pro quolibet posteriori et negatur consequentia **cc** *add. mg. infra MS* || (f) septimum] *om. MT* || (g) sed] non *add. MT* || (h) prius] plus *M* || (i) quod] *om. MST* ; *s.l. V* || (j) praecise] praece[ii] *M* || (k) instantia] eius *add. MST* || (l) illius] eius *V* || (m) similiter] aliter *M* || (n) firauf] sirauf' *M* ; fir[a]uf' *S* ; frauf' *T* ; ffirauf *V* || (o) ut – quia] videtur enim quod *MT* ; quia *S* ; videtur quia *a.c. s.l. V* || (p) merenti] *om. MT* ; *mg. S* || (q) illius] *om. MST* || (r) igitur] *om. MT* || (s) maius] magis *S* || (t) aut minus] *om. M* ; vel minus *V* || (u) argumentum] per divisionem sive *add. mg. V* || (v) esse] est *M* || (w) etiam] et *M* ; *om. V* || (x) praecisum] *p.c. S* ; praescium *a.c. mg. V* || (y) simul] similis *MST* || (z) immo] tantum *S* || (a) sequi videtur] sequitur *MT* ; *p.c. S* || (b) posse] *om. MT* ; *p.c. mg. V* || (c) nihil] *iter. a.c.. S* ; vel *ST* ; *p.c. V* || (d) praeterea] propterea *S* || (e) causatur] causetur *MT* || (f) causato] tanto *a.c. S* ; tanto *V* || (g) deberetur] debetur *MT*

1. Non invenimus.

2. RICCARDUS FITZRALPH, *Lectura in Sententias*, I, q. 11, a. 1, Paris 15853, f. 74rb : « Utrum intensio formae accidentalis fiat per additionam alicuius ».

quolibet instanti posteriori sicut[h] et pro primo aliquod praemium praecisum, et hoc – licet falso – supponit arguens primus sequi si possit[i] mereri in instanti[j].

[86] Quarto quaero ab isto respondente sic quomodo intelligit illud dictum, scilicet quod in quolibet instanti posteriori plus meretur quam prius, licet non merito totaliter distincto, etiam dato quod continue augeretur meritum semper, quod tamen ostensum est esse falsum : vel sic praecise quod in quolibet instanti habet plus de merito quam habuit in aliquo instanti praecedenti, ita tamen quod in nullo instanti posteriori aliquid sibi accrescat de merito, sicut nec aliquid
V 59v de[k] forma in motu augmentationis formae, immo quod si moreretur[l] | in aliquo instanti posteriori nihil minus haberet de praemio[m] quam si in[n] illo vixisset et non ultra vel non ultra[o] meruisset. Et sine dubio hoc habet in simili de augmento formae dicere Firauf[p] sicut et ego. Et si sic intelligit ille, tunc haberet[q] aliter quam facit[r] ad argumentum respondere, quia argumentum non deficit ubi ipse nititur instanter[s] negare, videlicet illud assumptum in probatione primae consequentiae, quam[t] negat et bene, scilicet quod sicut pro primo instanti extrinseco[u] debetur merenti aliquod meritum[v] praecise, ita[w] et[x] pro quolibet posteriori instanti[y]. Et sic respondeo[z] ego ad illam probationem, et[a] causam ego[b] prius assignavi.

T 31ra [87] Si autem aliter intelligit | ille quod[c] pro quolibet instanti posteriori plus meretur[d] quam prius, sic videlicet quod plus de praemio habebit[e] si mereatur usque ad illud instans, et in[f] illo etiam quam si mereretur[g] usque ad ipsum et moreretur[h] in ipso, et per consequens in ipso non[i] mereretur sicut nec in ipso viveret[j], tunc dicit falsum et oppositum in adiecto[k].

[88] Nec responsio in aliquo evadit argumentum. Addit enim quod in quolibet[l] instanti posteriori[m] plus meretur, licet non merito totaliter distincto. Si[n] enim plus habebit de praemio[o] ex hoc praecise adiecto quod in hoc instanti posteriori meretur quam si in ipso moreretur usque ad quod continue crevisset in merito, et Deus distinctissime novit quid de praemio sibi[p] dedisset si[q] in illo[r] instanti mortuus esset, igitur et novit quid superadderet pro hoc instanti. Cum enim meritum totale huius instantis sit certum et determinatum secundum quantitatem continens meritum primum[s] quod[t] habuisset si in instanti dato moreretur et excedens ipsum sicut totam partem suam, sequitur inevitabiliter quod in illo[u] instanti meretur aliquo merito partiali totius cuiusdam meriti totaliter[v] distincto a comparte. Et tunc clarissime procedit argumentum, et per consequens ille intellectus falsus est, cum argumentum inferat consequens impossibile et additur[w] oppositum suo

(h) sicut] *om. MT* ; *s.l. S* || (i) possit] posset *MT* ; *iter. (mg.) S* || (j) primus – instanti] posuisse simpliciter tenet *a.c. mg. S* || (k) de] *om. V* || (l) moreretur] mo[retur] *M* ; moveretur *T* || (m) praemio] primo *M* || (n) si in] sine *MT* || (o) vel non ultra] *om. M* || (p) firauf] staus' *M, p.c. T* ; taut' *a.c. T* ; firn[af]' *S* ; ffirauf *V* || (q) haberet] haberent *V* || (r) facit] fecerit *S* ; faciat *T* || (s) instanter] instare *MTV* || (t) quam] quod *MT* || (u) extrinseco] *om. S* || (v) meritum] praemium *MT* || (w) ita] *om. S* || (x) et] *om. V* || (y) instanti] *om. M* || (z) respondeo] respondeam *MT* ; responderem *S* || (a) et] rectam *MT* ; cuius *S* || (b) ego] *om. V* || (c) quod] *om. T* || (d) plus meretur] *tr. S* || (e) de – habebit] haberet de praemio *MST* || (f) in] *s.l. T* || (g) mereretur] meretur *SV* || (h) moreretur] mereretur *M* ; *p.c. V* || (i) non] *om. MT* || (j) viveret] vivet *V* || (k) adiecto] abiecto *S* || (l) quolibet] quocumque *T* || (m) posteriori] *om. SV* || (n) si] licet *MST* || (o) praemio] primo *M* || (p) sibi] si *V* || (q) si] licet *MT* || (r) illo] *om. V* || (s) meritum primum] *tr. V* || (t) quod] et *MT* || (u) illo] hoc *V* || (v) merito totaliter] meritoria *M* || (w) additur] addit *M* opposito, quae probanda erant. Et sic patet quod non similiter valet[x], sed valde[y] dissimiliter et absque colore bono ducitur argumentum primum ab illo contra facientem[z].

[89] Dico igitur, sicut[a] praedixi, quod assumptum in probatione consequentiae[b] falsum est. Nam sicut dat et bene responsio in argumento posita, primo instanti correspondet aliquod meritum praecisum et nullo[c] posteriori intrinseco saltem tempori minimo quod[d] vel maximo[e] quod non, infra quod ab actu elicito ceteris paribus cessare non posset. Sed in fine talis temporis bene potest mereri instantanee sicut primo, et in fine alterius tanti temporis ab illo instanti termino prioris inchoati iterato, et sic quotiens fuerint in tempore totali magno[f] talia parva tempora[g] contenta ab invicem totaliter distincta; sed illa sunt respective pauca, et ideo solvitur argumentum. Unde in tali processu talis non meretur nisi instantanee[h] et raro per oppositum augmentationi formae[i], quia ibi nihil accrescit[j] instantanee, sed successive solum[k], sed in casu isto non accrescit meritum successive, sed instantanee, licet volitio continuationis subita meritoria magis sit quam si non[l] vellet continuare actum huiusmodi meritorium consequenter[m], | ut prius dictum est[n]. **M 36vb**

[90→14] Ad decimum, quod Commentator ibi loquitur de actionibus causarum mere[o] naturalium, et de talibus verum est quod dicit Commentator quoad successionem. Tales enim, si nunc subito agunt et non prius[p], vel non fuerunt praesentes, et tunc movebantur ad invicem; vel aliqua[q] earum[r] ad aliam; vel aliquid impediens extrinsecum[s] a passo vel sibi intrinsecum erat amovendum[t] vel destruendum antequam posset sequi actio subita; et per consequens transmutatio subita huiusmodi[u], si esset, foret[v], secundum eum, finis[w] | talis motus praecedentis **S 44ra** ac[x] praesuppositi[y]. Verumtamen vix[z] umquam producitur in talibus aliquid[a] subito quin sit ibi successio vel secundum partes formae graduales vel secundum extensionem passi. Et ideo[b] Commentator quoad secundam partem dicti sui de subita productione falsum videtur dicere in naturalibus, si loquatur ad vim vocis. Et propter hoc, glossando Commentatorem, Commentator[c] et alii qui dicunt aliquid[d] causari[e] subito in huiusmodi actionibus causarum mere naturalium, et per consequens agentium[f] semper[g] secundum ultimum potentiae suae, sicut in causatione luminis vel in productione formae substantialis[h] et huiusmodi,

(x) valet] videlicet *MT* ; *om. S* || (y) valde] *om. T* || (z) facientem] responsio firf' *add. mg. S* ; opinio propria *add. mg. T* || (a) sicut] ut *p.c. V* || (b) consequentiae] consequens *M* || (c) nullo] termino *T* || (d) quod] *om. MST* ; *mg. V* || (e) maximo] ita *add. MT* || (f) magno] multa *MT* ; magna *S* || (g) parva tempora] *tr. MT* ; parva *a.c. s.l. V* || (h) instantanee] instantaneo *V* || (i) formae] fore *M* || (j) accrescit] accrescat *MT* ; *p.c. V* || (k) solum] subiectum *T* || (l) non] *om. MST* || (m) meritorium consequenter] meritum communiter *MT* || (n) est] quomodo intelligatur illud quod subita mutatio semper est finis alterationis praecedentis et illa forma substantialis subito inducitur cum tamen inducatur pars post partem **dd** *add. mg. infra MS* || (o) mere] *om. M* || (p) prius] plus *M, a.c. mg. V* || (q) aliqua] in altero *M* || (r) earum] illarum *T* || (s) extrinsecum] intrinsecum *MT* || (t) amovendum] ad movendum *T* || (u) subita huiusmodi] *tr. V* || (v) foret] for *M* ; *p.c. V* || (w) finis] sicut *M* || (x) ac] *om. V* || (y) praesuppositi] et *add. M* || (z) vix] et *add. M* || (a) aliquid] aliquod *S* || (b) passi – ideo] et passi et *M* || (c) commentatorem commentator] commentatorem *p.c. V* || (d) aliquid] *om. V* || (e) causari] et causas *M* ; causare *S* || (f) agentium] agere *M*, agere *p.c. S* || (g) semper] *om. MT* ; *mg. S* || (h) substantialis] simul *MST, a.c. V*

habent[i] intelligi quod sunt subitae non ut verba sonant, sed[j] sic subitae, id est, non successivae ex resistentia proprii susceptivi[k], sed tantum ex[l] successiva approximatione activi ad passum vel[m] econtra, vel ex successiva amotione impedimenti, vel[n] ex successiva vigoratione[o] causae, vel ex alia aliqua[p] causa simili[q]. Non autem habet intelligi auctoritas Commentatoris in argumento posita[r] de causatione effectus a causa libera, quia illa[s] potest omnibus aliis requisitis concurrentibus agere[t] vel dimittere sicut sibi placebit.

[91→15] Ad undecimum, quod infertur concedi potest loquendo de gravitate intensionis poenae, sed non de gravitate[u] eius secundum extensionem durationis. Et ita credo quod aliqui de facto plus torquentur[v] et gravius ad tempus in purgatorio quam quidam[w] alii aeternaliter in inferno.

[92→16] Ad duodecimum, neganda est consequentia et etiam assumptum ad probationem eiusdem, sicut patet ex supradictis.

[93→17] Et per idem patet[x] ad 13.

[94→18] Ad 14, satis patet etiam[y] ex dictis ad septimum.

[95→19] Ad 15, similiter[z] patet ex dictis, et consequentia ibi[a] facta nihil valet.

[96→21] Ad 16, dicendum quod tam de volitione[b] libere producta quam de illa quae[c] ante deliberationem causatur naturaliter est dare in casu saltem possibili primum instans quo voluntas tali volitione vel tali vult, puta si Deus simul imprimeret[d] intellectui claram sui[e] visionem[f] vel[g] ante oculos subito causaret obiectum multum placibile voluntati.

[97] Et cum hoc improbatur de volitione libere producta[h] per Commentatorem, respondendum est[i] ut supra ad decimum[1].

[98] Cum vero improbatur[j] hoc de volitione naturaliter producta, dicendum quod bene probat quod in casu potest volitio causari successive et quod in casu[k] **V 60r** non est[l] aliquod | primum instans in quo voluntas[m] velit, et hoc totum concedo. Sed non probat quin in casu possibili subito[n] causari possit talis volitio, utpote si Deus subito imprimeret[o] intellectui tali visionem solam[p] simplicem sui vel alterius naturaliter placibilis, sine omni deliberatione, tunc statim voluntas tali[q] naturaliter adhaereret[r] donec saltem deliberaret, ut patet ex declaratis alias. Finalis[s] autem ipsius Firauf[t] recapitulatio mediorum plenarius[u] solvitur in praedictis[v].

(i) habent] debent *T* || (j) sed] isti *M* || (k) susceptivi] suscepti *M* || (l) ex] *om. MST* || (m) vel] et *T* || (n) vel] et *M* || (o) vigoratione] rigoratione *M* || (p) aliqua] *om. MS* || (q) simili] sive *M* ; similiter *a.c. T* || (r) posita] nominata *M* || (s) illa] ita *S* || (t) agere] a se *M* || (u) gravitate] servitute *M* || (v) torquentur] torquerentur *MS* || (w) quidam] quod *M* || (x) patet] *om. ST* || (y) etiam] *om. S* ; *ante* satis *V* || (z) similiter] sicut *M* || (a) ibi] *om. MST* || (b) volitione] voluntate *MST* || (c) quae] quo *M* || (d) imprimeret] imprimat *M* ; imprimet *S* ; *p.c. V* || (e) sui] suam *M* ; *om. T* || (f) visionem] notitiam *T* ; volitionem *V* || (g) vel] licet *M* || (h) producta] productae *M* || (i) est] *om. MST* || (j) improbatur] iuxta *MT* ; *p.c. S* || (k) potest – casu] *iter. M*, *a.c. S* ; potest voluntas *add. T* || (l) est] *mg. S* ; sit *T* || (m) voluntas] non *add. T* || (n) subito] posito *MST* || (o) subito imprimeret] subito imprimet *M* ; *tr. T* || (p) solam] totam *M* || (q) tali] *om. MST* || (r) adhaereret] adhaeret *MTV* || (s) finalis] si alias *M* || (t) firauf] sira *M* ; firnaf' *S* ; frauf' *T* ; ffirauf *V* || (u) plenarius] plenarie *MS* ; plenius *T* || (v) predictis] quod ita potest (posset *M*) concedi Deus creat angelum malum et posito quod angelus peccaret in primo instanti sui esse *add. mg. MS* (*infra S*)

1. *Supra*, 90.

[99] 17 principaliter potest argui contra conclusionem quintam[w] sic[x] : si voluntas subito posset[y] producere liberam[z] volitionem, igitur, sicut supra[a], angelus posset peccare in primo instanti sui esse[b], igitur[c] esset malus in primo instanti sui esse, et tunc Deus crearet[d] angelum malum[e]. Sequitur enim : « Deus creat hunc angelum, et hic angelus est malus, igitur creat angelum malum et naturam malam ». | Consequens videtur[f] absurdum. T 31rb

[100→99] Ad illud dicendum quod conclusio illata est vera non per se, cum Deus non esset in illo[g] casu causa[h] quare[i] ille angelus malus esset, sed ipsemet angelus faciens vel committens aliquid[j] ad cuius oppositum tenetur, sed solum per accidens, sicut amo per accidens malum cum amo aliquem qui est malus, non tamen quia malus est, sed causa alia, utpote[k] quia propinquus est[l] vel[m] quia pulcher vel[n] familiaris mihi est.

### <Ad argumenta principalia quaestionis>

[101] Ad argumenta principalia satis[o] patet ex antedictis.

(w) quintam] ipsam *M* || (x) sic] istud argumentum superius in margine scripsi ignorans quod hic esset *add. mg. V* || (y) subito posset] *tr. T* || (z) liberam] libera *M* || (a) supra] alia *M* ; dictum est *add. T* || (b) esse] et tunc deus crearet angelum ma *add. et vacat S* || (c) igitur] sic *M* || (d) deus crearet] *tr. M* || (e) esset – malum] et tunc – malum + igitur – sui esse *tr. a.c. T* || (f) videtur] esse *add. S* || (g) illo] aliquo *T* || (h) causa] *ante* in illo *mg. V* || (i) quare] quia *MV* ; quia *a.c. S* (quare *P*) || (j) aliquid] aliud *add. M* || (k) utpote] *om. MS* || (l) est] *om. T* || (m) vel] et *M* || (n) vel] et *M* || (o) satis] *om. MS*

## DISTINCTIO 1, QUAESTIO 9

[M 36vb, S 44ra, T 31rb, V 60r]

[1] Utrum voluntas libere possit subito suspendere actum suum sive ab actu[a] habito[b] cessare.

[2] Videtur quod sic[c], quia voluntas potest subito actum suum[d] libere causare, ex proxima praecedenti quaestione[e] [1], igitur pari[f] ratione potest simul libere[g] et subito a tali actu causato cessare. Consequentia patet, quia est facilius[h] destruere quam construere agenti quod potest utrumque[i].

[3] Contra hoc argui[j] potest sic, quia non in instanti in quo est potest actus[k] instantanee productus simul totus cessare, quia tunc simul esset et non esset. Nec sine medio post[l], quia tunc[m] indivisibili[n] esset aliud indivisibile succedens
immediate[o], ex probatione | primae conclusionis praecedentis quaestionis[p] [2]. S 44rb
Igitur solum mediate[q] post posset voluntas cessare ab actu instantanee elicito,
et per consequens non esset in potestate voluntatis | quin si subito causet in se M 37ra
volitionem velit[r] postea per tempus aliquod antequam suspendat actum suum plene sive antequam plene a tali actu cesset. Sed hoc consequens videtur falsum, igitur primum antecedens.

[4] Falsitas ultimi consequentis probatur multipliciter[s]. Et probatur quod voluntas sic possit actum suum suspendere quod praecise per[t] instans velit[u]. Primo[v], quia aliter voluntas invite in casu[w] continuaret[x] actum suum, quia ponatur quod voluntas primo quando[y] elicit actum suum nolit illum[z] continuare per tempus aliquod. Aut igitur continuabit, et tunc invite, vel non, et habetur intentum.

(a) actu] actuali *M* || (b) habito] habuit* *T* || (c) sic] ista argumenta sunt Rod *add. mg. V* || (d) suum] potest *add. M* || (e) praecedenti quaestione] *tr. MS* || (f) igitur pari] *tr. MS* || (g) simul libere] simul et libere *T* ; *tr. V* || (h) est facilius] facilius *a.c. V* ; *tr. p.c. s.l. V* || (i) utrumque] utriusque *M* || (j) argui] arguitur *V* || (k) potest actus] *tr. MS* || (l) post] *om. MS* || (m) quia tunc] quia *MS* ; *mg. V* || (n) indivisibili] post indivisibile *T* ; indivisibile *a.c. V* || (o) succedens immediate] *tr. T* || (p) conclusionis – quaestionis] conclusionis *MT*, *a.c. s.l. S* ; quaestionis *V* || (q) mediate] mediatum *M* || (r) velit] nolit *add. T* || (s) probatur multipliciter] patet per magistrum *M* || (t) per] ait *add. T* || (u) velit] non *M* ; non *add. sed. exp. S* || (v) primo] post *M* || (w) in casu] *om. MS* || (x) continuaret] contrahit *M* || (y) quando] antequam *MS*, *p.c. T* ; quam *a.c. s.l. T* || (z) illum] ipsum *T*

---

1. *Supra*, q. 8, a. 1.
2. *Supra*, q. 8, a. 1, 5-6.

[5] **(2)** Praeterea, si volitio necessario durat[a] per tempus aliquod, sequitur quod in casu voluntas non possit se conformare iudicio intellectus, quia volo quod in medio[b] illius temporis iudicet intellectus quod volitio[c] non est[d] continuanda. Aut igitur tunc potest voluntas se[e] conformare illi iudicio, et tunc illa volitio non durat per tempus datum, aut non potest, et sequitur conclusio probanda.

[6] **(3)** Tertio[f], sequitur quod voluntas necessario meretur in casu, quia per tempus illam[g] volitionem inceptam bonam necessario continuaret, et sic post primum instans illius temporis[h] non esset in eius potestate quin mereatur[i] per totum illud tempus datum, et si ex necessitate, igitur non esset meritum.

[7] **(4)** Quarto, sequeretur[j] quod in casu viator aliquis[k] non posset poenitere de peccato suo[l], quia sit *b* ultimum instans temporis dati. Tunc si[m] actus de quo est sermo sit peccatum mortale, quaero an[n] ante *b* potest poenitere, et tunc[o] ante *b* potest ab illo actu cessare, cuius oppositum datur, vel non, et tunc[p] habetur conclusio probanda.

[8] **(5)** Praeterea, tunc in medio illius temporis non posset corrumpi ipsa voluntas, quia ita necessario sicut manet actus manet subiectum actus.

[9] **(6)** Praeterea, sequeretur quod in casu volitio esset respectu incogniti[q], quia ponatur quod in medio illius temporis fiat homo demens[r], ita quod corrumpatur cognitio respectu illius[s] obiecti, et ex quo adhuc[t] volitio ulterius[u] durat, sequitur propositum.

[10] In hac quaestione primo[v] respondebo in duabus conclusionibus ad quaesitum et solvam argumentum principale; secundo movebo duo dubia alia et solvam illa.

(a) durat] duraret *V* || (b) in medio] medius *a.c. s.l. et mg. T* || (c) volitio] voluntas *T* || (d) est] ulterius *add. V* || (e) voluntas se] *tr. V* || (f) tertio] item *T* || (g) illam] illud datum *V* || (h) illius temporis] *tr. M* ; temporis *V* || (i) mereatur] meretur *V* || (j) sequeretur] sequitur *S* || (k) viator aliquis] *tr. T* || (l) peccato suo] peccatis suis *T* || (m) tunc si] quia si *T* ; si igitur *V* || (n) an] aut *mg. T* || (o) tunc] tamen *M* || (p) tunc] *om. V* || (q) respectu incogniti] incognita *MS* || (r) demens] deviens *M* || (s) respectu illius] *tr. V* || (t) adhuc] est *add. V* || (u) ulterius] illius *T* || (v) primo] *om. M*

## PRIMUS ARTICULUS[a]

[11] Ad quaestionem igitur est dicendum quod voluntatem subito cessare ab actu suo vel subito suspendere actum suum potest dupliciter[b] intelligi, uno modo quod nunc habeat ipsum et immediate post[c] nec habeat ipsum nec aliquid eius, et hoc nego.

### <Prima conclusio[d]>

[12] Unde hic pono conclusionem quasi conversam primae primi articuli praecedentis quaestionis 8[e] [1] : Si voluntas in hoc instanti habeat actum aliquem, ipsa habebit illum vel partem illius.

[13] Et hoc probatur[f] sic, quia aliter esset[g] indivisibile immediatum indivisibili in successione vel[h] in continuo[i], quia si[j] simul cessaret, sic quod non partibiliter sed[k] instantanee destrueretur, et[l] non in instanti quo[m] producitur, quia tunc simul esset et non esset, igitur in alio : vel igitur immediato, et probata est consequentia probanda, vel mediato, et tunc manebit per tempus medium, quod est principale intentum[n].

### <Secunda conclusio[o]>

[14] Alio modo potest intelligi quod subito suspendat[p] actum suum vel[q] cesset ab eo, ita videlicet quod simul possit ac[r] subito ab actu per tempus praehabito vel ab actu[s] acquisito in fine huius temporis sic cessare simul quod tunc nec

(a) primus articulus] *mg. MST* ; *om. V* || (b) potest dupliciter] *tr. V* || (c) nunc – post] *om. hom. MST* || (d) prima conclusio (p.c. : *om. M*) quod si voluntas in hoc instanti habeat actum ad huc post habebit illum vel partem eius **a** *add. mg. infra MS* ; conclusio prima *add. mg. V* || (e) 8] scilicet *TV* || (f) probatur] probo *M* || (g) sic – esset] sicut illa quia aliter *V* || (h) vel] et *M* || (i) continuo] consequenter* (consequentes* *a.c.*) ens *add. mg. V* || (j) si] *om. M* || (k) partibiliter] parti[tur] *M* || (l) et] sed *MST* || (m) quo] alio *M* || (n) intentum] si vero partibiliter destruitur, igitur aliqua eius pars erit post hoc instans pro* simili* est intentum *add. mg. V* || (o) secunda conclusio quod si voluntas per aliquod tempus habuit actum in instanti terminante illud (illud : *om. S*) tempus potest cessare ab actu sic quod nec ipsum nec aliquid eius habet **b** *add. mg. infra MS* || (p) suspendat] suspendet *MS* ; *mg. V* || (q) vel] et *M* || (r) simul – ac] sic simul possit sic *T* || (s) ab actu] per tempus *V*

1. *Supra*, q. 8, a. 1, 5.

ille[t] actus nec aliquid ipsius[u] sit. Et[v] teneo quod sic, quia subito et simul ex[w]
discursu praehabito et deliberato consilio praehabito[x] potest sententiare, dictare,
seu iudicare illud esse malum quod prius credebatur esse bonum et illud[y] esse
V 60v nolendum | quod[z] prius volendum[a]. Nec videtur quin in instanti quo[b] primo
iudicabit intellectus illud esse malum et non expediens sibi, immo esse nolendum[c],
quod[d] prius dilexit, quin[e], inquam, possit desistere ab amore illius et nolle illud
et sic conformare se dictis iudiciis. Igitur videtur quod voluntas in casu subito[f]
et simul possit cessare ab amore vel odio per aliquod tempus usque tunc habito.

[15] Hic tamen est diligenter advertendum quoad causationes subitas
volitionum et nolitionum[g] et quoad suspensionem earundem[h], quia[i] aliter[j] est
S 44va quoad hoc de talibus | actibus ubi[k] ipsi sunt exsecutiones dictatae[l] debere haberi
vel[m] debere non haberi, et aliter de ipsis electionibus conformibus vel difformibus
ipsis dictaminibus seu[n] iudiciis practicis. Nam de secundis non video esse
instantiam quin in primo instanti evidentis[o] iudicii vel firmae credulitatis[p] possit[q]
se voluntas conformare talibus iudiciis immediate[r] principiando[s] libere talem
electionem conformem vel non conformare se, si occurrat[t] aliquid aliud[u] alliciens
vel movens ad oppositum[v], et eodem modo suspendere electionem conformem
iudicio contrario priori[w].

[16] Quando vero[x] dilectiones[y] vel odia seu nolitiones[z] de quibus est sermo
non sunt electiones ipsae[a] conformes huiusmodi iudiciis[b], sed solum sunt
exsecutiones dictatae[c] debere poni vel suspendi, non est hic ita facile voluntati,
T 31va immo oportet ibi plus laborare inveniendo | causas motivas[d] ad hoc exsequendum.
M 37rb Verbi gratia, cum iudico me aliquem quem odio debere[e] diligere | vel econverso[f],
vel me debere ferventius diligere Deum quam facio, non possum hoc semper[g]
subito[h] velle vel[i] exsequi, sed ponam me in conceptionibus requisitis ad[j]
exsecutiones dictatas quae[k] aliae sunt saepae quam illa dictamina, ut potest patere
in exemplo adducto de odiente quem deberet[l] diligere. Debet enim cogitare quod
ipse est Dei creatura et praeparata ad bonum supernaturale[m] secum et[n] redempta
eodem sanguine, et quod non debet sibi dimitti nisi aliis dimittat, et huiusmodi
multa. Et sic mediate poterit exsequi. Similiter, habita forte[o] carnali delectatione[p]

(t) ille] *om. MS* || (u) ipsius] eius *T* || (v) et] *om. M* || (w) ex] et *M* || (x) praehabito – praehabito] deliberato consilio *M* ; *om. T* || (y) illud] id est *M* ; idem *S* || (z) nolendum quod] volitum quia *T* || (a) volendum] fuit volitum *V* || (b) quo] illo *T* || (c) immo – nolendum] nunc esse volendum *S* || (d) quod] quidem *T* || (e) quin] *om. M* || (f) subito] sibito *T* || (g) et nolitionum] *om. S* || (h) earundem] eorumdem *M* || (i) quia] quod *V* || (j) aliter] omnes *M* || (k) ubi] si *MS* || (l) dictatae] dictare *M* || (m) vel] et *M* || (n) seu] vel *T* || (o) evidentis] *om. M* || (p) firmae credulitatis] in fine redu[ter] *M* || (q) possit] posset *S* || (r) immediate] mediate *T* || (s) principiando] praelibando* *M* || (t) occurrat] et *add. M* || (u) aliud] *om. V* || (v) movens – oppositum] in omnem ad propositum *M* || (w) priori] primi sibi *M* || (x) vero] nec *M* || (y) dilectiones] electiones *T* ; executiones *add. s.l. T* || (z) nolitiones] volitiones *T, a.c. V* || (a) ipsae] *om. MS* ; ipsi *a.c.. T* || (b) huiusmodi iudiciis] *tr. T* || (c) dictatae] dictare *M, a.c. V* || (d) motivas] nocivas *T* || (e) debere] deberem habere *T* || (f) econverso] econtra *T* || (g) hoc semper] de semper *a.c. V* ; *tr. p.c. mg. V* || (h) subito] ut *add. T* ; tunc *add. V* || (i) vel] et *T* ; *om. V* || (j) conceptionibus – ad] contemptionibus requisitis *M* || (k) quae] vel *M* ; aliquae *a.c. V* || (l) deberet] debent *a.c. S* ; deberent *T* || (m) supernaturale] naturale *T* ; essentiale *V* || (n) et] *om. M* || (o) forte] forti *T* || (p) delectatione] dilectione *MST, a.c. mg. V* indeliberata, cum volo[q] illam[r] suspendere, oportebit forsan in casu hoc facere sic[s] mediate quod avertatur[t] intellectus vel cogitatio ab illa[u] ad aliud vel alia et huiusmodi.

[17] Si autem amores vel[v] volitiones illae quae sunt exsecutiones dictatae[w] sint[x] etiam quaedam[y] electiones prioribus dictaminibus adhuc[z] stantibus conformes, tunc est[a] satis facile habere vel[b] suspendere illas pro libito[c] ad imperium electionum vel[d] volitionum reflexarum[e] conformium dictaminibus reflexis super electiones ac iudicia illa[f] praevia quae sunt obiecta sequentium[g], sicut si uno iudicio iudicem esse tali tempore eundum ad ecclesiam et alio iudicem me debere conformiter velle[h] illi iudicio[i] de eundo ad ecclesiam, ecce[j] iudicia duo[k] quorum utrique[l] potest haberi[m] conformis electio libera, et tamen prima[n] est[o] exsecutio dictata et electa prosequens[p] iudicium reliquum et electioni[q] illi sequenti dictamini[r] conforme[s].

## <Solutio ad rationem principalem>

[18→3] Ad rationem[t] igitur praesentem[u] principalem, concedo[v] quod voluntas non potest per instans praecise[w] habere actum quin postea habebit illum vel[x] aliquam eius partem, licet[y] possit ad alium intellectum datum suum actum[z] subito[a] suspendere.

[19→4] Ad[b] primam probationem in oppositum, concedo primum consequens illatum[c]. Et[d] ad primam ipsius improbationem, dico quod voluntas potest velle impossibile sibi, immo impossibilia potest voluntas velle, et ita voluntas in proposito, posito casu[e] argumenti, vult[f] sibi impossibile, quia, ut dictum est[1], non est in potestate[g] voluntatis in hoc instanti causantis actum aliquem quin ipsum vel[h] aliquam eius partem[i] retineat per tempus. Nec tamen sequitur quod invite volet vel[j] quod invite continuabit actum in illo puncto, quia non sequitur quod

(q) volo] nolle *M* || (r) illam] eam *T* || (s) sic] si *T* || (t) avertatur] avertitur *M* || (u) illa] illo *MST* || (v) vel] et *M* || (w) dictatae] dictare *M* || (x) sunt] fiunt *MT* ; *mg. V* || (y) quaedam] est *add. M* || (z) adhuc] ad hoc *MS* || (a) est] *om. M* || (b) vel] et *M* || (c) libito] debito *M* || (d) vel] et *M* || (e) reflexarum] reflexato *T* || (f) illa] illam *M* ; iam *ST, a.c. s.l. V* || (g) sequentium] sequentia *MT* || (h) conformiter velle] *tr. V* || (i) iudicio *coni.*] iudicem me *M* ; iudio + *spatium S* || (j) ecce] mea *add. MS* || (k) iudicia duo] *tr. V* || (l) utrique] uterque *MST* || (m) haberi] habere *MST, a.c. V* || (n) prima] utraque *M* ; ipsa *ST* || (o) est] conformis *add. MS* || (p) prosequens] per sequens *V* || (q) et electioni] dilectioni *MS* ; deliberationi *T* || (r) rectum – dictamini] *om. M* || (s) conforme] conformem *V* || (t) ad rationem] quomodo potest esse quod voluntas eliciens actum in hoc instanti necessario continuabit illum per tempus et tamen non continuabit invite sed merebitur, licet non novo merito, et quod in medio illius temporis non potest cessare ab illo actu stantibus omnibus aliis (aliis : *om. S*) dispositionibus **c** *add. mg. infra MS* ; ad rationem principalem Rodinton *add. mg. V* || (u) praesentem] *om. V* || (v) concedo] teneo *T* || (w) per – praecise] praecise per instans *V* || (x) vel] et *M* || (y) licet] *sed M* || (z) datum – actum] creatum suum datum actum *T* ; datum actum suum *V* || (a) subito] *om. M* ; *mg. S* || (b) ad] et *a.c. V* ; et ad *p.c. s.l. V* || (c) illatum] illa cum *M, a.c. S* || (d) et] esset *M* || (e) casu] possibili *add. MS* || (f) vult] *om. T* || (g) in potestate] impossibile *M* || (h) vel] et *M* ; ad *a.c. s.l. V* || (i) eius partem] *tr. S* ; eius *a.c. mg. V* || (j) vel] et *MT*

1. *Supra*, 12-14.

tunc volet quando nolet[k] efficaciter[l] velle, et tamen hoc requireretur[m] ad hoc quod invite deberet velle[n]. Assumptum patet. Modo enim non vult invite eo ipso quod vult per actum reflexum velle rectum esse. Et sicut[o] modo vult ipsum esse et ideo non invite habet illum, ita quia[p] volet ipsum[q] immediate post hoc instans, non invite[r] immediate post hoc instans[s] habebit eum. Non enim plus est in potestate voluntatis habentis nunc[t] actum reflexum quin ille vel aliqua eius pars sit post hoc instans quam de actu volendi recto. Non igitur[u] valet consequentia : « Habebit eum, igitur invite », sed tantum sequitur quod aliter erit quam nunc vellet quod foret. Non autem aliter quam modo vult quod sit quoad hoc quod[v] nunc vult ipsum esse, nec aliter quam[w] volet[x] quoad hoc quod volet ipsum esse.

S 44vb [20→5] Ad | secundam improbationem[y], dicendum quod consequens illatum verum est de damnatis qui sciunt Deum non esse odiendum[z], et tamen ab eius odio modo[a] per seipsos cessare non possunt. De voluntate tamen viatoris non est hoc concedendum absolute[b], quod scilicet voluntas non poterit volendo vel nolendo conformare se intellectui iudicanti volendum esse vel nolendum. Potest enim statim conformare se voluntas per electionem, licet[c] non fortassis per exsecutionem vel quoad velle seu[d] nolle dictata[e] seu imperata, ut prius declaravi[1], et ideo[f] dixi illud diligenter notandum[g].

[21] Et ad probationem consequentiae, cum ponitur[h] quod intellectus in medio[i] temporis infra quod dictum est[j] voluntatem non posse stantibus omnibus eisdem condicionibus cessare totaliter ab actu dato si iudicet actum non esse ulterius continuandum, est ut sic et est ut non, ut visum est. Tamen quantum[k] est pro isto argumento, quaero ab opponente[l] an velit quod[m] intellectus tunc noviter iudicet hoc, vel a principio electionis actus de quo est sermo. Si primo modo, receditur a pacto[n], quia[o] ibi est nova condicio[p], scilicet novum iudicium, et certe tale novum iudicium nec[q] poterit de se habere in medio[r] talis temporis parvi dati nisi sibi a Deo immitteretur vel[s] extrinsece[t] proveniret. Et bene volui a principio quod in tali casu poterit infra tempus datum ab actu volendi cessare infra tempus
V 61r infra quod non posset si praecise mansissent omnes priores dispositiones | praeter

(k) volet – nolet] volet *MT, a.c. S* ; quando volet (*s.l.*) nolet *p.c. mg. S* ; volet quando volet *a.c. V* || (l) efficaciter] effi^lis *M* || (m) tamen – requireretur] cum hoc requiretur *M* || (n) velle] nolle *V* || (o) sicut] sic *MST* || (p) quia] quod *MT* || (q) volet ipsum] *tr. T* ; esse *add. s.l. V* || (r) invite] *om. M* ; *scr. sed exp. S* (*def. T*) || (s) non – instans] invite *add. mg. S* ; *om. hom. T* ; non invite immediate post hoc *mg. V* || (t) voluntatis – nunc] voluntaria habentis non *M* || (u) recto – igitur] certo igitur non *T* || (v) quod] volo *add. M* ; volo *add. sed exp. ST* || (w) quam] quod *M* || (x) volet] vult *MS* || (y) improbationem] probationem *M* || (z) odiendum] ad illud *M* ; *p.c. V* || (a) modo] divino *M* ; amodo *p.c. S* ; dum modo *a.c. T* ; nullo modo *p.c. s.l. T* ; a divino* *a.c. V* || (b) hoc – absolute] absolute concedendum *V* || (c) licet] sed *M* || (d) quoad – seu] ad velle vel *V* || (e) dictata] dicta *T* || (f) et ideo] nam *MS* || (g) notandum] diligendum *M* || (h) ponitur] probatur *V* || (i) medio] medietate *V* || (j) est] quod *add. S* || (k) quantum] quod *MT, a.c. S* ; *p.c. V* || (l) opponente] o (!) opposito noviter *M* || (m) quod] autem *M* ; *s.l. T* ; talis *add. V* || (n) receditur a pacto] vel reditur a puncto *M* || (o) quia] quod *T* || (p) condicio] cognitio *M* || (q) nec] *post* certe *V* || (r) in medio] *mg. S* || (s) immitteretur vel] immittes et *M* || (t) extrinsece] ab extrinseco *MS*

---

1. *Supra*, 15.

tempus. Si autem sic iudicabit[u] a principio, tunc minus tempus a dato esset ab ipso perceptibile[v] secundum dispositiones tunc[w] habitas, contra superius probata et hic supposita.

[22→6] Ad tertium, concedo quod infra tempus[x] datum et per[y] totum[z] illud tempus, si sibi relinquatur cum communi Dei adiutorio, necessario meretur, non novo merito, sed priori, necessario[a], inquam, id est[b], non libere libertate[c] propria ad utrumque oppositorum. Verum est autem[d] quod Deus posset illud tempus praedictum breviare[e] pro libito suo.

## <AD RATIONES CAMSALIS[f]>

[23] Ex his duabus responsionibus praesentibus patet ad rationes multas Camsalis[g] [1] per quas nitebatur probare quod voluntas libere potest velle praecise per instans, quia[h] si non, voluntas non esset[i] libera, immo[j] cogeretur ad peccandum. Quia pono quod intellectus iudicet non esse bonum, immo malum, velle tale obiectum[k] in secunda medietate temporis dati, aut igitur potest tunc[l] ab actu[m] | cessare ante finem temporis dati[n], et tunc illud non erat[o] ita parvum citra cuius finem non potuit cessare ab actu, contra te, vel non, et habetur intentum. **M 37va**

[24→23] Dicendum, ut prius, quod si a principio illius temporis sic iudicat distincte discernendo unam medietatem temporis dati ab alia, tempus illud erat[p] maius[q] quam dandum[r]. Si noviter sic iudicatur, hoc est aliunde, et ab extra provenit, et tunc[s] receditur a | pacto, quia tunc habetur[t] alia dispositio praevia secundum naturam cessationi ab actu illo quam prius. **T 31vb**

[25] **(2)** Idem[u] arguit sic[2] : in quocumque instanti vel tempore obiectum apparet bonum, potest voluntas se convertere ad illud, vel si apparet malum, avertere se ab ipso, aliter oporteret exspectare antequam vellet in casu[v] ubi nihil sibi deficeret ad agendum ; sed in quolibet instanti temporis dati posset aliud[w] obiectum concurrere sub ratione melioris vel illud idem sub ratione mali ; igitur.

(u) iudicabit] iudicabilis *M* || (v) perceptibile] imperceptibile *T* || (w) tunc] inter *M* || (x) tempus] *om. MS* || (y) et per] *om. MST* || (z) totum] ratum *M* || (a) sed – necessario] *om. MS* || (b) id est] quod *M* || (c) libertate] si potestate *M* || (d) autem] *om. M* || (e) breviare] *p.c. M* || (f) Camsalis] ad respondens Camesalle *add. mg. T* ; Camsalis *add. mg. V* || (g) Camsalis] Tamtale *M* ; Camassale *T* ; Campsale *V* || (h) quia] quod *M* || (i) esset] vellet *a.c. T* || (j) immo] quia tunc *MS* || (k) obiectum] oppositum *T, a.c. V* || (l) tunc] nunc *M* (*def. V*) || (m) actu] intellectu *T* (*def. V*) || (n) aut – dati] *om. hom. V* || (o) erat] erit *MT, a.c. S* || (p) erat] erit *MT* ; *p.c. S* || (q) maius] magis *MST* || (r) dandum] datum *MT* || (s) tunc] etiam *add. V* || (t) habetur] *om. MT* ; *mg. S* || (u) idem] item *TV* || (v) in casu] *om. MT* ; *mg. S* || (w) aliud] ad *a.c. S, T* ; aliquod *p.c. S*

1. Riccardus Campsall, *Quaestio theologica*, a. 2, ed. K. H. Tachau, « Richard Campsall as a Theologian : New Evidence », in *Historia Philosophiae Medii Aevi : Studien zur Geschichte der Philosophie des Mittelalters*, ed. B. Mojsisch and O. Pluta, vol. 2, Amsterdam-Philadelphia, 1991, p. 979-1002, p. 997.178-183.

2. Riccardus Campsall, *Quaestio theologica*, a. 2, ed. Tachau, p. 997.184-189.

[26→25] Dicendum ad hoc sicut prius quod per nullum tempus necessario continuat actum datum[x], posito possibili. Positis tamen[y] praecise circumscriptis[z] praehabitis[a], non est in eius[b] libera potestate non continuare ipsum per certum tempus.

[27] **(3)** Tertio arguit sic[1], quod illo dato, voluntas cogeretur in casu ad merendum et in casu ad demerendum, quia actu incepto non posset se[c] retrahere ab eo infra tempus datum.

[28→27] Dicendum quod non cogitur ad primam causationem, sed cogitur, id est, necessitatur, continuare ipsum, si causet[d], nisi aliud noviter occurrens vel
**S 45ra** impediens ob|stet[e]. Per hoc patet ad tertiam[2] probationem principalem.

[29] **(4)** Praeterea[f], arguit sic[3] : tunc totum residuum a primo instanti non esset sibi imputandum, sicut nec proiectio lapidis post primum instans.

[30→29] Dicendum quod et[g] causatio actus et etiam continuatio est sibi imputanda propter liberam[h] causationem, sed non nova imputabilitate[i] infra tempus dandum praecise propter continuationem, et ideo argumentum verum concludit[j].

[31] **(5)** Item[4], arguit quod, cum « nihil sit tam in potestate voluntatis sicut ipsa voluntas »[5], et per impedimenta extrinseca potest[k] eius actus incurtari, videtur multo fortius quod a seipsa, aliter nihil esset ita prompte ab ipsa causabile vel[l] destruibile sicut ab extrinseco[m].

[32→31] Dicendum quod Augustinus intelligit quod nullus actus exterior ita est in potestate voluntatis sicut intrinseca volitio. Ex hoc tamen non sequitur quod, licet actus posset tolli vel incurtari a voluntate cum illis casualiter concurrentibus per[n] concurrentia extrinseca, non sequitur, inquam, quod ipsa sine talibus virtute propria et priorum tantum dispositionum[o] possit infra tempus illud[p] parvum ipsum tollere.

[33→7] Ad quartam improbationem principalem, concedo quod, si quis in principio[q] temporis minimi ab eo perceptibilis vel maximi quod ab eo percipi non potest demeritorie inceperit[r] velle, si moriatur ante finem temporis huius vel infra ipsum, et nulla nova dispositio sufficiens[s] ad actum poenitentiae concausandum

(x) actum datum] *tr. MS* || (y) posito – tamen] dispositionibus tamen illis positis tantum *MS* || (z) circumstantiis] cui communiter *M* ; circumscriptis *ST* || (a) praehabitis] plurimis *MS* || (b) eius] eis *M* || (c) se] eum *M* ; rem *a.c. S* ; rationem *p.c. S* || (d) ipsum – causet] si causet ipsum *V* || causet] esset *M* || (e) obstet] *om. M* ; obstaret et *V* || (f) praeterea] tunc *add. V* || (g) et] *om. M* || (h) liberam] novam *M* || (i) imputabilitate] imputatione *T* || (j) concludit] contradicit *T* || (k) potest] post *T* || (l) vel] et *M* || (m) extrinseco] extrinsecis *V* || (n) per] post *MT* ; post *a.c. S* || (o) dispositionum] *a.c. S* ; disponentium *p.c. S, T* || (p) illud] et *add. M* || (q) principio] privatio *M* || (r) inceperit] percipit *M* ; incipit *p.c. T* || (s) sufficiens] diffiniens* *M*

1. Riccardus Campsall, *Quaestio theologica*, a. 2, ed. Tachau, p. 997.194-195.
2. *Supra*, 6.
3. Riccardus Campsall, *Quaestio theologica*, a. 2, ed. Tachau, p. 997.208-998.210.
4. Riccardus Campsall, *Quaestio theologica*, a. 2, ed. Tachau, p. 997.196-198.
5. Augustinus, *De libero arbitrio*, III, c. 3, n. 7, ed. Green (CCSL 29), p. 279.63-64.

ab extra proveniat, ipse se impossibilitat libere ne valeat infra tempus[t] sibi debitum[u] poenitere.

[34→33] Contra : sancti dicunt quod de nullo dum est in vita ista[v] desperandum est, cum semper sit in via misericordiae divinae.

[35→34] Dicendum quod verum[w] dicunt, quamdiu superest sibi possibilitas ad deliberandum et scienter volendum conformiter deliberationi, quod non est in proposito, quamvis illa morula[x] talis momentaria[y] sit et[z] brevis. Nec credo de cursu communi hominem ita tarde ante mortem aliquem actum deliberate[a] et ex certa scientia posse elicere, immo iudicio hominum[b] a mortuo distingui[c] non posse.

[36→8] Ad quintam improbationem principalem[d], neganda est consequentia, quia voluntas destrui non potest nisi a Deo tantum[e]. Ipse autem[f] distinctissime novit minus tempus, non sic voluntas creata, quae deberet ab actu cessare. Et falsum etiam supponit quod actus maneat[g] necessario per tempus huiusmodi certum, nisi loquendo solum de necessitate opposita libertati condicionatae huius voluntatis, si causet videlicet actum.

[37→9] Ad sextam[h] dicendum quod casus[i] aufert condicionem pacti, quia si fiat demens[j], non manent praecise circumstantiae et dispositiones eaedem quae ante in principio huius[k] temporis parvi, ideo non est argumentum contra prius dicta.

(t) tempus] vitae *add. V* || (u) debitum] determinatum *M* || (v) ista] ita *S*, *a.c. V* || (w) verum] oppositum* *M* || (x) morula] in horula *M* || (y) momentaria] momentanea *V* || (z) et] *om. T* || (a) deliberate] deliberare *M* || (b) hominum] homini *V* || (c) distingui] desti^tur^ *T* || (d) principalem] dicendum *M* ; *p.c. S* ; *om. T* || (e) tantum] tamen *S* || (f) ipse autem] quia ipse *MS* ; omni tempore *add. mg. V* || (g) maneat] in alia nec *T* ; *p.c. V* || (h) ad sextam] ad secundum *S* ; ad aliud *mg. T* ; *mg. V* || (i) casus] actus *S* || (j) demens] deviens *M* || (k) huius] illius *T*

## SECUNDUS ARTICULUS[a]

### PRIMUM DUBIUM[b]

[1] Quantum[c] ad secundum articulum illius quaestionis, ad primam conclusionem[1] potest esse dubium utrum sequatur : « Sortes[d] in hoc instanti meretur, igitur Sortes[e] immediate post hoc[f] merebitur ».

[2] Videtur quod non, quia si[g] non possem rescindere[h] actum meum ita quod non maneret post illud instans[i], sequeretur, ut praetactum[j] [2] est, quod magis[k] esset in potestate mea retrahere digitum meum[l] quam rescindere[m] actum meum volendi, quod est contra Augustinum[3], qui dicit « quod nihil est in potestate voluntatis » etc.

[3] **(2)** Item, si sic, sequitur[n] : « Voluntas habet *a* actum volendi, igitur immediate post habebit illum vel aliquid eius ». Et ex isto sequitur ulterius quod ille actus erit immediate post hoc instans, igitur hoc sequetur[o] ex primo, igitur primum falsum sicut et illud. Falsitas huius patet, quia si iste actus erit immediate post hoc instans, igitur[p] erit in aliquo instanti immediate post hoc instans. Hoc[q] falsum, quia infert falsum, quia sequitur : « Ille actus erit in aliquo instanti immediate[r] etc., igitur ille actus erit[s] in aliquo instanti ante[t] quodlibet[u] instans futurum ». Consequens impossibile. Et consequentia patet ex una parte[v], quia sequitur : « Ille actus erit, igitur in aliquo instanti erit ». Et ex alia parte arguitur per locum a convertibilibus, quia isti termini convertuntur cum verbo de praeterito : « *A* | immediate ante hoc instans fuit » et « *A* post quodlibet instans ante hoc **M 37vb**

(a) secundus articulus] *mg. MSTV* || (b) primum dubium] *mg. ST* ; primum dubium an sequatur sortes in hoc instanti meretur, igitur sortes immediate post hoc merebitur, dicitur quod sic **d** *add. mg. MS* || (c) quantum] exemplum *M* || (d) sortes] idem *M* || (e) sortes] scilicet *M* || (f) hoc] instans *add. T* || (g) si] *om. M* || (h) rescindere] retinere *a.c. mg. S* ; retindere *a.c. mg. V* || (i) illud instans] *tr. T* || (j) praetactum] pertactum *M* || (k) magis] minus *M* ; non minus *ST* ; non magis *a.c. V* || (l) meum] quando moveretur *add. T* || (m) rescindere] retinere *MST, a.c. mg. V* || (n) sequitur] sequeretur *S* || (o) sequetur] sequitur *T* || (p) hoc sequetur – igitur] *mg. (hom.) V* || (q) hoc] *om. S* || (r) immediate] post hoc instans *add. T* || (s) erit] est *MT* || (t) ante] tantum *M* || (u) quodlibet] quod habet *M* || (v) ex – parte] quia *M* ; *mg. S*

1. *Supra*, q. 9, a. 1, 12.
2. *Supra*, q. 9, a. 1, 31.
3. AUGUSTINUS, *De libero arbitrio*, III, c. 3, n. 7, ed. Green (CCSL 29), p. 279.63-64.

V 61v instans[w] fuit », et isti similiter termini cum verbo de | futuro : « *A* immediate post hoc instans erit » et « *A*[x] ante quodlibet instans post hoc instans erit ». Utrobique enim isti termini modo exposito inferunt se mutuo, igitur convertuntur.

[4] **(3)** Praeterea, si immediate post hoc instans erit iste actus, igitur immediate S 45rb post hoc[y] potest ille actus esse[z], et immediate etiam post | hoc instans[a], ut videtur, potest ille actus non esse, quia ante quodlibet instans post hoc instans potest[b] Deus illum actum destruere[c], nam huius universalis quaelibet singularis est vera. Igitur ita cito post hoc instans[d] poterit non esse sicut esse ille actus[e] et econverso. Igitur simul poterit esse et non esse, vel una istarum propositionum ita cito esse[f] vera sicut reliqua, quia utraque immediate post hoc[g], igitur.

[5] **(4)** Item, ex hoc contra primam conclusionem[1] sic : hoc quod nunc est sine medio potest non esse vel ante omne instans post hoc[h] potest non esse secundum quodlibet sui, igitur immediate post potest non esse, igitur non sequitur : « Est, igitur erit ».

T 32ra [6→5] Contra : non | contingit dare ultimum rei permanentis in esse.

[7→6] Ad illud dubium dicendum quod sic. Sequitur enim hoc ex prima conclusione[2] huius quaestionis nonae.

[8→2] Ad primum in contrarium, neganda est consequentia, quia a primo possum ab extrinseco cohiberi contra voluntatem meam, a secundo non.

[9→8] Dices : in quolibet instanti[i] possum motum digiti rescindere[j].

[10→9] Dicendum quod hoc non est verum nisi a casu, cum[k] secundum impetum factum[l] a voluntate, si nihil novum obstet, procedet[m] motus, et si voluntarie debet motus[n] praescindi[o], hoc erit mediante actu voluntatis alio ab illo quo imperabatur motus, et ita ille actus erit immediate[p] in potestate voluntatis, sicut dicit auctoritas allegata[3].

[11] Aliter etiam[q] dicendum quod exemplum illud magis est ad oppositum. Licet[r] enim Deus saltem[s] in quolibet instanti possit[t] motum inchoatum digiti sistere, tamen hoc erit sic quod tunc in illo instanti erit verum dicere quod digitus non movetur. Unde etiam per nullam potentiam fieri potest quin in quocumque instanti movetur adhuc movebitur[u], igitur similiter hoc[v] est in proposito, si actus qui[w] est, erit. Sequitur tamen quod[x] bene possit dare[y] primum instans sui[z] non-esse sicut ex alia parte[a] de motu.

(w) instans] *om. MST* || (x) a] *om. M* || (y) se – hoc] *mg. V* || (z) ille – esse] esse ille actus *MST, a.c. s.l. V* || (a) erit – instans] *iter. M* || (b) potest] post (*mg.*) *V* || (c) illum – destruere] destruere istum actum (*mg.*) *V* || (d) potest – instans] *mg. (hom.) V* || (e) esse – actus] esse *MS* ; ille actus *T, a.c. s.l. V* || (f) esse] esset *MS* || (g) hoc] instans *add. T* || (h) post hoc] *scr. sed del. V* || (i) a primo – instanti] *mg. V* || (j) rescindere] recindere *SV* || (k) cum] quod *M* ; quia *S* || (l) factum] suum *M* || (m) procedet] procederet *S* ; *s.l. V* || (n) debet motus] *tr. T* || (o) praescindi] praecindi *SV* || (p) immediate] immediatius *V* || (q) etiam] *om. V* || (r) licet] si *M* || (s) saltem] *om. MST* ; *mg. V* || (t) possit] posset *MS* || (u) movebitur] movetur *M* || (v) hoc] hic *M* || (w) qui] *om. MS* || (x) sequitur – quod] quin argui et *T* ; quam aliter licet *V* || (y) dare] dari *V* || (z) sui] *om. M* || (a) parte] *om. MTV* ; *mg. S*

1. *Supra*, q. 9, a. 1, 12.
2. *Supra*, q. 9, a. 1, 12.
3. Augustinus, *De libero arbitrio*, III, c. 3, n. 7, ed. Green (CCSL 29), p. 279.63-64.

[12] Aliter etiam responderi potest concedendo[b] quod plus est in potestate voluntatis retrahere digitum quam rescindere[c] actum proprium, sed[d] actus[e] magis est in potestate quantum[f] ad causationem suam.

[13→3] Ad secundum[g] argumentum, primam consequentiam concedo et consequens quod infertur, sed secundam consequentiam nego. Sed bene sequitur quod immediate post hoc[h] erit ille actus vel aliquid eius, et hoc concedo, et causa[i] huius exprimitur in argumento. Sequitur enim : « Erit, igitur[j] in aliquo instanti erit », sive ly « erit » praeponatur huic adverbio « immediate » sive postponatur. Sed[k] si praeponatur[l], est propositio impossibilis[m]. Si sequatur, vera. Et causa est quia ly « immediate » confundit terminum communem[n] sequentem confuse tantum, sicut patet in exemplo[o]. Haec enim est vera : « Immediate post hoc erit instans »[p], id est[q], sine medio post hoc erit instans, id est[r], nullum tempus praecedit omne instans, et tamen haec est falsissima : « Instans erit immediate post hoc », quia quaelibet singularis est falsa. Mihi autem placet convertibilitas quae ponitur de ly « immediate » quando coniungitur cum verbo de praeterito et de futuro – non[s] simpliciter, quoniam non respectu verbi de praesenti[t], nam praesens[u] instans, quod vocetur *a*, est ante[v] quodlibet instans futurum, et tamen constat quod non sequitur : « Tu es ante quodlibet instans post *a*, igitur tu es immediate post *a* », quia antecedens est[w] verum et consequens[x] falsum.

[14→4] Ad tertium[y], dicendum quoad formam quod[z] non sequitur : « Ita cito potest una esse vera sicut alia, igitur simul possunt esse verae », non plus quam sequatur : « Una erit ita[a] cito vera[b] sicut alia, igitur simul erunt verae ». Quod autem secunda consequentia non valeat patet, posito[c] quod illius horae medietas remotior ab isto instanti sit prima pars proportionalis istius horae, et sit *a*, et prima pars secundae medietatis[d] versus illud instans sit *b*, et sic[e] semper alternatim una pars proportionalis sit *a* et alia *b*[f]. Hoc, inquam, posito[g], ita cito erit illa vera « *A* est » sicut « *B* est » et econverso, et tamen numquam erunt simul verae, quia tunc[h] contradictoria forent simul vera, quia ad *a* esse sequitur[i] *b* non esse et ad *b*[j] esse sequitur *a* non esse.

(b) concedendo] concedo *M* || (c) rescindere] recindere *SV* || (d) sed] bene sequitur quod immediate post hoc *scr. sed exp. M* || (e) actus] *om. M* || (f) quantum] quam *M* || (g) ad secundum] licet ista sit concedenda immediate post hoc erit actus non tamen ita (ista *M*) actus erit immediate post hoc, quia ly immediate confundit terminum sequentem **e** *add. mg. infra MS* || (h) hoc] instans *add. T* || (i) causa] tamen *M* || (j) igitur] *om. T* || (k) sed] *om. S* || (l) huic – praeponatur] *mg. (hom.) M* || praeponatur] praeponitur *V* || (m) impossibilis] et *add. M* || (n) communem] *om. MT*; *mg. S* || (o) exemplo] communi *add. V* || (p) erit instans] *tr. MST* || (q) id est] instans *M*; o *a.c. mg. S*; *om. T* || (r) id est] et *M* || (s) non] autem *add. mg. S* || (t) praesenti] praeterito *M, a.c. S* || (u) praesens] privatur *M* || (v) est ante] dante *M*; est quando *T* || (w) est] *om. ST* || (x) consequens] est *add. T* || (y) ad tertium] quod illa (ista *M*) est concedenda immediate post hoc potest actus esse et immediate post hoc potest idem actus non esse, et per consequens ita cito potest non esse sicut esse, et tamen non sequitur quod simul possit esse et non esse **f** *add. mg. infra MS*; ad tertium *add. mg. T* || (z) quod] *om. T* || (a) ita] *om. M*; *scr. sed del. V* || (b) vera] *om. M*; *mg. SV* || (c) posito] ponendo *S*; vel *add. M* || (d) medietatis] medietas *V* || (e) sic] tunc *MS* || (f) et alia b] *om. MT*; et altera b *mg. S* || (g) posito] iam *add. M* || (h) tunc] *om. MST* || (i) esse sequitur] *tr. M* || (j) b] non *add. M, a.c. S*

[15→14] Contra[k] : omnia quae immediate erunt post hoc instans erunt simul ; *a* et *b* erunt immediate post hoc instans ; igitur erunt simul.

[16→15] Dicendum[l] quod minor est falsa.

[17] Ad rationem autem argumenti huius, quantum videlicet ad propositum, dicendum quod, licet iste actus qui nunc est immediate post hoc instans possit
S 45va | totaliter non esse, tamen haec[m] est impossibilis[n] : « Hoc[o] est et[p] immediate post non erit nec aliquid ipsius », sive « Ille actus est et per totum aliquod tempus immediatum huic instanti non erit nec aliquid ipsius »[q]. Et licet etiam ante quodlibet instans futurum posset[r] ille actus qui nunc est a Deo destrui et sic totaliter non esse, quia tamen nunc est[s], ideo non videtur concedendum quod ita cito possit non esse sicut esse[t].

[18→5] Ad quartum, dico quod non sequitur : « Immediate post hoc instans potest ille actus non esse, igitur non[u], si est, erit », sicut nec sequitur : « Immediate
M 38ra post hoc instans potest hoc quod movetur et movebitur | etiam non moveri, igitur non, si movetur, movebitur »[v], quia antecedens est verum et consequens impossibile.

## SECUNDUM DUBIUM[w]

[19] Secundum dubium huius articuli[x] est contra secundam conclusionem[1]. Videtur enim quod ipsa sit vera per argumentum quo probatur et videtur iterum quod ipsa non sit vera. Nam si voluntas subito possit dimittere actum praehabitum, sicut dicit illa conclusio[y], praecipiatur igitur Sorti quod cesset subito[z] ab[a] actu volendi habito citra[b] *a* instans meridiei, et non cesset[c]. Hoc posito, sequuntur contradictoria ; et non ex casu, cum sit satis possibilis ; igitur ex primo dato, scilicet quod[d] voluntas potest actum praehabitum subito[e] dimittere. Quod[f] autem contradictoria sequuntur videtur[g], quia sequitur quod talis primo peccet in *a* et non primo peccet in *a*. Primum patet, quia numquam ante[h] *a* fuit verum dicere : « Ille peccat contra praeceptum sibi datum », quia ex quo[i] potest instantanee ab actu[j] praehabito cessare, et post quodlibet instans ante *a* et ipsum *a* mediet tempus, et per consequens instantia infinita, sequitur quod post quodlibet instans

(k) contra] obiectio *add. mg. T* || (l) dicendum] quod illa (ista *M*) consequentia non valet immediate post hoc potest iste actus totaliter non esse (non esse totaliter *M*), igitur non (nam *M*) si est, erit vel aliquid (ad *M*) ipsius **g** *add. mg. infra MS* ; solutio *add. mg. T* || (m) haec] hoc *MT* || (n) impossibilis] impossibile *T* || (o) hoc] haec *S* || (p) et] etiam *M* || (q) ipsius] proprius *T* || (r) posset] esse *add. T* ; possit *V* || (s) est] et erit *add. V* || (t) esse] sicut esse *mg. S* || (u) non] sequitur *add. T* || (v) etiam – movebitur] *mg. (hom.) V* || (w) secundum dubium] *mg. MSV* ; vide dubium *mg. T* ; secundum dubium an (*om. S*) si sorti praecipitur (praecipiatur *M*) elicere aliquem actum ante a vel incipere agere ante a et ipse omittat (omittit *M*) quando erit verum dicere quod ipse peccat **h** *add. mg. infra M(37vb)S* || (x) huius articuli] argumenti *V* || (y) dicit – conclusio] illa conclusio dicit *T* || (z) subito] *om. MT* ; *mg. SV* || (a) ab] illo *add. MST* ; isto *add. sed del. V* || (b) citra] circa *MS* ; *om. T* || (c) cesset] continuet *M, a.c. mg. S* ; *illeg. s.l. T* || (d) scilicet quod] *tr. MS* ; scilicet *T* || (e) subito] summo* *M* ; *post* potest *V* || (f) quod cum *T* || (g) sequuntur videtur] sequantur ibi patet *T* || (h) ante] *om. M* || (i) quo] alio *M* || (j) actu] sibi *add. T*

1. *Supra*, q. 9, a. 1, 14.

ante *a*[k] potest sicut sibi[l] praecipitur ab actu praehabito[m] cessare[n]. Videtur igitur[o] quod talis in *a* primo peccet contra praeceptum huiusmodi. Quod autem non primo[p] peccet in *a*[q] videtur, quia[r] in *a* non tenetur cessare ab actu, sed ante *a*.

[20] Istud argumentum fieri solet communiter de actu instantaneo : si praecipiatur alicui quod talem causet ante *a* et omittat usque post *a*, ille peccavit, quia inobediens fuit, et non peccavit, quia nec in *a*, nec post *a*, nec ante[s] *a*; igitur numquam peccavit contra praeceptum illud. Quod non in *a* nec post *a*[t] primo videtur quia[u] non tenebatur actum huiusmodi causare in *a* nec post *a*, quia hoc sibi non fuit praeceptum. Nec ante *a* peccavit[v], quia in nullo instanti ante *a* tenebatur actum illum causare. Igitur in nullo instanti ante *a* omisit Sortes facere quod | debuit. | Igitur non[w] peccavit ante *a*. **V 62r T 32rb**

[21→20] Sed hic forte dicetur[x] quod praedictae formae procedunt contra illos qui ponunt false[y] tales actus subito posse[z] causari vel suspendi a voluntate, non autem[a] contra illos qui ponunt quod successive solum[b] sint[c] causabiles a voluntate.

[22] Ideo addenda est tertia forma contra sic dicentes[d], quia saltem talis potest incipere causare talem actum in aliquo instanti, ita quod in illo instanti – quod vocetur *a* – non causet[e] et immediate post causet[f] subito vel successive. Hoc igitur Sorti praecipiatur[g], quod scilicet in *a* instanti incipiat causare dilectionem Dei super omnia[h], et quod de facto non incipiat in *a* instanti causare dilectionem huiusmodi. Cedat igitur tempus. Et quod sequantur[i] contradictoria contra sic dicentes, sicut[j] contra alios, videtur, quia[k] in casu sic posito Sortes peccat[l], ita quod postea est haec[m] propositio vera, si formetur : « Sortes peccavit », quia non fecit illud ad quod tenebatur[n], et haec similiter est vera post *a*, si formetur[o] : « Sortes non peccavit in *a* », quia non tenebatur aliquid facere in *a*, sed tantum incipere facere in *a*[p]; igitur nihil omisit in *a*[q] quod tunc debuit facere[r]. Nec peccavit[s] post *a*[t], quia non tenebatur incipere volitionem vel eius causationem[u] post *a*, igitur numquam post *a* omisit quod erat sibi iniunctum. Igitur nec[v] post *a* nec in[w] *a* peccavit ille primo. Et constat, ut videtur, quod ante *a* non peccavit[x], igitur non peccavit. Peccavit igitur et non peccavit[y], quae sunt contradictoria.

(k) ante a] *mg. V* (*vide infra*) || (l) sibi] *om. M* || (m) praehabito] ante a *add. MV* || (n) cessare] et si post quodlibet instans ante a potest sicut sibi praecipitur ab actu praehabito ante a cessare *add. S* || (o) igitur] sic *M* || (p) non primo] *tr. T* || (q) praeceptum – a] *om. hom. M* ; *mg. (hom.) S* || (r) quia] quod *M* || (s) post – ante] ante a nec post *MST* || (t) igitur – a] *om. hom. MST* || (u) quia] quod *MS* || (v) peccavit] peccat *MST* || (w) non] potest *add. M* || (x) dicetur] diceretur *T* || (y) false] *om. T*; falso *V* || (z) posse] posset *V* || (a) non autem] *om. M* || (b) solum] tantum *T* || (c) sint] sunt *V* || (d) dicentes] ponentes *V* || (e) causet] esset *T* || (f) causet] et *add. M* || (g) praecipiatur] praecipitur *MS* || (h) super omnia] *scr. sed del. V* || (i) sequantur] sequatur *MT* ; sequuntur *V* || (j) sicut *coni.*] si tamen *MTV*, *p.c. S* ; sic tamen *a.c. S* || (k) quia] quod *T* || (l) peccat] peccavit *p.c. S* || (m) haec] *om. M* || (n) tenebatur] et quod erat sibi inunctum *add. MS* || (o) sortes – formetur] *om. hom. M* ; *mg. S* || (p) in a] *om. V* || (q) in a] ita *MT* ; *s.l. S* || (r) facere] *om. MT* ; *mg. SV* || (s) peccavit] peccat *MT* ; peccat *a.c. S* || (t) a] *om. MST* ; *s.l. V* || (u) volitionem – causationem] *om. MST* ; *mg. V* || (v) nec] *s.l. S* ; *om. T* || (w) post – in] in a nec post *M* || in] ante *a.c. s.l. S, T* ; *s.l. V* || (x) peccavit] *iter. p.c. V* (*vide infra*) || (y) igitur non – peccavit] igitur peccavit et non peccat *M* ; peccavit igitur et non peccavit *T*, *a.c. mg. SV*

[23] Quarta[z] forma est similior prioribus formis contra sic dicentes, supponendo quod Sortes praecipiatur quod ante *a* incipiat causare huiusmodi dilectionem et quod non exsequatur[a]. Tunc possunt fieri formae priores vel similes omnino quod ille peccaverit et non peccaverit sicut ibi.

## PRIMA CONCLUSIO[b]

[24] Hic pono tres conclusiones. Prima est quod Sortes, cui praecipitur quod[c]
**S 45vb** ante *a*[d] causet actum, vel dimittat actum praehabitum, vel quod ante | *a*[e] incipiat facere aliquid, et[f] non faciat nec exsequatur ante *a*, quod Sortes non primo[g] peccat in *a*.

[25] Quod probatur[h], quia Sortes in *a* nec committit primo[i] nec primo[j] omittit aliquid contra praeceptum sibi datum, quia[k] non praecipitur sibi quod in *a* aliquid subito causet[l] vel incipiat causare, vel subito cesset in *a* ab actu praehabito, igitur tunc non primo peccat contra praeceptum sibi datum.

[26] Praeterea, Sortes illo casu[m] posito[n] peccavit[o] ante *a*, sicut patebit ex probatione tertiae conclusionis[1]. Non igitur primo[p] peccat in *a*.

[27] Tertio[q], quia tunc primo est sibi impossibile implere quod praecipitur sibi[r], potest sic argui : Sortes in *a*, supposito primo casu[s], si sibi infunderentur[t] cognitiones a Deo vel naturaliter perciperet[u] quod ante *a* non fecisset quod sibi praecipiebatur facere vel[v] incipere ante *a*, posset conteri et dolere de hoc, et per consequens in *a*[w] habere caritatem, et per consequens non in *a*[x] primo peccat[y] mortaliter, quia peccatum mortale et gratia non compatiuntur[z] se in eodem secundum legem Dei ordinatam.

[28] Quarto[a], quia cum toto casu illo[b] staret quod Sortes moreretur in *a* habens miraculose usum[c] liberi arbitrii usque ad *a*, et per consequens tunc anima Sortis non primo[d] peccaret in *a*, quia nullus peccat quando non est in statu viae; sed in *a* est anima Sortis extra statum viae, et tunc tamen esset digna poena[e] aeterna, quia verum est tunc[f] quod inobediens fuit, non faciens nec facere incipiens ante *a* quod debuit et potuit; igitur in casu argumenti non est[g] dicendum quod Sortes primo peccat in *a*.

(z) quarta] quae *MST* || (a) exsequatur] in actum exeat *MS* || (b) prima conclusio] *mg. MSTV* ; prima conclusio quod in (isto *M*) casu posito sortes non peccat in a **j** *add. mg. infra MS* || (c) sortes – quod] si sortes *M* ; si praecipiatur quod sortes *S* ; sortes *T* || (d) ante a] *om. T* || (e) causet – a] actum et dimittit actum praehabitum quod ante a *mg. (hom.) M* || (f) et] tunc *add. MS* || (g) primo] *om. MT* ; *mg. S* ; *s.l. V* || (h) quod probatur] *om. V* || (i) primo] *om. M* || (j) primo] *om. MT* ; *s.l. S* || (k) quia] quod *M* || (l) subito causet] causat subito *V* || (m) illo casu] in illo casu primo (*mg. infra*) *S* (*def. MT*) || (n) tunc – posito] *om. MT* ; *mg. infra S* || (o) peccavit] sortes non peccat *M* ; sic non peccat *T* ; sortes non peccavit *S* || (p) primo] *om. M* || (q) tertio *coni.*] secundo *MST* ; tertia *V* || (r) sibi] tertio *add. MST* || (s) casu] potest *add. codd.* || (t) infunderentur] infundentur *MS* || (u) perciperet] percipiet *T* || (v) vel] et *M* || (w) in a] *om. MST* || (x) a] peccatum *add. M* || (y) primo peccat] *tr. MST, a.c. s.l. V* || (z) compatiuntur] compatitur *T* || (a) quarto] quarto *add. mg. T* || (b) casu illo] *tr. M* || (c) usum] visum *M* || (d) primo] *om. M* || (e) poena] vita *V* || (f) tunc] *om. M* ; *illeg. V* || (g) est] *om. M*

1. *Infra*, 73-74.

[29] Et cum arguitur quod immo, quia tunc primo et non ante[h] est Sortes non potens[i] facere[j] quod sibi praecipitur vel incipere[k] facere, patet ex praecedenti quaestione[l][1] et patebit infra circa tertiam conclusionem[2] quod[m] non | est verum **M 38rb** illud assumptum.

[30→29] Sed contra[n] illud stat altera pars principalis argumenti, cui parti argumenti[o] innituntur contrarium opinantes, sicut patet non solum per modernos illud tenentes sed per illum antiquum[p] doctorem Altissiodorensem in *Summa* sua[3], ubi ponit casum[q] illum[r] et argumentum etiam[s] libro[t] 2[u], capitulo[v] 63[w], dicens quod « si praeceptum esset alicui quod cogitaret de Deo ante terminum huius diei, sed non cogitat, non est culpabilis ante » finem[x] seu[y] « terminum diei. Nec[z] potest dici quod contrahat maculam omissionis ante terminum huius diei ita quod in aliquo instanti ante, quia[a] inter illud instans et terminum huius diei est aliquod totum tempus in quo potest cogitare de Deo[b] et implere illud praeceptum ». Et ideo, secundum eum, « talis argumentatio non valet : 'Ille tenebatur cogitare de Deo ante terminum huius diei, et non cogitat, igitur omisit[c] ante terminum huius diei'[d]. Debet enim addi », secundum eum, « 'vel contraxit[e] maculam omissionis[f] in termino huius[g] diei', quod verum est », secundum eum, « quia », ut dicit, « tunc primo fuit culpabilis »[h]. Et ita in hoc concordat in opinione quorundam tenentium contradictoriam propositae conclusionis.

[31→30] Huic[i] rationi dicendum quod supponit unum falsum, sicut patet ex responsione[j] ad septimum[k] contra ultimam conclusionem proxime[l] praecedentis quaestionis[m][4]. Supponit enim quod libere ultra quodlibet instans citra[n] *a* posset differre et velle differre causationem talis actus[o] subito causabilis sibi praecepti, et tamen[p] sicut sibi praecipitur causare[q] ipsum ante *a*, quod non est verum. Et illud confirmatur, quia ille cui praecipitur[r] quod sic agat non implet quod sibi[s] praecipitur sicut debet et tenetur nisi hoc scienter et advertenter exsequatur. Talis

(h) et – ante] et non *a.c. T* ; et non ultimo *p.c. s.l. T* ; non *a.c. V* ; *om. p.c. V* || (i) non potens] potens *MT*, *a.c. s.l. S* ; praesens *a.c. mg. V* || (j) facere] *om. T* || (k) incipere] incipiens *V* || (l) quaestione] conclusione *T* || (m) quod] et *M* || (n) sed contra] recitatur opinio Magistri Guillelmi Antissiodorensis qui tenet in uno (*om. M*) loco quod talis primo peccat in a et tunc primo contrahit maculam, quia post omne instans citra a potuisset inplevisse praeceptum (et tunc – praeceptum : *om. M*) **k** *add. mg. infra MS* ; oppositum *add. mg. T* || (o) parti argumenti] *om. MST* || (p) illum antiquum] *tr. MST* || (q) casum] primum *add. sed del. S* || (r) illum] *om. M* ; istum *S* || (s) etiam] in *add. S* ; *illeg. V* || (t) libro] 1² *V* || (u) 2] 6 *MT*, *a.c. s.l. S* ; *p.c. V* || (v) capitulo] *s.l. S* || (w) 63] 363 *M* ; 36 3 *T* || (x) finem] speciem *M* || (y) seu] sive *T* || (z) nec] non *M* || (a) ante quia] ante *T* ; antequam* *a.c. V* ; ante quantum* *p.c. V* (ante quoniam *ed.*) || (b) deo] diligendo *add. T* || (c) omisit] omittit *S* || (d) diei] *om. M* || (e) vel contraxit] et contraxi *T* || (f) omissionis] *om. M* || (g) huius] illius *V* || (h) secundum – culpabilis] *om. MST* || (i) huic] solutio huius rationi praecedenti *add. mg. T* || (j) patet – responsione] *om. MS* ; dictum est *T* ; patet *a.c. mg. V* || (k) septimum] a *T* || (l) proxime] proximo *ST* || (m) quaestionis] a *T* || (n) citra] circa *M* || (o) talis actus] *om. T* || (p) tamen] tunc *T* || (q) causare] causaretur *V* || (r) causare – praecipitur] *om. hom. M* || (s) sibi] sic *T*

---

1. *Supra*, q. 8, a. 2, 71-79.
2. *Infra*, 73-79.
3. GUILLELMUS ALTISSIODORENSIS, *Summa aurea*, II, tract. 17, c. 2, ed. J. Ribailler (Spicilegium Bonaventurianum 17b [vol. 2]), Grottaferrata 1982, p. 574.146-575.155.
4. *Supra*, q. 8, a. 2, 9.

autem deliberatio et recollectio[t] sui requirit aliquod certum tempus secundum naturam voluntatis et intellectus correspondenter et proportionabiliter et secundum aliquas condiciones praesentialiter[u] habitas[v]. Igitur vel ipse incipit[w] ante *a* deliberare per maius tempus quam requirat sui recollectio[x] et deliberatio talis, vel, si non, ad ultimum in principio tanti temporis[y] ante *a* erit vituperabilis.

[32→31] Sed hic dicetur quod forte stare poterit continue per totum tempus huiusmodi[z] in eadem deliberatione, nolle[a] tamen exsequi adhuc[b], sed velle[c] ulterius differre.

[33] Et est[d] dicendum quod tunc diligenter oportet eum cavere ne habeat
actum volendi differre causationem actus qui praecipitur ultra principium, immo
T 32va nec in principio minimi temporis ab eo perceptibilis | citra *a* vel maximi quod ab
eo percipi non potest distincte, quia ex tunc non erit in sua potestate nec facere
nec velle libere et scienter facere quod sibi praecipitur, ut prius[e] [1] visum est. Sic
S 46ra | igitur patet ad illud quod concludit[f] conclusionem iam positam.

[34→30] Ad Altissiodorensem, dicendum est primo quod loquitur imaginando
quod omnem partem temporis in infinitum dividendo versus minus possit
V 62v intellectus creatus distincte | cognoscere. Et illo supposito, non viderem[g] fugam meliorem quam suam, nisi forte diceretur[h] quod talis creatura simpliciter eligeret non facere quod sibi praecipitur, et tunc sic volendo contempneret[i] et peccaret peccato commissionis[j] in instanti illo et deinceps a quo[k] sic eligeret[l]. Si vero non nollet[m] exsequi illa imaginatione supposita, sed vellet semper adhuc[n] differre, et per illum modum se haberet donec totum tempus usque ad[o] *a* laberetur[p], peccaret sic[q] volendo differre[r], quia exponeret se[s] periculo sicut rei eventus tunc edoceret[t]. Et ideo vere vel saltem interpretative contempneret, vel saltem[u] non haberet se erga impletionem praecepti sicut teneretur se habere. Et per consequens ab illo instanti et deinceps quo fatue[v] sic praesumeret, nolens[w] adhuc, sed postea[x], ante tamen *a*, exsequi quod sibi praecipitur, peccaret. Quia tamen haec sua responsio non potest evadere argumenta omnia pro mea conclusione proposita[y], ideo non sufficit[z] illa responsio, dicens scilicet[a] quod primo peccat in *a*.

(t) recollectio] praecollectio *MS* || (u) praesentialiter] principaliter *MS* || (v) habitas] habendas *M* || (w) incipit] incipiat *MT* ; incipiet *a.c. S* || (x) recollectio] collectio *V* || (y) tanti temporis] caritatis *M* || (z) tempus huiusmodi] *tr. MS* ; tempus *V* || (a) nolle] nollet *MS* || (b) adhuc] ad hoc *M* ; *iter. mg. V* || (c) velle] vellet *MS* || (d) et est] rem *M* || (e) prius] supra *V* || (f) illud – concludit] illud quod includit *M* ; responsionem quae est contra *V* || (g) viderem] videret *MT* || (h) diceretur] dicerentur *T* || (i) contempneret] contempnere *M* || (j) commissionis] omissionis *V* || (k) a] *om. MS* ; in *T* || (l) eligeret] diligeret T || (m) non nollet] vellet *V* || (n) vellet – adhuc] adhuc semper *MST* || (o) a] *om. V* || (p) laberetur] labentur *M* || (q) sic] si *T* || (r) et – differre] *mg. (hom.) V* || (s) exponeret se] *tr. MS* ; se *T* || (t) tunc edoceret] tunc educeret *S* ; doceret tunc *T* || (u) interpretative – saltem] *om. hom. M* || (v) quo fatue] *om. MST* || (w) nolens] volens *M* || (x) sic – postea] volens adhuc sed postea sicut praesumeret *a.c. T* || (y) proposita] praeposita *V* ; et *add. MST* || (z) sufficit] *om. T* || (a) scilicet] *om. V*

---

1. *Supra*, 31.

[35] Secundo[b] dico quoad[c] illum doctorem quod non innititur firmiter nec absolute omnino inhaeret dictae suae[d] responsioni. Quod patet ex eius responsione ad illud[e] argumentum[f] satis bonum in materia hac[g] iuxta formam tertiam superius[1] arguendo positam in principio dubii secundi huius[2] : « Quilibet », inquit, qui mortaliter peccavit[h] « tenetur conteri de peccatis suis quoniam illud est praeceptum, et illud praeceptum », inquit, « potest quis[i] omittere[j], non[k] est dubium ». Sit igitur *a* instans in quo vel prius tenetur habere actum conterendi, et ille non conteritur in *a* nec prius, supponatur, igitur in *a* est peccator. Si concedatur, contra[l] : « Aut tenetur[m] conteri in *a* aut non. Si non, igitur non omittit in *a* ex hoc quod non conteritur in *a* ». Si sic, hoc est impossibile sibi, cum *a* sit et non conteritur per casum ; tunc enim teneretur[n] ad impossibile. Ad hoc respondet[o] hoc modo[3] : « Concedo », inquit, « quod aliquis potest omittere ex hoc quod non conteritur in hoc instanti. Nec tamen dico », inquit, « quod tenetur conteri in hoc instanti, quia hoc esset impossibile », quia sicut omne quod est necesse[p] etc., ita[q] omne quod non est, quando non[r] est[s], necesse est non esse[t]. « Sed ideo omittit, id est, maculam omissionis contrahit, quia non conteritur in hoc instanti. Nec prius est contritus, cum prius continue[u] teneretur conteri in hoc instanti[v] vel ante ».

[36] Unde[w] notandum[x], secundum illum, quod « cum homo[y] peccavit[z], non statim omittit ex hoc quod non conteritur, quoniam impossibile esset quod statim conteretur, quoniam[a] ad hoc quod aliquis[b] conteratur oportet quod prius deliberet cogitando de peccato suo et de poena aeterna et iustitia Dei[c] et huiusmodi. Dantur enim indutiae[d] a Deo, id est, tempus deliberationis, sed quantum tempus praecise detur, nemo scit[e]. Tenetur igitur[f] conteri[g] in tempore indutiarum vel in termino illius temporis. Et si non conteritur in tempore illo[h] vel in termino | illius, **M 38va**
omittit, id est, peccatum omissionis seu maculam contrahit. Tunc enim primo est vituperabilis, et omittit ex hoc quod non conteritur tunc[i], cum[j] non fuerit prius contritus[k] et tenebatur prius conteri in hoc instanti vel ante ». Et tunc addit ad hoc[l] quod est directius ad propositum pro quo totum hoc ponitur : « Si tamen », inquit, « fiat vis in hoc quod contritio[m] exigit tempus, quoniam ad hoc quod aliquis

(b) secundo] de tempore ubi quo qui tenetur* *add. mg. M* || (c) quoad] ad *MS* ; quod ad *T* || (d) inhaeret – suae] adhaeret suae dictae *T* || (e) illud] *om. MST* ; *s.l. V* || (f) argumentum] aliquod *add. T* || (g) materia hac] *tr. V* || (h) peccavit] peccat *MST* ; *p.c. V* || (i) potest quis] *tr. V* || (j) omittere] et *add. MT, a.c. S* || (k) non] ideo *MT* || (l) contra] consequentia *M* || (m) tenetur] teneretur *V* || (n) teneretur] tenetur *M* || (o) respondet] et *add. S* || (p) necesse] *om. MS* || (q) ita] quod *add. S* || (r) non] bonum *M* || (s) quando – est] *om. T* || (t) quia – esse] *scr. sed del. V* || (u) continue] *om. ST* (*def. M*) || (v) nec – instanti] *om. hom. M* || (w) ante] nota *add. mg. S* || (x) notandum] negandum *T* ; est *add. MS* || (y) homo] hoc *T* || (z) peccavit] peccat *MS* || (a) quoniam] quia *MST* || (b) aliquis] aliquando *MST* || (c) et – dei] et misericordiae *MS* ; cavere *T* || (d) indutiae] indicia *M, a.c. S* || (e) detur nemo] deus scit *alia manu M, S* ; detur sic *T* || (f) igitur] *om. T* || (g) conteri] continuo *M* || (h) conteritur – illo] conteratur in illo tempore *MST* || (i) tunc] *om. MST* || (j) cum] quod *M* || (k) contritus] *om. M* || (l) ad hoc] *om. V* || (m) contritio] cum triuo *M*

1. *Supra*, 22.
2. GUILLELMUS ALTISSIODORENSIS, *Summa aurea*, II, tract. 17, c. 2, ed. Ribailler, p. 573.97-101.
3. GUILLELMUS ALTISSIODORENSIS, *Summa aurea*, II, tract. 17, c. 2, ed. Ribailler, p. 575.157-184.

conteratur oportet multa praecedere, ut dictum est, secundum hoc dicendum est quod ille non omittit in termino temporis indutiarum, sed in instanti in quo primo efficitur impotens conteri in tempore indutiarum[n]. Est enim »[o], inquit, « generalis doctrina quod, si aliquis tenetur ad aliquam actionem in hac die, si illa actio non[p] exigit tempus ad sui completionem, sed[q] potest impleri[r] in instanti, tunc contrahitur omissio, non tamen[s] in termino, non citra. Si autem actio exigit tempus a sui expletionem, tunc contrahitur omissio non in termino[t], sed citra, in instanti in quo efficitur primo[u] impotens ad illam actionem in hac die ». Haec ille in *Summa*[v] quantum ad propositum spectat.

[37] Cum igitur prius[1] visum est, si Sortes velit differre exsecutionem
S 46rb praecepti, illud velle[w] remanebit per tempus | secundum se vel secundum aliquid sui, et hoc per tempus certum secundum exigentiam dispositionum tunc praesentialiter[x] habitarum[y], et quamdiu remanebit velle dilationis, non ponetur velle efficax exsecutionis, et sine[z] tali velle efficaci, non poneretur exsecutio sicut deberet secundum exigentiam praecepti, igitur si in principio parvi temporis supra descripti immediate praecedentis *a* velit differre[a] exsecutionem actus sibi praecepti[b], impossibile sibi est[c], quantum est ex parte sui, ex tunc citra *a*[d] exsequi. Et per consequens ab initio illius temporis et post est in peccato vel citius[e] forte. Et per consequens, secundum veritatem, oportet ire, secundum istum etiam[f], ad secundam[2] suam responsionem in his argumentis, non ad primam[3], etiam per artem[g] suam.

[38] Ad formam suae rationis, quae est quinta[4] principalis forma in isto dubio, dicetur quando solventur formae quae prius tactae sunt[5].

*<Responsio Altissiodorensis ad argumenta pro prima conclusione*[h]>

[39] Sed hic est dubium qualiter evadere posset quis argumenta pro[i] mea conclusione superius posita innitendo primae imaginationi[6] huius doctoris, scilicet imaginando quod post omne instans citra *a* posset Sortes implere quod sibi praecipitur sicut debet[j] et tenetur.

(n) sed – indutiarum] *om. hom. MST*; *mg. V* || (o) enim] *om. M* || (p) non] *om. MS*; si *a.c. s.l. V* || (q) sed] nec *MS* || (r) impleri] compleri *M*; o *add. sed del. S* || (s) omissio] non tamen *add. M*; non *add. ST* || (t) non citra – termino] *om. hom. MST* || (u) primo] *om. MST*; *s.l. V* || (v) summa] sententia *MS* || (w) velle] vel *M* || (x) praesentialiter] principaliter *MT* || (y) habitarum] habitat *M* || (z) sine] cum *M* || (a) differre] defere *M* || (b) igitur – praecepti] *mg. (hom.) V* || (c) sibi est] *tr. V* || (d) a] *om. M*; *mg. S* || (e) citius] citra *V* || (f) etiam] et *M* || (g) artem] et regulam *add. mg. S* || (h) per quem modum responderet (respondetur *M*) ad argumenta sua qui teneret imaginationem illius (istius *M*) doctoris Guillelmi Antissiodorensis I *add. infra mg. MS* || (i) pro] quod *T* || (j) debet] dicitur *T*

1. *Supra*, 31.
2. *Supra*, 35-36.
3. *Supra*, 30.
4. *Supra*, 30.
5. *Infra*, 80-86.
6. *Supra*, 34.

[40→25] Ad primum potest dici, secundum eum, quod licet Sortes nihil teneatur facere in *a*, tamen[k] primo imputatur sibi ad culpam et ad poenam[l] quod ante *a* non fecit quod ante *a* facere tenebatur, et hoc et[m] non aliud debet intelligi per Sortem in *a* primo contrahere maculam deformitatis peccati omissionis[n] ad modum loquendi illius doctoris[o].

[41→26, 29] Secundum et quintum fundantur[p] super principia[q] secundae imaginationis[1] verae in hac materia, quae principia[r] oporteret eum negare, licet sint[s] multum evidentia apud me.

[42→27] Ad | tertium[t], cum accipitur quod Sortes posset in *a* instanti conteri, **T 32vb** et per consequens esse in caritate, dicendum esset, secundum imaginationem illam, quod non est in potestate sua naturali cum generali Dei influentia tunc conteri de[u] hoc, quia, secundum istum[v], contritio plura praesupponit, et propterea, secundum eum, nec potest conteri in instanti in quo peccat nec statim post.

[43→42] Sed in contrarium stat fortiter quarta ratio[w] [2], quia aliquis, secundum viam istam, posset iuste damnari etiam secundum ordinatam Dei iustitiam, ut videtur, qui[x] numquam in tota vita sua peccasset mortaliter peccato omissionis vel[y] commissionis, quia ponatur quod non peccaverit alio[z] peccato mortali ab illo de quo est casus positus, immo[a] praecipiatur[b] sibi sub poena mortis temporalis in *a* infligendae[c] nisi faciat quod praecipitur sibi[d] citra *a* et etiam sub[e] poena damnationis aeternae. Ponatur igitur iuxta talem comminationem factam quod[f] Sortes in instanti *a* absque infirmitate[g] praecedente de potentia Dei moriatur. Hoc posito, ille damnabitur perpetuo, et tamen numquam dum vixit mortaliter peccavit. Consequens hoc[h] est inconveniens, igitur etc.

[44] Et in[i] hoc videtur aliunde oportere illum[j] dicere. Ex quo enim plene habuit usum liberi arbitrii usque ad *a*, et veniente *a* lapsum est totum tempus in quo potuit[k] et tenebatur implere praeceptum et non fecit, igitur in *a* imputabatur sibi ad culpam et damnationem, etiam secundum istum, et tamen secundum istum in vi|ta sua[l] non peccavit[m], quia[n] ante *a* non peccavit. **V 63r**

[45] Melius igitur videtur, cum hoc illatum sit inconveniens magnum[o] et clare deductum, refugere[p] ab hac imaginatione.

(k) in – tamen] iam cum *M* || (l) imputatur – poenam] sibi reputatur ad poenam et ad culpam *MST* || (m) et] *om. V* || (n) peccati omissionis] *tr. MST* || (o) illius doctoris] doctorum *MS* || (p) fundantur] fundatur *M* || (q) principia] principalia* *M*; principium *S* || (r) principia] principalia* *M* || (s) sint] fuit *M* || (t) tertium] secundum *M* || (u) de] cum *MT* || (v) istum] istis *MS* || (w) quarta ratio] *tr. S* || (x) qui] quia *V* || (y) vel] peccato *add. V* || (z) alio] aliquo *M* || (a) immo] nunc *T* || (b) praecipiatur] precipitur *MS* || (c) infligendae] inflagendae *M* || (d) praecipitur sibi] *tr. T* || (e) sub] fuisset *M* || (f) quod] quia *M* || (g) infirmitate] dicitur *add. T* || (h) hoc] *om. S* || (i) in] *a.c. S*; etiam *p.c. S* || (j) illum] eum *T*; istum *a.c.* * *V*; ipsum *p.c.* * *V* || (k) potuit] ponitur *MS* || (l) sua] *om. T* || (m) peccavit] peccat *S* || (n) quia] nec *add. sed exp. S* || (o) magnum] masum* *M* || (p) refugere] vel fugere *M*

1. *Supra*, 35.
2. *Supra*, 28.

[46] Ad secundam[q] imaginationem[r 1] tactam in quinta[s] ratione contra[t] primam, quia illa via hanc difficultatem non incurrit consequenter, videretur tamen[u] dicendum secundum istum doctorem[v 2], sustinendo primam imaginationem[3], quod in vita sua ille omisit facere sibi praeceptum ad hunc intellectum, id est, caruit actu quem tenebatur habuisse aliquo tempore quo vixit, sed quod maculam omissionis non contraxit usque ad[w] *a*, in quo non vixit. Tunc enim primo imputatur sibi ad culpam et poenam quod actu tali[x] caruit usque ad *a*.

[47] Unde sciendum est, secundum eum[y], quod omissio dupliciter accipitur, quia « principaliter », ut dicit, ille terminus « omissio »[z] « significat carentiam actus[a] debiti »[b]. Alio modo, secundum eum, importat deformitatem culpae omissionis[c], et aliquando, etiam secundum eum[d], non compatiuntur se carentia actus debiti et deformitas quae inde provenit, sicut est, secundum eum[e], in exemplo de cogitatione habenda de Deo citra *a*, quia, secundum eum, nec in *a*
**S 46va** nec ante *a*[f] omittit ille omissione quae | sit carentia actus debiti, quia pro nullo instanti citra *a* tenetur habere illum actum. Nec in *a*, quia in *a* est sibi[g] impossibile reddere illum actum[h] ex quo de facto tunc non habet eum, immo nec a principio tenebatur tunc habere eum.

[48] Aliud exemplum[i] ponit[4] de illo qui « tenetur reprimere motum libidinis antequam sit mortalis[j] et non » facit[k]. Sit enim ita quod talis motus semper citra *a* sit venialis et in *a*[l] primo mortalis, si non reprimatur citra *a*. In quo
**M 38vb** casu, secundum eum, « non valet | haec argumentatio[m] : 'Iste tenetur reprimere motum libidinis antequam sit mortalis[n], et non reprimit antequam sit mortalis[o], igitur omittit antequam sit mortalis'[p], sed[q] secundum quod hoc verbum 'omittit' importat deformitatem. Principaliter enim »[r], inquit[s], « significat carentiam actus debiti ». Nec in proposito compatiuntur se « carentia actus debiti et deformitas quae inde provenit ». Unde « impossibile est », inquit, « omittere in proposito secundum hanc significationem. Sed si[t] omittere importet tantum deformitatem omissionis, dicendum est », inquit, « quod ille qui non reprimit motum libidinis omittit[u] in illo instanti in quo iste motus incipit esse mortalis, id est, deformitatem omissionis contrahit ». Haec ille.

(q) secundam] tertiam *M* || (r) imaginationem] *om. TV* || (s) quinta] quadam *MS* ; hac *V* || (t) contra] propter *M* || (u) videretur tamen] cum videretur *M* ; *tr. S* ; tunc videretur *V* || (v) istum doctorem] *tr. T* || (w) ad] *om. MSV* || (x) tali] *om. V* || (y) secundum eum] *om. M* || (z) dupliciter – omissio] *om. hom. MST* || (a) actus *coni.*] alicuius *codd.* || (b) debiti] inesse *add. T* || (c) omissionis] commissionis *ST* || (d) eum] eum *add. mg. S* || (e) non – eum] *om. hom. MTV* ; *mg. infra S* || (f) nec – a] *om. M* || (g) sibi] simpliciter *T* || (h) nec – actum] *om. hom. M* ; [va]nec in a quia in a est sibi impossibile[cat] *add. sed del. per vacat V* || (i) aliud exemplum] ad quartum *M* || (j) mortalis] mortuus *T* || (k) facit] faciat *V* || (l) in a] iam *M* || (m) haec argumentatio] *tr. V* || (n) mortalis] mortuus *T* || (o) mortalis] mortuus *T* || (p) mortalis] mortuus *T* || (q) sed] scilicet *MS* || (r) enim] sed *M* ; *om. T* || (s) inquit] secundum quod *M* || (t) si] secundum *M* || (u) omittit] concurrit *T*

---

1. *Supra*, 35.
2. Cf. GUILLELMUS ALTISSIODORENSIS, *Summa aurea*, II, tract. 17, c. 2, ed. Ribailler, p. 574.127-575.156.
3. *Supra*, 30.
4. GUILLELMUS ALTISSIODORENSIS, *Summa aurea*, II, tract. 17, c. 2, ed. Ribailler, p. 574.127-143.

[49] Igitur consimiliter[v], ut videtur, haberet dicere ad quartum[1] argumentum meum[w] contra se quod in instanti mortis, illo casu posito, primo contrahit[x] deformitatem[y] seu reatum culpae[z] vel obligationem ad poenam debitam illi culpae.

[50→49] Quod[a], quia mihi ultimate non videtur concedendum, sed omnino negandum, et simul me movent multum[b] argumentum secundum[2] et quintum[3], quae fundantur super principia alterius imaginationis verae, ideo teneo sicut prius conclusionem prius[4] positam et probatam.

## SECUNDA CONCLUSIO[c]

[51] Secunda conclusio in hac materia ponenda est quod, retento principali[d] casu, haec copulativa non est vera, si formetur[e] : « Sortes[f] peccavit ante *a*, et tamen numquam ante *a* vel in nullo instanti[g] ante *a*[h] fuisset verum dicere 'ille peccat' ».

[52] Et huiusmodi contradictionem diversi diversimode tenuerunt, aliqui dicentes quod Sortes peccavit[i] et tamen in nullo instanti peccavit, et quod licet in nullo instanti peccavit[j], peccavit[k] tamen in aliquo instanti. Aliqui vero tenuerunt et[l] tenent quod in nullo instanti peccavit[m] ante *a*, nec etiam peccavit in aliquo instanti ante *a*, sed in toto tempore continuato ad *a*, sumendo[n] ly « totum » categorematice.

[53] **(1)** Contra[o] quos omnes et pro mea conclusione arguo primo sic, quia talis continue, secundum istos, usque ad *a* fuit in caritate, ut probo[p] : sit ita quod non habeat aliud peccatum mortale quam[q] de quo est sermo hic[r], et prius fuit[s] in gratia, igitur non peccavit mortaliter ante *a*. Antecedens probatur, quia continue fuit in gratia vel in culpa mortali ; igitur si citra *a* perdidit suam caritatem, sive fuerit dare ultimum instans esse talis[t] gratiae sive primum instans non-esse illius, inter illud instans[u] et *a* cecidit tempus medium, quoniam si non fuit usque *a*, altero illorum duorum modorum, oporteret[v] quod in aliquo instanti citra *a* desineret[w] et in toto illo tempore, ex quo non fuit in gratia, fuit in culpa ; igitur in quolibet instanti[x] illius temporis fuit ille in culpa ; igitur in aliquo instanti ante *a* peccavit,

(v) consimiliter] conformiter *T* || (w) meum] *om. M* || (x) contrahit] contrahet *V* || (y) deformitatem] deformitate *M* || (z) culpae] tale *M* || (a) quod] *om. M* || (b) me – multum] moveret *M* || (c) secunda conclusio] *mg. MSTV* ; secunda conclusio quod in hoc casu ista copulativa non est vera sortes peccat (peccavit *M*) ante a et tamen in nullo instanti vel tempore ante a fuisset verum dicere sortes peccat **m** *add. mg. infra M(38vb)S* || (d) principali] *om. T* || (e) si formetur] *om. MST* ; *mg. V* || (f) sortes] non *add. T* || (g) instanti] vel tempore *add. mg. S* || (h) et – a] *iter. M* || (i) peccavit] peccat *ST* || (j) et – peccavit] *om. hom. MST* || (k) peccavit] *om. M* || (l) tenuerunt et] *om. S* || (m) peccavit] *a.c. S* ; peccat *p.c. S, T* || (n) sumendo] accipiendo *T* || (o) contra] probatio secundae conclusionis *add. mg. T* || (p) ut probo] *om. MST* || (q) mortale quam] mortale *MT, a.c. S* || (r) sermo hic] *tr. T* || (s) prius fuit] quod prius fuerit *V* || (t) esse talis] principalis *T* || (u) ultimum – instans] *om. M* ; *mg. infra S* || (v) oporteret] oportet *M* ; oportuit *V* || (w) desineret] esse desie[t] *V* || (x) quolibet instanti] aliquo instanti quolibet *T*

---

1. *Supra*, 28.
2. *Supra*, 26.
3. *Supra*, 35-36.
4. *Supra*, 24.

et verum etiam fuit[y] dicere : « Ille peccat », immo[z] in[a] infinitis instantibus. Igitur patet conclusio.

[54] Confirmatur haec ratio[b], quia sequitur : « Peccavit[c] ante *a* mortaliter[d], igitur ante *a*[e] privabatur gratia ». Et si ante *a* caruit gratia, vel igitur[f] in aliquo instanti ante *a* ultimo habuit gratiam, vel in aliquo instanti ante *a*[g] primo non habuit eam. Et sive sic sive illo modo, igitur per tempus certum interceptum[h] inter illud instans et *a* Deo et naturae notum fuit sine gratia. Et per nullum tempus caruit ille gratia quam praehabuit nisi pro culpa sua[i] contra praeceptum illud sibi datum. Igitur toto tempore illo ante *a* quo[j] caruit ille gratia ipse fuit in peccato, et per
**T 33ra** consequens in quolibet instanti temporis intercepti inter esse[k] gratiae | Sortis et *a* fuisset[l] haec vera, si formaretur : « Ille peccat »[m], contra datum ab eis, igitur[n] etc.[o]

[55] **(2)** Praeterea, secundum istam responsionem[1], Sortes[p] fuit peccator in *a* et ante *a* etiam. Cum igitur istud suum peccatum numquam fuerit[q] interruptum, sequitur quod ipse fuerit peccator per aliquod certum tempus et Deo notum terminatum ad *a*. Consequens falsum, secundum eos. Et[r] consequentia[s] patet, quia generaliter[t] omne quod nunc est aliquale[u] et prius fuit tale sine interruptione aliqua, per tempus aliquod fuit tale. Et[v] falsitas consequentis patet per viam
**S 46vb** sic opinantium, quia adhuc[w] in | principio secundae[x] medietatis temporis cuiuscumque[y] dandi vel[z] quantumcumque Deo noti[a] parvi potuit[b] Sortes praeceptum implere, igitur non a principio illius temporis fuit[c] Sortes peccator, alioquin, posito possibili illo inesse quod in principio illius[d] medietatis secundae[e] temporis illius dandi impleat praeceptum, sequitur quod ille[f] a principio[g] illius temporis dandi[h] et Deo noti peccavit, et etiam[i] non[j] a principio temporis[k] illius peccavit, et ita contradictoria. Nec potest[l] impletio praecepti in principio secundae medietatis facere quod ille qui de facto a principio illius temporis[m] peccavit[n] non a principio illius temporis[o] peccaverit, quia hoc esset[p] facere de eo quod transiit[q] in praeteritum[r] quod non fuerit, et « Hoc solo privatur Deus », secundum Aristotelem et Agathon[s][2].

(y) fuit] fuisset *V* || (z) immo] *om. MS* || (a) in] *om. V* || (b) haec ratio] *tr. T* || (c) peccavit] peccat *T* || (d) mortaliter] *om. MST*; *mg. V* || (e) igitur – a] *om. M* || (f) vel igitur] *tr. V* || (g) ultimo – a] *om. hom. T* || (h) interceptum] inceptum *M, a.c. S* || (i) pro – sua] per culpam suam *V* || (j) quo] conclusio *S* || (k) inter esse] interesse *M* || (l) fuisset] gratia *add. M* || (m) peccat] peccant *M* || (n) igitur] *om. T* || (o) sortis – etc.] *mg. infra f. 32vb et in textu f. 33ra T* || etc.] om. *SV* || (p) sortes] *om. M* || (q) fuerit] fuit *M* || (r) et] *om. T* || (s) consequentia] probatur (patet *a.c.*) et *add. S* || (t) generaliter] sicut aliter *M* || (u) nunc – aliquale] aliquale nunc est *T* || (v) et] *om. V* || (w) adhuc] ad hoc *V* || (x) secundae] secundo *M* || (y) temporis cuiuscumque] cuiuscumque *a.c. V*; *tr. p.c. s.l. V* || (z) vel] et *MS* || (a) quantumcumque – noti] deo noti quantumcumque *V* || (b) potuit] poneretur *T* || (c) fuit] facit *T* || (d) illius] secundum *V* || (e) secundae] *om. MV* || (f) ille] qui *add. V* || (g) principio] *om. T* || (h) impleat – dandi] *mg. (hom.) V* || (i) et etiam] *om. MSV* || (j) non] igitur *add. MS* || (k) temporis] *om. MSV* || (l) potest] modo *M* || (m) illius temporis] *tr. T* || (n) peccavit] peccat *S* || (o) temporis] *om. MSV* || (p) esset] *om. M* || (q) transiit] transit *V* || (r) praeteritum] praeterito *MS* || (s) agathon] agatham *T*; agaton *V*

1. *Supra*, 52.
2. Aristoteles, *Ethica*, VI, c. 1 : 39b5-10, ed. Gauthier (AL XXVI. 1-3), p. 480.3-6.

[56→55] Sed hic dicetur forte quod, licet[t] secundum veritatem iste peccaverit a principio temporis dandi, tamen[u] hoc semper remanet contingens[v] usque ad *a*, vel usque[w] quod[x] impleat[y] praeceptum ille peccat. Et si non impleat, tunc in *a* primo est haec necessaria : « Ille peccavit »[z]. Et si ante *a* impleat praeceptum[a], numquam[b] fuit haec vera : « Ille peccat »[c]. | **V 63v**

[57→56] Sed[d] contra istam cavillationem arguo sic : iste de facto, ut probavi[e], peccavit a principio cuiusdam temporis dandi[f] vel Deo noti. Vel igitur peccato commissionis vel omissionis[g]. Si peccato commissionis, hoc fuit per causationem alicuius positivi contra praeceptum. Sed ab instanti talis causationis non potest contingere quin praeceptum[h] fuerit datum, nec etiam quin causaverit[i] illud quod causavit, non plus[j] quam possit contingere quod Deus non creaverit[k] caelum et terram, vel quam possit contingere quod ille | qui voluerit[l] fornicari non voluerit[m] **M 39ra**
fornicari, et sic de similibus. Igitur nec ab instanti causationis potest contingere quod talis non commiserit[n] contra praeceptum absolutum sibi prius datum. Igitur[o] nihil quod Sortes facere[p] poterit primo in principio secundae medietatis illius temporis poterit tunc[q] primo vel ex tunc facere quod ille non peccaverit[r].

[58] Nec iterum potest dici quod[s], si[t] de facto a principio illius temporis dandi vel Deo noti peccavit[u] Sortes peccato omissionis, tamen quod[v] in principio secundae medietatis temporis potest Sortes facere quod numquam sic peccaverit. Quia si a principio illius temporis peccavit peccato omissionis, igitur a principio caruit actu aliquo vel aliquo positivo quod tenebatur a principio illius habere. Et si a principio illius temporis[w] caruit illo actu et a principio tenebatur eo tunc non carere, et hoc est eum[x] a principio peccasse omittendo[y], igitur si[z] in principio secundae medietatis non potest facere quin prius caruerit[a] actu sibi praecepto pro tunc debito haberi, quia nullus peccat omittendo nisi tunc quando sic peccat[b] teneatur habere vel facere quod omittit[c], et ita per nihil factibile ab eo in principio secundae medietatis tolletur quin a principio temporis[d] dati peccaverit omittendo, quod erat probandum.

(t) licet] *om. T* || (u) tamen] cum *M, a.c. S* || (v) contingens] continuabile *M* || (w) usque] ad hoc *add. T* || (x) quod] quo *p.c. V* || (y) impleat] adimpleat *T* || (z) peccavit] peccat *T* || (a) et si non – praeceptum] et si non impleat praeceptum *a.c. mg. infra (hom.) V* || (b) numquam] numquid *M* || (c) peccat] peccavit *V* || (d) sed] arguit contra illam evasionem quae diceret quod in quolibet instanti ante a peccavit, sed tamen cum hoc in quolibet instanti post potuit facere quod numquam peccavit **n** *add. mg. infra M(38va)S* || (e) de – probavi] *mg. supra V* || (f) dandi] *om. M* || (g) commissionis – omissionis] *tr. S* ; peccato omissionis *a.c. V* ; peccato commisionis vel peccato omissionis *p.c. mg. V* || (h) sed – praeceptum] *mg. (hom.) V* || (i) causaverit] creavit *M* ; creaverit *T* || (j) non plus] et non (et non] nam *a.c. S*) quod non causaverit (creavit *M*) non plus potest contingere *MS* || (k) creaverit] creavit *MST* || (l) qui voluerit] voluit *M* || (m) voluerit] voluit *M* || (n) commiserit] omiserit *V* || (o) sibi – igitur] si prius daret* omnes *M* || (p) nihil – facere] quod nihil (*tr. T*) potest facere sortes *MT* || (q) tunc] *om. MST* ; *p.c. V* || (r) peccaverit] peccavit *S* || (s) quod] *om. V* || (t) si] *om. S* || (u) peccavit] peccat *M* ; *p.c. V* || (v) tamen quod] tum quia *MST, a.c. V* || (w) illius temporis] *om. SV* || (x) eum] tantum *M* ; *p.c. s.l. T* || (y) omittendo] omittendum *M* || (z) si] sicut *V* || (a) caruerit] caruit *V* || (b) sic peccat] peccet sic *a.c. S* ; *tr. p.c. S* || (c) omittit] omittitur *T* || (d) temporis] dandi *add. sed del. T*

[59→56] Item, secundo contra dictam cavillationem arguo sic : si[e] Sortes ab instanti *b* peccavit mortaliter – sit *b* primum instans temporis illius Deo noti et *c* instans eius[f] medium – si[g], inquam[h], Sortes ab instanti *b* mortaliter peccavit, tunc in quolibet instanti inter *b* et *c*, in quo ponitur adhuc posse implere[i] quod praecipitur sibi, moreretur Sortes, ipse damnaretur perpetuo, igitur in quolibet instanti intermedio dignus est poena aeterna; sed de nullo qui ante *c* fuit dignus poena aeterna potest in *c* fieri quod ipse non fuerit dignus poena aeterna[j]; igitur nec quin mortaliter peccaverit. Ultima minor patet, quia si ante *c* fuit dignus poena aeterna[k], igitur ante *c* caruit gratia, immo nisi ante *c* caruerit gratia, non est verum quod a[l] principio temporis dati[m] peccaverit mortaliter, quia peccatum mortale et gratia non compatiuntur[n] se in eodem, secundum legem Dei. Sed per[o] nullam causam potest contingere in *c* instanti[p] ut ille qui ab instanti *b*[q] caruerit[r] gratia ipsa non caruerit, quia sicut in *c* instanti[s] non potest per aliquam causam fieri ut illud non fuerit quod vere[t] fuit, quia pari ratione posset adhuc contingere quod caelum et terra numquam fuerint[u] – quod secundum quemdam doctorem[v] bene in hoc sententientem[w], ut mihi videtur, est asininum[x] (probatur hoc, quia[y] etiam[z] philosophis[a], ut praetactum est, fuit contrarium huius evidenter notum) – ita etiam et pari ratione non potest in *c* instanti per aliquam causam fieri ut illud quod de facto a principio *b* usque tunc non fuit fuerit[b]. Patet igitur quod dicta cavillatio est falsa et omnino irrationabilis[c].

*<Secundo principaliter pro secunda conclusione>*

[60] Secundo principaliter arguo pro dicta conclusione sicut quarto[1] loco arguebam et reducebam pro conclusione mea[d] prima[e]. Pono quod Sortes moriatur **S 47ra** in *a*. | Pono etiam simul casum principalem et simul etiam quod ab initio praecepti dati usque ad *a* et post fuerit haec propositio scripta in libro vel[f] pariete : « Ille non[g] peccat », et[h] similiter eius contradictoria[i] : « Ille[j] peccat ». Ex his[k] arguo quod[l] ille non peccavit ante[m] *a* quin haec fuerit vera ante *a* : « Iste peccavit ». Si enim haec affirmativa : « Iste peccavit »[n], non fuit vera ante *a*, igitur eius contradictoria continue fuit vera usque ad *a*, haec scilicet[o] : « Iste non peccavit »[p].

(e) si] nisi *MST* || (f) eius] *om. MST* || (g) si] sit *MT* || (h) inquam] igitur *S* || (i) posse implere] *tr. MST* || (j) sed – aeterna] *om. hom. MT* ; igitur non potest esse quin caruerit gratia (*ut corr. om. hom. ?) S* ; (*mg. V*) || (k) sed – aeterna] *mg. (hom.) V* || poena aeterna] *tr. MST* || (l) a] in *MT* || (m) dati] quod *add. M* || (n) compatiuntur] compatitur *M* || (o) per] propter *MS* || (p) instanti] primo *add. V* || (q) b] *om. MS* || (r) caruerit] caruit *T* || (s) in – instanti] scilicet c *M* ; instans c *S* ; in c *T* || (t) vere] vero *S*, *p.c. T* ; ante *a.c. T* || (u) fuerint] fuerunt *V* || (v) doctorem] et *add. s.l. V* || (w) sentientem] sentit *V* || (x) asininum] *p.c. SV* || (y) quia] quod *MTV* || (z) etiam] ut *add. MT* || (a) philosophis] prohibens* *M* || (b) ita – fuerit] *om. MST* ; *mg. V* || (c) omnino irrationabilis] non irrationabilis *a.c. V* ; non rationabilis *p.c. V* || (d) mea] *om. MV* || (e) prima] primum *S* || (f) vel] in *add. V* || (g) non] *om. MS* || (h) et] non *add. M* || (i) contradictoria] *om. M* || (j) ille] non *add. S* || (k) his] autem *add. V* || (l) quod] quia *M* || (m) ante] in *MST* ; *p.c. V* || (n) peccavit] peccat *V* || (o) haec scilicet] his *M* || (p) peccavit] peccat *SV*

---

1. *Supra*, 28.

Igitur et haec, si formetur[q] : « Iste non est peccator »[r]. Igitur et[s] haec : « Iste non est obligatus ad poenam aeternam ». Igitur et[t] haec : « Ille est[u] in gratia ». Numquam enim fuit haec falsa : « Iste est in gratia », nisi quando[v] fuit haec vera : « Ille peccat »[w] vel « est peccator ». Tunc sic : illa continue fuit vera usque ad *a*[x] : « Iste est in[y] gratia », igitur continue usque ad *a* fuit[z] iste gratus Deo. Et tamen, per te, ipse[a] damnabitur, quia mortaliter, per te[b] adversarium, iste peccavit. Igitur qui continue fuit gratus Deo usque ad instans mortis suae damnabitur[c], nulla lege Dei communi mutata. Consequens inconveniens hic sicut et supra, igitur conclusio probanda vera.

[61→60] Hic forte respondebitur : concedo quod iste continue usque ad *a* fuit in gratia et quod in | **T 33rb** quolibet instanti ante *a* fuit iste in gratia. Cum hoc tamen stat[d], dicetur tibi, iuxta principalem[e] proterviam contra quam ponitur secunda conclusio, quod haec sit[f] falsa : « Iste fuit in gratia in quolibet instanti usque ad[g] *a* ».

[62→61] Contra[h] : si in quolibet instanti ante *a* fuit Sortes in gratia et in nullo instanti ante *a* peccavit, igitur habuit gratiam continue usque ad *a*. Hoc igitur retineatur in memoria. Pono igitur simul cum casu priori quod Deus[i] dederit praeceptum Platoni de causando vel suspendendo similem actum subito in *a*, et quod ipse hoc non[j] fecerit. Et sint[k] Sortes et Plato pares in omnibus aliis[l] secundum dispositiones naturales vel gratuitas. Tunc sic : uterque istorum[m] fuit in gratia usque ad *a*, igitur uterque illorum primo privabatur gratia in *a* ; sed nunc est ita quod Plato, quia primo in *a* privabatur gratia[n], ideo primo in *a*[o] peccavit vel fuit peccator ; igitur pari ratione, cum circa Sortem maneat eadem ratio, scilicet quod primo in *a* privabatur[p] gratia[q], sequitur quod etiam[r] Sortes primo peccavit[s] in *a*. Si tamen usque ad *a* fuit in gratia, sicut deductum est illos oportere dicere, igitur non possunt[t] dicere rationabiliter quod Sortes mortaliter peccat ante *a* nisi simul concedant vere potuisse dici ante *a* : « Sortes peccat ». Igitur conclusio est[u] danda.

[63] Similiter hoc aliunde probatur, scilicet quod Sortes primo privabatur[v] gratia[w] in *a*, secundum | **M 39rb** illam viam ut supra, quia si *a* non sit primum instans non-esse gratiae Sortis[x], igitur aliquod aliud[y] instans est primum instans non-esse gratiae Sortis vel ultimum instans sui esse. Sed hoc non potest dicta via ponere, quae tenet quod in nullo instanti ante *a* Sortes peccavit, quia tunc in quolibet instanti temporis | **V 64r** intercepti inter desitionem gratiae et *a* fuisset in culpa, et per consequens ante *a* Sortes peccavit.

(q) si formetur] *om. MST* ; *mg. V* || (r) peccator] peccatum *M* || (s) et] *om. V* || (t) et] *om. S* || (u) est] fuit *MS* || (v) quando] *om. V* || (w) peccat] peccavit *MST* || (x) a] fuit *add. V* || (y) in] *om. M* || (z) iste – fuit] *mg. (hom.) V* || (a) ipse] iste *V* || (b) te] adversantem *add. sed del. V* || (c) quia – damnabitur] *om. hom. MST* ; *mg. V* || (d) tamen stat] *tr. V* || (e) principalem] *om. MST* || (f) haec sit] *tr. MST* || (g) ad] *om. V* || (h) contra] sed contra *V* || (i) deus] determi *add. M* || (j) ipse – non] non ipse *M* ; non ipse hoc *TV* || (k) sint] sicut *M* || (l) aliis] *om. V* | (m) istorum] istarum *M* || (n) privabatur gratia] *om. MT* || (o) a] *s.l. T* || (p) privabatur] scilicet *add. MS* || (q) ideo – gratia] *iter. mg. V* || scilicet gratia] *tr. M* || (r) quod etiam] *tr. V* || (s) peccavit] peccat *MST* || (t) possunt] posset *S* || (u) est] erit *MS* || (v) privabatur] privabitur *M* || (w) gratia] *om. MT* ; *mg. V* || (x) sortis] sorte *M* || (y) aliud] *om. MTV*

[64→63] Sed[z] forte diceretur[a] quod non est magis inconveniens quod ante *a* Sortes peccaverit et tamen quod ante *a* non fuisset verum dicere[b] : « Sortes peccat » quam quod hoc album fuit in *a* et tamen quod numquam fuit verum dicere ante[c] *a* : « Hoc album est » ; sed hoc est satis possibile ; igitur illud[d].

[65→64] Istud[e] non valet, quia subiectum non ita[f] appellat formam suam[g] sicut praedicatum. Verum est[h] quidem quod non sequitur : « Iste peccator vel iste peccans fuit, igitur haec fuit vera, si fuit formata : 'Iste peccator vel iste peccans[i] est' », quia antecedens potest esse verum sine consequente, sicut patet in exemplo. Sed sic non erat[j] in proposito argutum, sed ponendo[k] in praedicato peccantem vel peccatorem vel aequipollens et ex una[l] in praesenti de praeterito inferendo unam de praesenti fuisse veram in praeterito[m]. Et[n] hoc est generaliter verum[o] ubi[p] aliqua adverbialis determinatio vel simile[q] expressum vel implicitum non impedit consequentiam. Et hoc quia praedicatum appellat formam suam[r]. Unde etiam in terminis exempli bene valet ponendo ly « album » ex parte praedicati : « Hoc fuit album, igitur verum fuisset hoc[s] dicere : 'Hoc est album'». Aliqua tamen adverbialis determinatio praecise significans cum determinata temporis differentia posset bene[t] huiusmodi consequentiam impedire. Verbi gratia, non sequitur : « Tu fuisti[u] heri albus[v], igitur haec fuit vera[w] : 'Tu es heri albus'», sed sequitur tunc aliter sic : « Igitur heri[x] fuisset verum dicere[y] 'Tu es albus'», et sic de similibus.

### <*Evasio Rodington*[z]>

[66] Alia tamen evasio poneretur hic ad rationes iam factas pro conclusione secunda et contra contrarium opinantes mihi mirabilis et vix imaginabilis, scilicet
**S 47rb** quod Sortes ante *a* peccavit vel[a] | gratiam perdidit, in nullo tamen instanti ante *a*, sed immediate ante *a*, ita quod[b] in quolibet instanti *a* habuit gratiam, et etiam econtra gratia sua fuit in quolibet instanti ante *a*, et tamen sine medio ante *a* corrumpebatur gratia Sortis. Imaginatur[c] enim[d] quasi unum medium inter omnia instantia praeteriti temporis continuati ad *a* et ipsum *a*.

[67→66] Sed contra istam responsionem est ista[e] ratio praetacta[1] contra priores evasiones, quia scilicet si caritas Sortis corrumpebatur ante[f] *a*, vel[g] igitur successive corrumpebatur ante *a*, et hoc falsum, quia nulla umquam[h] caritas sic

(z) sed] quod inconveniens est dicere quod ante a sortes peccaverit et tamen numquam ante a fuerit (fuit *M*) verum dicere sortes peccat **o** *add mg. infra MS* ; evasio *add. mg. T* || (a) diceretur] dicetur *V* || (b) dicere] quod *add. M* || (c) ante] eum *T* || (d) illud] etc. *S* || (e) istud] contra *add. mg. T* || (f) non ita] in ista *MT* ; in illa *S* ; non *a.c. s.l. V* || (g) istud – suam] *iter. M* || (h) verum est] *tr. M* || (i) fuit igitur – peccans] *mg. (hom.) V* || (j) erat] est *MT* || (k) argutum – ponendo] argumento sed posito *V* || (l) ex una] verbum *S* || (m) inferendum – praeterito] *om. hom. MS* || (n) et] etiam *T* || (o) est – verum] generaliter verum est *MT* || (p) ubi] nisi *MS* || (q) simile] silbem* *V* || (r) formam suam] *tr. V* || (s) hoc] *om. SV* || (t) posset bene] *tr. V* || (u) fuisti] vere *add. T* || (v) albus] albedo *M* || (w) vera] haec *add. T* || (x) heri] eri *T* || (y) dicere] *om. V* || (z) rodington] *mg. S* ; ponitur a quibusdam quod in casu posito sortes in nullo instanti ante a peccavit (peccavit ante a *M*) et tamen immediate ante a peccavit **p** *add. mg. infra MS* ; evasio *add. mg. T* ; L(ibro) 2 Rod quasi verb(atim)* *add. mg. V* || (a) vel] et *V* || (b) ita quod] *om. M* || (c) imaginatur] imaginabatur *MT* || (d) enim] *om. SV* || (e) ista] *om. SV* || (f) ante] in *MST* ; *p.c. V* || (g) vel] simul *M* || (h) nulla umquam] numquam nulla *MT, a.c. S*

---

1. *Supra*, 62.

corrumpitur de lege communi Dei[i], et casus totus est possibilis de communi lege Dei ; vel subito illo modo corrumpebatur, et hoc non, quia quod simul ac subito corrumpitur, instantanee seu in instanti corrumpitur ; si igitur caritas corrumpitur ante *a* vel corrumpebatur subito, et non in instanti immediato, igitur mediato, et per consequens per totum tempus interceptum et in quolibet instanti illius temporis[j] fuisset sine gratia ante *a*, cuius oppositum dicit dicta evasio[k].

[68] **(2)** Similiter[l], si caritas Sortis corrumpebatur ante *a*, vel igitur sic quod habuit ultimum sui esse vel primum sui non-esse ; si primum instans sui non-esse, et hoc non est *a*, per eos, igitur aliud[m] ante *a* ; et non immediatum, ut prius, igitur mediatum, et sequitur idem quod pridem. Si habuit ultimum sui esse[n], multo fortius sequuntur[o] ea[p] quae prius et plura etiam inconvenientia contra eos, sicut satis patet cuilibet attendenti. Alii autem modi non videntur[q] imaginabiles quibus illa potuerit corrumpi in *a* quam alter istorum, igitur etc.

[69] **(3)** Praeterea, caritas Sortis, si corrumpebatur ante *a*, desinebat esse ante *a*. Vel igitur exponendo ly « desinebat » sic : « Nunc non est et prius immediate fuit », vel sic : « Nunc est et sine medio non erit »[r]. Et sive sic sive sic desinebat ante *a* esse[s], sequitur quod inter desitionem gratiae Sortis et *a* cadebat tempus medium[t] in quo et[u] quolibet eius instanti intrinseco Sortes caruit gratia, et per consequens in quo et[v] quolibet eius instanti[w] Sortes fuit peccator seu peccavit, cuius oppositum tenet dicta evasio[x] etc.

[70] **(4)** Praeterea, capio totum tempus quo Sortes habuit gratiam antequam[y] peccavit peccato de quo est hic sermo, quia[z] circumscribamus omne[a] aliud peccatum. Et capio iterum totum tempus quo ille peccavit contra dictum[b] praeceptum. Et constat quod inter ista tempora[c] nullum tempus fuit interceptum, quia tunc per totum illud[d] tempus Sortes non fuisset in culpa nec in gratia, quod est impossibile secundum communem legem Dei, secundum[e] quam procedit totum argumentum, cum secundum istam communem Dei legem[f] gratia et mortalis culpa sint sic opposita immediata per se vel per accidens quod nec circa idem obiectum[g] compatiuntur se nec idem subiectum[h] aptum natum[i] esse sub utroque posset esse et sine gratia et sine culpa[j]. | Igitur totum tempus[k] in quo Sortes fuit **T 33va** in gratia et totum tempus in quo Sortes fuit in culpa per inobedientiam, ex quo fuerunt immediata, sine scilicet interruptione alicuius temporis medii, copulantur[l] per aliquod instans unicum. De illo ego quaero utrum fuerit *a* vel instans aliud ab *a*. Si illud instans fuit *a*, non igitur ante *a* corrumpebatur gratia eius ; igitur[m]

(i) communi dei] *tr. V* || (j) interceptum – temporis] *om. hom. MT* || (k) evasio] evacuatio *V* || (l) similiter] secundo *add. mg. T* || (m) aliud] *om. M* || (n) sui esse] *om. MST* || (o) sequuntur] sequitur *V* || (p) ea] illa *MT* ; *om. V* || (q) videntur] habentur *M* || (r) sic nunc non – erit] tunc non erat et immediate ante fuit vel quia tunc erat et immediate post non fuit *MST*, *a.c. partim mg. V* || (s) esse] *om. S* || (t) medium] mediato *M* || (u) et] *om. V* || (v) quo et] *scr. sed del. V* || (w) eius instanti] *tr. T* || (x) instanti – evasio] *mg. V* ; igitur *add. mg. V* || (y) gratiam antequam] aliquam gratiam *M* ; gratiam aliquam *T* || (z) quia] quod *M* || (a) omne] esse *M* || (b) dictum] praedictum *V* || (c) tempora] tempore *MT* || (d) totum illud] *tr. V* || (e) secundum] per *V* || (f) secundum quam – legem] *om. hom. M* || (g) obiectum] subiectum *V* || (h) subiectum] obiectum *V* || (i) natum] est *add. MT* || (j) esse sub – culpa] cum *add. MS* ; esse et sine gratia et sine culpa *a.c. mg. V* || (k) tempus] *ante* igitur (*a.c. et p.c. mg.*) *V* || (l) copulantur] copulatur *MST* || (m) igitur] *om. M* ; sortes *add. T* ; immo *V*

vel eius gratia[n] tunc primo non est vel tunc ultimo est – oppositum enim non est conceptibile[o] – quorum utrumque est contra praedictam evasionem. Si autem[p] M 39va instans copulans duo praedicta tempora sit instans aliud ab *a*, et non | est aliquod instans post *a*, certum est tam mihi quam[q] sic respondentibus[r], igitur est instans vel[s] fuit instans praecedens *a*; et non immediatum, quia instans instanti sine medio succedere includit repugnantiam, sicut et[t] indivisibile indivisibili in continuo, ut alias demonstrabo[1]; igitur illud instans praecedens *a* fuit instans[u] mediate[v] praecedens *a*. Et per consequens per totum medium interceptum fuisset corrupta gratia Sortis, contra sic evadentes ponentes eam fuisse in omni instanti ante *a* et tamen quod[w] corrumpebatur ante *a*. Igitur illa evasio est irrationabilis et falsa. Igitur stant rationes prius factae et conclusio[x] antedicta.

[71] **(5)** Praeterea, secundum quosdam sic opinantium, sicut[y] caritas et gratia Sortis fuit in proposito casu in quolibet instanti ante *a* et tamen corrumpebatur ante *a*[z] impartibiliter[a], ita potuit Deus fecisse unum angelum qui vere fuisset ante *a* et tamen qui nec in *a* nec in aliquo instanti ante *a*[b] fuisset, sed in toto V 64v S 47va tempore continuato ad *a*, | categorematice sumendo ly « totum » | quasi[c] post omnia instantia ante *a*, et tamen ante[d] *a*, immo sine quasi[e], quia ita ad punctum est imaginatio eorum. Et eodem modo ponunt quod sine medio post *a* Deus posset producere unum angelum alium[f] simul totum, ita quod non per partem ante partem, qui angelus nec esset in *a* nec in aliquo instanti post *a*, sed inter *a* et inter omnia instantia sequentia[g] in quodam[h] – nescio in quo[i] – latibulo mensurae[j] nec a Deo nec ab homine, ut mihi videtur, imaginabili[k], istorum duorum angelorum neuter esset in *a* nec in aliquo instanti alio ab *a*, sed unus ante *a* et alius post *a*. Et constat omnibus quod in *a* instanti potuisset Deus unum angelum tertium[l] producere. Ponatur quod ita fecerit, et tunc habebimus tres angelos consequenter[m] se habentes et indivisibiliter productos, nullum cum alio. Hoc autem falsum est et omni causae ad[n] faciendum sic impossibile, tum quia pari ratione posset[o] Deus indivisibiliter et sine medio producere quartum post tertium, et sine medio post quartum producere quintum, et sic sine fine in quovis[p] numero finito, et sic haberemus unam moram vel durationem compositam ex indivisibilibus consequenter se habentibus, cuius oppositum evidentissime, ut aestimo, alias in materia de continuo demonstrabo[2]. Tum quia tertius angelus ex eis simul esset et non esset, quia esset in *a* et non esset in *a*, quae sunt incompossibilia. Quod esset

(n) eius gratia] culpa eius *M* ; *om. S* || (o) conceptibile] conteplabile (!) *M* || (p) si autem] *a.c. V* ; nam* si *p.c. V* || (q) quam] quod *T* ; quia *V* || (r) respondentibus] quod *add. T* || (s) igitur – vel] igitur *MST*, *a.c. mg. V* || (t) et] *om. MT* || (u) instans] instantis *S* || (v) mediate] medium *M* || (w) quod] *s.l. TV* || (x) conclusio] contra *MST* || (y) sicut] sic *MT* ; si *S* || (z) et – a] *om. S* || (a) impartibiliter] impartiali* *M* || (b) ante a] *om. MST* || (c) quasi] a *M* || (d) ante] *om. T* ; *s.l. V* || (e) quasi] a *M* ; gratia *a.c. s.l. V* || (f) angelum alium] *tr. M* || (g) sequentia] sequantur *M* || (h) in quodam] *om. MST* || (i) quo] quodam *S* || (j) mensurae] mensuro *M* || (k) imaginabili] imaginabile *SV* || (l) tertium] *om. MST* || (m) consequenter] continualiter* *M* || (n) et – ad] et omnium esse *M* ; cum hoc ad *S* || (o) posset] possit *MST* || (p) quovis] quodam *M*

---

1. Adam Wodeham, *Tractatus de indivisibilibus*, q. 1, a. 1, ed. Wood, passim.
2. Adam Wodeham, *Tractatus de indivisibilibus*, q. 1, a. 1, ed. Wood, p. 34.11-36.5.

in *a* probo[q], quia sicut in continuo, secundum[r] Philosophum, VI *Physicorum*[1], indivisibile additum indivisibili non facit maius[s], et ideo si sumantur, ut dicit, tria indivisibilia sine medio divisibili consequenter se[t] habentia in continuo, primum illorum non partim tangeret[u] secundum[v] et partim non, quia tunc[w] haberet partem et partem et non esset indivisibile, igitur totum totaliter tangeret totum, et pari[x] ratione secundum totaliter tangeret tertium[y], igitur et primum[z] sic tangeret tertium, et per consequens non essent mediata[a], ita arguam in proposito de tribus illis factionibus indivisibilibus et sic sine medio divisibili consequenter se habentibus in duratione, quoniam[b] tertia indivisibilis[c] productio erit immediata[d] primae sicut et secunda est sibi immediata. Et si hoc, igitur tertius angelus fit[e] in *a*, si valet ratio Philosophi contra indivisibilia in continuo consequenter se habentia. Immo quia valet, ut alias declarabo[2], valet[f] et mea[g], quae omnino similis est de indivisibilibus succedentibus sicut[h] de[i] indivisibilibus permanentibus. Aliam[j] autem, quod tertius ille angelus[k] non erit in *a*, dant adversarii. Erit igitur in *a* et[l] non erit in *a*, et per consequens simul esset et non esset, quod erat probandum ; sed hoc constat esse[m] impossibile ; impossible est[n] igitur et[o] illud ex quo sequitur, scilicet quod angelus possit indivisibiliter produci et esse ante[p] *a* vel post *a*, qui tamen nec esset in *a* nec in aliquo instanti ante *a* vel post[q] *a*.

[72] **(6)** Sexto[r] et ultimo contra ultimam evasionem[3] arguo sic : si gratia seu[s] caritas Sortis fuit in omni instanti ante *a*, et tamen corrumpebatur ante *a*[t], et omne corruptum ante *a* potest Deus in *a* reproducere, posset Deus facere quod caritas aliqua, puta *b*, fuerit in omni instanti huius diei ante *a*, et cum hoc etiam in *a*, et tamen quod semel[u] in hac die fuerit corrupta ante *a*. Et pari ratione potest facere quod caritas quae est in hoc instanti *a* corrumpatur sic[v] sine medio post *a* et tamen sic reproducatur quod ipsa sit in omni instanti huius diei post *a*, et per consequens quod caritas *b* fuerit[w] bis adnihilata in hac die, et tamen quod ipsa fuerit in omni instanti huius diei. Et sicut argutum est respectu *a* instantis, ita potest argui de omni instanti inchoante partes proportionales huius diei, quarum prima sit prima medietas diei, secunda prima[x] medietas residui, et sic deinceps. Et tunc sequitur quod simul starent quod caritas *b* esset in omni instanti huius diei, et tamen quod infinities corrumpetur in[y] hac die. Et pari ratione per eadem

(q) probo] probatio *S* || (r) secundum] s *a.c. V* ; *om. p.c. V* || (s) maius] magis *S* || (t) consequenter se] *tr. V* || (u) tangeret] tangitur *M* || (v) secundum] et secundum *M* ; istum *S* || (w) tunc] *om. T* || (x) pari] in *M* || (y) tertium] secundum *M* || (z) primum] et *add. S* || (a) mediata] et *add. S* || (b) quoniam] *mg. et in textu S* ; quod *V* || (c) indivisibilis] divisibilis *MT* || (d) erit immediata] *tr. MT* || (e) fit] sit *MT* ; *p.c. V* || (f) valet] hoc *V* || (g) mea] me *MT* || (h) sicut] sue *V* || (i) de] in *S* || (j) aliam] *om. M* || (k) ille angelus] *tr. V* || (l) et] *om. M* || (m) esse] omne *M* || (n) impossible est] *tr. MST* || (o) et] *om. V* || (p) ante] quando *M* || (q) ante – post] post a vel ante *MST* || (r) sexto] sexto *add. mg. ST* || (s) seu] et *MT* || (t) et – a] *mg. (hom.) V* || (u) semel] simul *MST* || (v) corrumpatur sic] corrupta sit *S* || (w) fuerit] fuit *S* || (x) prima] *om. MST* || (y) in] *om. S* ; *s.l. V*

1. Aristoteles, *Physica*, VI, c. 1 : 231a30-b15, ed. Bossier et Brams (AL VII. 1.2), p. 216-217.
2. Adam Wodeham, *Tractatus de indivisibilibus*, q. 2, a. 2, ed. Wood, p. 138-142.
3. *Supra*, 66.

media probatur contra eos quod[z] simul possent haec[a] stare econverso : quod *b*
caritas in nullo instanti huius diei esset et tamen quod *b*[b] caritas esset infinities
M 39vb in hac die[c]. | Et[d] deductiones istorum patent ex iam dictis cuilibet advertenti. Et
forte, immo sine « forte », sicut notum est mihi, aliqui eorum[e] concederent haec[f]
illata. Quia tamen, meo iudicio[g] et[h] iudicio omnium qui ratione sapiunt, utrumque
S 47vb illatum hic ultimo et similiter utrumque | primo illatum, ex quibus haec ultima
inferuntur, includit incompossibilia[i], igitur et antecedens ex quo haec[j] sequuntur[k]
est impossibile, scilicet quod *b*[l] caritas fuerit in omni instanti ante *a*[m] et tamen
quod corrumpebatur non in *a*, sed ante *a*. Igitur illa evasio non est bona.

## TERTIA CONCLUSIO[n]

[73] Conclusio tertia principalis in principali dubio[o] est quod Sortes, posito
T 33vb casu principali, peccavit ante *a* et quod[p] per tempus[q] aliquod | et per infinita
instantia illius temporis fuit Sortes peccator ante *a*.

[74] Ex quo enim certum est Sortem peccasse in *a* vel ante, et probatum est pro prima conclusione[1] quod non primo in *a*, ex quibus iunctis[r] evidenter sequitur quod Sortes peccavit ante *a*. Probatum est autem pro secunda[s] conclusione[2] quod non stant simul quod Sortes peccavit ante *a*[t] et tamen[u] quod in nullo instanti ante *a* peccavit, et multo fortius per consequens quod non stant simul quod Sortes peccavit[v] ante *a*[w] et tamen quod Sortes non peccavit in aliquo instanti ante *a*. Et si Sortes peccavit ante *a*[x], et cum hoc non stet quod in nullo instanti ante *a* peccavit, sequitur[y] quod Sortes in aliquo instanti ante *a* peccavit. Et cum inter[z] quodlibet instans ante *a* et *a* fuerit tempus medium, in quo Sortes non emendavit se nec implevit praeceptum sibi, ex casu, igitur per tempus aliquod perseveravit Sortes in peccato, et hoc est ipsum peccasse per tempus aliquod[a] ante *a* et per infinita instantia illius temporis. Patet igitur illata conclusio[b].

(z) quod] quia *M* || (a) haec] *om. MST* || (b) quod b] quaelibet *MT* || (c) hac die] *tr. V* || (d) et] *om. V* || (e) eorum] illorum *S* || (f) haec] *om. MST* || (g) meo iudicio] *om. MST* ; *mg. V* || (h) et] in *S* || (i) incompossibilia] impossibilia *V* || (j) haec] *om. MST* ; *s.l. V* || (k) sequuntur] sequitur *MT* || (l) b] *om. M* || (m) a] et tamen quod corrumpebatur ante a *add. M* || (n) tertia conclusio] tertia conclusio in proposito *M*, *mg. S* ; conclusio tertia principalis *mg. TV* ; ponitur tertia conclusio quod sortes in casu proposito peccavit ante a per aliquod tempus et per infinita instantia illius temporis **q** *add. mg. infra MS* || (o) principali dubio] *tr. V* || (p) quod] *om. MST* || (q) tempus] consequens *M* || (r) iunctis] cunctis *S* ; *mg. V* || (s) secunda] tertia *M* || (t) probatum est – a] *mg. (hom.) V* || (u) et tamen] tamen *om. MT* ; *mg. S* || (v) quod in – peccavit] *iter. M* || (w) ante a] *om. MT* ; *mg. S* || (x) et tamen – a] *mg. (hom.) V* || (y) sequitur] similiter *MT*, *a.c. S* ; *s.l. V* || (z) cum inter] communiter *MT* || (a) perseveravit – aliquod] *om. hom. MT* ; *mg. infra S* || (b) illata conclusio] conclusio certa *M* ; *tr. T*

---

1. *Supra*, 24.
2. *Supra*, 51.

[75] **(2)** Praeterea, sicut prius pro prima conclusione quinto loco[1] fuit argutum respondendo ad argumentum sumptum ex Altissiodorensi, ubi probavi quod non primo peccavit in *a*, sed in principio vel a principio minimi temporis ab eo perceptibilis[c] secundum dispositiones illas praecise quae tunc praesentialiter habentur, vel maximi temporis ab eo non perceptibilis terminati ad *a*, ad[d] ultimum peccavit Sortes, quia vel in principio illius temporis voluit efficaciter, eo modo quo loquitur saepe Magister[e] *Sententiarum*, distinctione 46 primi libri[2] de voluntate Dei efficaci, vel[f], inquam, in principio illius parvi temporis voluit efficaciter exsequi quod sibi erat iniunctum, vel non voluit[g]. Si voluit[h], et potuit[i], igitur fecit et non peccavit. Si voluit et non potuit, excusatus est et non peccavit.

[76] Si vero non voluit tunc exsequi cum effectu, vel hoc fuit quia adhuc[j] tunc voluit differre, et tunc non est in eius potestate quin perseverabit[k] in tali velle usque ad *a*, et per consequens non est tunc in eius potestate quod habeat velle[l] efficax exsequendi[m] | citra *a*, quia cum effectu sive efficaciter velle et velle[n] **V 65r** differre habent ad invicem naturalem repugnantiam. Igitur si in principio illius temporis vult[o] differre, ita quod tunc libere causet in se tale velle dilationis vel libere eligit[p] tale velle ulterius continuare, scilicet[q] velle huiusmodi dilationem, ipse libere[r] impossibilitat se ad exsequendum ante *a* illud quod sibi[s] praecipitur ut faciat ipsum ante *a*. Et per consequens vel prius vel saltem ad ultimum ab initio illius parvi temporis[t] peccavit Sortes in casu argumenti. Et multo fortius ex tunc peccavit si tunc noluit[u] illud praeceptum umquam[v] ante *a* implere.

[77] Vel secundo, si tunc[w] non voluit, hoc fuit quia erat[x] distractus[y], non cogitans de hoc, sed de impertinentibus[z], et pari ratione[a] sicut de velle dilationis, ita et de illis actibus distractivis[b], non est nec erit[c] in sua potestate secundum praecisas dispositiones et circumstantias[d] alias tunc praesentialiter[e] habitas[f] quin taliter distrahatur usque ad *a*. Igitur iam sibi defuit[g] diligentia requisita, et per consequens iam[h] vere vel interpretative contempsit[i] vel neglexit implere sibi praeceptum.

(c) ab – perceptibilis] perceptibilis ab eo *MT* || (d) ad] *om. T* || (e) saepe magister] *tr. S* || (f) vel] etiam *T* || (g) vel – voluit] et non potuit vel potuit sed non potuit vel potuit vel voluit et potuit *M* ; et non potuit vel potuit sed non potuit vel voluit et potuit *T* || (h) voluit] sic *add. mg. V* || (i) et potuit] *iter. T* || (j) adhuc] ad hoc *V* || (k) perseverabit] perseveraverit *S* || (l) velle] *om. M* || (m) exsequendi] exequen *M* ; *p.c. V* || (n) velle – velle] velle et nolle *M* ; nolle et velle *p.c. S* || (o) vult] voluit *MS* || (p) eligit] elicit *MT* ; *p.c. V* || (q) scilicet] si *M* || (r) libere] loquitur *M* || (s) sibi] si *V* || (t) parvi temporis] *tr. V* || (u) noluit] novit *M* ; voluit *a.c. s.l. V* || (v) umquam] *ante* illud *V* || (w) si tunc] scitum *M* || (x) fuit – erat] fuit quod erat *S* ; erat quia fuit *V* || (y) distractus] distractans *M* || (z) impertinentibus] pertinentibus *MT*, *a.c. s.l. S* || (a) ratione] velle *MST* || (b) ita – distractivis] ita (*om. M*) et de illis actibus discursivis *MST*, *a.c. mg. V* || (c) nec erit] nunc *MS* ; nec*T* || (d) circumstantias] circumscriptas *MT* || (e) praesentialiter] principaliter *MST* || (f) habitas] habitus *M* || (g) defuit] *om. MT* ; *mg. S* || (h) iam] tam *M* || (i) contempsit] contempnit *MT*

1. *Supra*, 31-33.
2. PETRUS LOMBARDUS, *Sententiae*, I, d. 46, c. 1, ed. Brady, vol. 1, p. 312.15-19.

[78] Vel tertio modo[j] et ultimo, quoniam quartum modum non reducibilem[k] ad aliquem istorum nullus[l] inveniet, si[m] ab initio illius parvi temporis ad ultimum non voluit exsequi, et tamen tunc nec voluit adhuc differre nec fuit distractus, sed actu habuit omnem[n] cognitionem ad executionem praecepti requisitam, hoc erit suspendendo adhuc omnem[o] actum vel in[p] nullum actum volendi[q] aut nolendi[r] circa[s] executionem dati sibi praecepti exeundo seu nullum talem adhuc habendo. Et si hoc, igitur nec[t] habebit citra *a*, quia velle efficax sive imperium voluntatis efficax[u] respectu praecepti exsequendi[v] deberet[w] esse unum tale velle : « Fac hoc nunc », vel : « Velis hoc nunc »[x], vel simile ; sed tale[y] non potest habere[z] citra *a* ex quo non habet eum in principio parvi temporis dandi[a], quia si sic, tunc[b] S 48ra M 40ra tempus[c] datum non esset secundum praesentes | dispositiones | minimum tempus ab eo[d] perceptibile, nec etiam[e] maximum ab eo[f] non-perceptibile, quia hoc est tempus aliquod distincte percipi[g], ex IV *Physicorum*[1], ipsum scilicet concludi inter duo nunc percepta et per conceptionem[h] adverti concludi inter illa ; igitur[i] cum iste[j] per casum habeat in principio dati temporis omnem[k] cognitionem requisitam ad executionem praecepti sine distractione repugnante executioni, igitur in principio illius temporis, cum tunc de facto praeceptum non exsequatur[l], adhuc bene advertit quod tunc non exsequitur ; igitur[m] si simul cum hoc citra *a* instans haberet imperium efficax tale : « Fac nunc » – quoniam « Fac cras » vel « Fac alias » non esset imperium efficax, sed solum tale[n] : « Fac[o] nunc »[p] vel « Incipe nunc » – et nihil est volitum nisi sit cognitum[q], si virtuose imperaret : « Fac nunc »[r], iudicaret nunc faciendum[s], et per consequens distincte perciperetur illud nunc citra *a* dandum, quoniam[t] tale imperium pro nunc, quod est ipsum *a*, vel pro nunc posteriore ipso, nimis tarde veniret. Igitur intellectus Sortis distincte advertisset[u] primum nunc temporis dati et aliud[v] eius nunc distincte citra *a*. Igitur tempus datum non fuit[w] minimum distincte perceptibile ab ipso nec maximum ab eo non-perceptibile, nam perceptis[x] ipsis nunc leve est illud[y] tempus interceptum attendere, secundum imaginationem Philosophi[z], IV *Physicorum*[2].

(j) modo] *om. S* || (k) reducibilem] reduicibilem *S* || (l) nullus] non *MT* || (m) si] sed *M* || (n) omnem] omniam *M* || (o) omnem] omni *M* || (p) in] *om. MT* ; *s.l. SV* || (q) volendi] ponendi *MT* ; nolendi *V* || (r) nolendi] volendi *V* || (s) circa] *om. MT* ; *mg. S* || (t) nec] non *M* || (u) voluntatis efficax] *tr. V* || (v) exsequendi] exeundo *ST* || (w) deberet] doceret *M* || (x) velis – nunc] *om. MT* ; *mg. S* || (y) tale] simile *MT* || (z) habere] haberi *S* || (a) dandi] dando *M* || (b) tunc] *om. MT* ; *s.l. S* || (c) tempus] cuius *M* || (d) ab eo] habeo *V* || (e) etiam] in *V* || (f) perceptibile – eo] *om. MT* ; *s.l. S* || (g) aliquod – percipi] distincte percipi aliquod *MT, a.c. S* ; aliquod *p.c. mg. S* || (h) per conceptionem] perceptionem *S* || (i) igitur] *om. MST* ; *s.l. V* || (j) iste] ipse *S* ; ille *V* || (k) omnem] omniam *M* || (l) repugnante – exequatur] *om. M* || (m) exsequitur igitur] exsequatur *M* || (n) fac nunc – tale] *om. hom. MST* ; *mg. V* || (o) fac] fiat *S* || (p) nunc] *om. V* || (q) sit cognitum] *tr. T* || (r) et – nunc] *om. hom. M* || (s) nunc faciendum] *tr. MS* ; faciendum *T* || (t) quoniam] quando *MST* || (u) advertisset] avertisset *V* || (v) aliud] *ad MST, a.c. V* || (w) fuit] fit *MT, a.c. S* || (x) nam perceptis] iam perceptum *T* || (y) illud] id *S* || (z) philosophi] *om. MST* ; *s.l. V*

1. Aristoteles, *Physica*, IV, c. 10 : 218b25, ed. Bossier et Brams (AL VII. 1.2), p. 173.5-10.
2. Aristoteles, *Physica*, IV, c. 10 : 218b25, ed. Bossier et Brams (AL VII. 1.2), p. 173.5-10.

[79] Et forte illud argumentum concludit quod non est dare aliquod tempus maximum non-perceptibile ab intellectu isto creato[a], habitis praecise his condicionibus[b] et circumstantiis, sed potius[c] minimum ab eo perceptibile quoad[d] qualitates sensibiles. Sed hoc per certitudinem iudicare relinquo ingeniis aliorum[e]. Apparet tamen[f] mihi quod[g], loquendo de tempore imaginato, non est aliquod maximum non-perceptibile[h], sed minimum perceptibile. De vero autem tempore, qui est motus caeli[i], apparet mihi quod[j] ibi est dare maximum non-perceptibile distincte mediante cognitione intuitiva sensus, non autem ibi minimum tale sic distincte perceptibile.

## <AD RATIONES PRINCIPALES SECUNDI DUBII>

[80→19, 20, 23] Per praedicta satis patet ad tres formas | principales in **T 34ra** principio praesentis dubii propositas[k], scilicet ad primam[1], secundam[2], et quartam[3]. Dicendum est enim in omnibus illis casibus et similibus quod Sortes ante *a* peccavit, sicut declaratum est sufficienter. Et cum[l] probatur quod non, quia[m] post quodlibet instans ante *a* poterat implere quod sibi praecipitur, illud est negandum[n], quia hoc[o] non posset sine circumstantia alia nondum[p] habita, nec quae sit in potestate voluntatis Sortis[q] haberi a principio illius[r] temporis parvi praenotati citra[s] *a*.

[81→22, 30] Ad tertiam[4] formam principalem et ad quintam[5], quae[t] quinta est forma Altissiodorensis, et ad omnes tales in quibus Sortes tenetur in *a* facere vel incipere[u] vel in quibus praeciperetur[v] quod Sortes aliquid faceret vel inciperet ante *a* vel in *a*, et tamen non faceret, si[w] fiant tales formae de faciendo aliquid[x] simul in *a* vel[y] de simul cessando in *a* ab actu aliquo per tempus praehabito[z], dicendum[a] quod talis non faciens in *a* nec[b] ante quod sic sibi praecipitur pro *a* vel ante primo peccat in *a*, quia obligabatur per praeceptum vel votum vel huiusmodi facere in *a* vel ante[c], vel dimittere in *a* vel ante, quod non[d] fecit vel quod non dimisit in *a* vel[e] ante sicut tenebatur; talis igitur peccat in *a* primo.

(a) creato] dato *MS* || (b) condicionibus] minimus (*sed. del.)* omnibus *add. V* || (c) potius] post *M* || (d) quoad] econverso ad *V* || (e) aliorum] aliquorum *MST* || (f) tamen] enim *V* || (g) quod] *om. T* || (h) non-perceptibile] nec perceptibile *V* || (i) caeli] tunc *S* || (j) quod] qui *T* || (k) propositas] praepositas *V* || (l) cum] *s.l. M* || (m) quia] plus *add. MT* || (n) illud – negandum] est illud negandum (notandum *a.c.*) *S*; est negandum illud *V* || (o) hoc] hic *M* || (p) nondum] non *M* || (q) sortis] *om. V* || (r) illius] *om. SV* || (s) citra] circa *M* || (t) quae] an *a.c. mg. S* || (u) sortes – incipere] tenetur sortes facere vel incipere in a *MT* || (v) praeciperetur] praecipitur *T* || (w) si] autem *add. MST, a.c. V* || (x) aliquid] ad *M* || (y) vel] et *MST* || (z) praehabito] praehabitum *MT*; praehabitio *S* || (a) dicendum] est *add. V*; inprobatur (improbatur *M*) solutio Filii Radulphi dicentis quod licet dum aliquis peccavit peccato commissionis fuerit aliquotiens verum dicere iste peccat, non sic tamen de peccato omissionis **r** *add. mg. infra MS* || (b) nec] vel *MST* || (c) primo – ante] *om. hom. MST*; *mg. V* || (d) non] *scr. sed del. V* || (e) vel] et *M*

1. *Supra*, 19.
2. *Supra*, 20.
3. *Supra*, 23.
4. *Supra*, 22.
5. *Supra*, 30.

[82] Sed si argumentum fiat de incipere sicut fiebat tertia[1] forma principalis, tunc est difficilius, quia[f] tunc talis nihil tenetur facere in *a*, sed tantum incipere, et incipere facere non semper est aliquid facere.

[83→82] Et huic respondet Firauf[g] in opere correcto[2] : « Pro isto », inquit, « argumento et similibus est sciendum quod aliter dicitur aliquis peccare peccato omissionis et aliter peccato commissionis, quia peccatum commissionis est actus aliquis, et ideo per illum actum[h] aliquando[i] dicitur peccans actualiter peccare. Sed peccatum omissionis est pura privatio actionis quae fieri deberet, et ideo non oportet quod ille in quo est illa privatio dicatur aliquando peccans actualiter, sed verius dicitur de eo quod est in peccato et quod[j] numquam peccavit, quia nullum actum peccati habuit ratione peccati[k] omissionis. Unde dico », inquit[l], « quod Sortes non peccavit, quia tantum[m] tenebatur incipere unam volitionem[n] in *a* et
**V 65v** non incepit, et[o] ideo tunc non omisit[p] aliquid, sed[q] incepit[r] omittere. | Incipere enim agere non est[s] agere. Et tunc incepit esse in peccato, ita quod tunc non fuit in peccato et sine medio postea fuit in peccato[t], et tamen numquam peccavit. Immo
**S 48rb** dico », inquit, « quod[u] si Deus creasset in ipso gratiam sine | medio post *a*, tunc ipse numquam fuisset in peccato, sed Deus praevenisset culpam ». Haec ille, sine pluri, in opere correcto quoad solutionem talium.

[84→83] Verum est autem[v] quod casus posset poni in quo punctus[w] suae solutionis, scilicet quod in *a* non omittit sed incipit omittere, nec in *a* peccat[x] sed incipit peccare, esset[y] verus et dandus, puta in casu quo dato praecepto de eligendo[z] actum volendi respectu alicuius obiecti[a] Deus suspenderet actum pro solo primo instanti, et consequenter sine medio secum coageret successive ad productionem volitionis praeceptae vel quod ex tunc peractus est sic[b] coagere voluntati[c] et[d] ipsa non facit quod deberet.

**M 40rb** [85] Si tamen Deus praeciperet alicui quod in *a* instanti | inciperet moveri vel aliquid aliud facere quod moram requireret, nisi ultimo in *a* vel ante *a*, immo nisi in ipsomet *a*, haberet efficax imperium faciendi vel movendi, talis peccaret in *a* peccato omissionis[e] primo, quia sine tali volitione efficaci in *a* non exsequeretur statim sine medio post *a*, et ipse sicut tenetur ad exsecutionem exteriorem, ita etiam ad interiorem sine quo non potest sicut tenetur in exteriorem[f].

(f) quia] quod *V* || (g) firauf] frauf' *T* ; ffirauf' *V* ; firefauf *add. mg. V* || (h) actum] *om. V* || (i) aliquando] a[n] *M* || (j) quod] quid *M* || (k) peccati] *om. T* ; peccandi *a.c. mg. V* || (l) inquit] inquam *S* || (m) tantum] cum *M* ; tamen *ST* || (n) incipere – volitionem] unam volitionem incipere *S* || (o) et] *om. MST* ; *s.l. V* || (p) omisit] commisit *MT* || (q) aliquid sed] aliquod si *V* || (r) incepit] incipit *MST* || (s) est] *om. V* || (t) et – peccato] *om. hom. MT* ; *mg. infra S* || (u) quod] *om. V* || (v) autem] *om. M* || (w) quo punctus] peccato *M* ; *p.c. S* ; in quo peccato *T* || (x) peccat] *om. M* || (y) esset] esse *V* || (z) eligendo] eliciendo *V* || (a) obiecti] instanti *T* || (b) sic] *om. MT* || (c) voluntati] voluntatis *V* || (d) et] vel *S* || (e) omissionis] commissionis *MTV* || (f) ita – exteriorem] *om. hom. M*

---

1. *Supra*, 22.
2. Riccardus FitzRalph, *Lectura in Sententias*, I, q. 10, a. 2, Paris 15853, f. 68rb.

[86] Et in alio etiam dicit irrationabiliter, nisi quod voces sunt ad placitum, quia[g] scilicet dicit nullum actualiter peccare ex hoc praecise quod omittit quod debet facere[h], quia peccatum communiter primo dividitur in peccatum originale et actuale, et actuale ultra in peccatum omissionis et commissionis[i]. Similiter, aliquis ultra[j] actu omittit[k] quod facere deberet[l], aliquis nondum omittit sed potest omittere[m]. Si igitur primus actualiter omittit, igitur et actualiter peccat, quia non solum ante actum in potentia[n]. Si autem ille vocet « actualiter peccare » causare unum actum qui sit peccatum, non est contra eum de significatione vocabuli contendendum[o].

## <AD ARGUMENTA PRINCIPALIA QUAESTIONIS>

[87→9.1. 2] Ad primum argumentum principale, dicendum[p] quod tantum probat secundam conclusionem[1] primi articuli, et ideo unum verum[q].

[88→9.1. 3] Ad argumentum pro alia[r] parte, quod vadit directe contra primam conclusionem[2], responsum est in primo articulo.

(g) quia] quod *V* || (h) facere] *om. SV* || (i) omissionis – commissionis] *tr. V* || (j) ultra] ultimo *MT* ; *om. V* || (k) actu omittit] tr. *MT* ; actum omittit *S* || (l) facere deberet] *tr. MT* || (m) omittere] committere *M* || (n) ante – potentia] in potentia ante actum *a.c. S*, *V* ; in potentia in actu *p.c. S* || (o) contendendum] concedendum *M* ; *p.c. V* || (p) dicendum] *om. M* || (q) ideo – verum] *mg. S* ; ideo in oppositum *add. S* || (r) alia] *om. SV*

1. *Supra*, q. 9, a. 1, 14.
2. *Supra*, q. 9, a. 1, 12.

APPENDIX

## RICCARDI FITZRALPH
## UTRUM ACTUS VOLUNTATIS FIAT SUBITO IN INSTANTI VEL FIAT IN TEMPORE

[First transcribed by Girard J. ETZKORN as Anonymous, Vat. lat. 943 = *E* 49ra]

[1] Utrum actus voluntatis fiat subito in instanti vel fiat in tempore.

### QUOD ACTUS VOLUNTATIS FIAT IN TEMPORE[a]

[2] Et sunt motiva multa pro utraque parte. Primo ostendo quod actus voluntatis fiat in tempore, ita quod non sit dare aliquod primum instans in quo actus voluntatis ponatur in esse, sed quod fiat successive sicut et quaelibet qualitas quae non inducitur tota simul. Imaginor enim quod actus voluntatis sit quaedam qualitas cuius generatio non potest esse sine augmento et intensione, ita quod suum noviter generari sit de necessitate successive et in tempore cum quadam intensione et quod habeat suum esse completum, non quidem pro aliquo uno instanti in quo talis qualitas fiat subito tota simul, sed pro aliquo instanti terminante tempus quo qualitas illa fit. Et ita videtur esse dicendum de quolibet actu hominis sive sit volitio, sive cognitio, sive sensatio. Nec oppositum intelligit Aristoteles, sicut infra videbitur[1].

[3] Et quod actus voluntatis fiat successive in tempore sicut et qualitas caloris in aqua probo primo sic. Si actus voluntatis fieret in instanti et non in tempore, sequeretur quod aliquis posset peccare in eodem instanti in quo primo esset. Sed consequens est falsum, ergo et antecedens. Patet primo consequentia, quia qua ratione quis potest pro eodem instanti pro quo primo est habere aliquem actum voluntatis, potest habere actum cognitionis de bono et malo, et pro illo instanti habet libertatem arbitrii; et pari ratione pro illo instanti potest aeque bene libere velle male vel bene sicut pro quocumque alio, ex quo volitio potest esse instantanea quantum ad suum totale esse, et ita pro illo primo instanti poterit male velle et ita peccare.

(a) quod – tempore] *mg. E*

1. *Infra*, 53–54.

[4] Sed[1] probo falsitatem consequentis multipliciter. Primo sic : ponatur quod aliquis angelus peccet in primo instanti in quo habet esse, ex quo istud ponitur esse possibile. Constat quod illud peccatum est vitium voluntatis ; ergo
**E 49rb** nocet voluntati ; ergo adimit aliquid a voluntate ; et per consequens voluntas | in qua fuit[b] illud bonum praefuit. Ergo illud non fuit primum instans sui esse ; sed ponitur primum ; ergo contradictoria erunt simul. Et istum modum arguendi tenet Augustinus, XII *De civitate Dei*, capitulo 7[2], ubi probat quod nulla voluntas potuit esse mala ab aeterno. Et arguit sic : « Quaero utrum illa mala voluntas, quam tu dicis fuisse malam ab aeterno, fuerit in aliqua natura vel in nulla natura. Si dicatur quod in nulla natura fuit, ergo omnino non fuit. Si autem in aliqua, ergo illam vitiabat et illi noxia erat, et per consequens aliquo bono privabat, alias vitium non fuisset ; ergo natura, cum illo bono quo mala voluntas eam privavit[c], praecessit, et per consequens mala voluntas aeterna non fuit ». Et eodem modo ego arguam in proposito.

[5] Praeterea[3], ad illud Augustinus, XI *De civitate Dei*, capitulo 15[4], dicit quod angelus malus qui cecidit aliquando fuit in veritate, sed non permansit. Et hoc probat Augustinus per Scripturam, reprobans opinionem illorum qui dicunt ipsum pro eodem instanti peccasse in quo habuit primo esse, propter auctoritatem illam prima canonici Iohannis capitulo 3[5] et Iohannis 8[6] : *Ab initio diabolus peccat.* Contra quos dicit Augustinus quod ipsi non intelligunt, quia si naturale est, nullo modo videtur esse peccatum. Et expresse ostendit Augustinus quod omne quod convenit rei pro primo[d] instanti pro quo habet esse, dummodo illud ex naturalibus suis possit, est sibi naturale, et per consequens non est sibi peccatum. Et ideo vult quod nulla creatura potest habere peccatum in primo instanti in quo primo habet esse.

[6] Praeterea[7], ad idem est intentio Augustini, XII *De civitate Dei*, capitulo 1[8], 3[9], et 7[10]. Iterum, *Enchiridion* 7 et 8[11]. Iterum, III *De libero arbitrio*, capitulo 19[e], 21, et 23[12], ubi dicit quod non adhaerere Deo est vitium, et omne peccatum est vitium, et omne vitium est nocens naturae et adimens naturae bona.

(b) fuit] h *add. sed del. E* || (c) privavit *coni.*] praevavit *E* || (d) pro primo *coni.*] proprio *E* || (e) 19] xx *add. sed del. E*

1. Riccardus FitzRalph, *Lectura in Sententias*, I, q. 10, a. 2, Paris 15853, f. 59ra.
2. Augustinus, *De civitate Dei*, XII, c. 6, ed. Dombart et Kalb (CCSL 48), p. 360.15-43.
3. Riccardus FitzRalph, *Lectura in Sententias*, I, q. 10, a. 2, Paris 15853, f. 59ra.
4. Augustinus, *De civitate Dei*, XI, c. 15, ed. Dombart et Kalb (CCSL 48), p. 335.1-3.
5. 1 Io. 3 : 8.
6. Io. 8 : 44.
7. Riccardus FitzRalph, *Lectura in Sententias*, I, q. 10, a. 2, Paris 15853, f. 60va-b.
8. Augustinus, *De civitate Dei*, XII, c. 1, ed. Dombart et Kalb (CCSL 48), p. 356.50-56.
9. Augustinus, *De civitate Dei*, XII, c. 3, ed. Dombart et Kalb (CCSL 48), p. 357.19-21.
10. Augustinus, *De civitate Dei*, XII, c. 7, ed. Dombart et Kalb (CCSL 48), p. 362.1-4.
11. *Recte* Augustinus, *Enchiridion de fide, spe et caritate*, c. 4, n. 12, ed. M. P. J. Van den Hout, E. Evans, J. Bauer, S. D. Ruegg, M. V. O'Reilly, R. Vander Plaetse, et C. Beukers (CCSL 46), Turnhout 1969, p. 54.1-26 ; c. 8.24, p. 63.9-19.
12. *Recte* Augustinus, *De libero arbitrio*, III, c. 13, n. 36, ed. Green (CCSL 29), p. 297.1-9 ; c. 13, n. 38, p. 298.49-56.

Ergo si in primo instanti in quo primo fuit peccasset, pro tunc adimisset aliquod bonum quod prius fuisset, et per consequens non in primo instanti peccasset, et ita in primo et non in primo.

[7] Praeterea[1], Magister, II libro, distinctione 3[2], fecit istud argumentum ad probandum quod angeli non peccaverunt in primo instanti sui esse : quia omne quod illis erat in primo instanti a Deo erat, et ideo bonum erat, quia Deus auctor mali non est. Sed ista ratio nihil probaret si aliquis posset peccare in primo instanti sui esse. Et per istud dicit Magister ibi quod omnes angeli creati fuerunt boni.

[8] Praeterea[3], probo quod angelus, si peccasset in primo instanti sui esse, non sponte peccasset, et per consequens non peccasset. Patet, quia numquam ante illud instans potuit vitasse illud peccatum, nec in illo instanti potuit non facere, quia tunc fecit, ergo simpliciter ille angelus necessario peccasset. Sed hoc posito, non peccasset, sicut deducit Augustinus, III libro *De libero arbitrio*, capitulo 20[4].

[9] Praeterea[5], si actus voluntatis possit fieri in instanti, ergo angelus potuisset mereri in primo instanti sui esse. Consequens est falsum. Probatio : ponamus, per te, quod meruerit in primo instanti. Tunc arguo : iste non potuit iustitiam amittere[f] in primo instanti illo eodem. Iterum, nec prius potuit illam amittere[g], immo non magis laudandus esset de iustitia quam de rationalitate quam non potest amittere, sicut arguit Anselmus, *De casu diaboli*, capitulo 5[6], probans quod boni angeli potuerunt quandoque peccare, aliter non plus meruissent[h] servando iustitiam quam servando rationalitatem.

[10] Secundo[7] arguo ad principale sic : si actus voluntatis posset fieri subito, sequeretur quod posito casu possibili aliquis angelus invitus et necessario peccaret. Probo : suppono quod Deus crearet in hoc instanti unum angelum dando sibi perfectam cognitionem et libertatem arbitrii. Et praecipiat sibi quod statim cum poterit diligat Deum quantum potest, ita quod statim ab illo instanti exclusive in quo creatus est, diligat ita cito sicut possibile est sibi et intensive quantum potest – immo etiam si nullum daret praeceptum, adhuc ille angelus teneretur hoc facere. Et ultra[i] : tu dicis quod actus dilectionis fiet subito et in instanti. Quaero ergo : in quo instanti ? Constat quod non in illo in quo est primo creatus, quia pono quod praeceptum sit ei factum quod diligat statim cum potest post illud instans. Ergo in quodam alio instanti. Sed inter illa duo instantia cadit tempus medium ; ergo pro illo tempore medio non dilexit, sed potuit diligere. Ergo <si> ante illud instans in quo primo dilexit, ita quod prius, ut a te positum

(f) amittere *coni.*] admittere *E* || (g) amittere *coni.*] admittere *E* || (h) meruissent *coni.*] meruisset *E* || (i) ultra] d *add. sed del. E*

1. RICCARDUS FITZRALPH, *Lectura in Sententias*, I, q. 10, a. 2, Paris 15853, f. 59rb.
2. PETRUS LOMBARDUS, *Sententiae*, II, d. 3, c. 4, ed. Brady, vol. 1, p. 345.20-25.
3. RICCARDUS FITZRALPH, *Lectura in Sententias*, I, q. 10, a. 2, Paris 15853, f. 59rb.
4. AUGUSTINUS, *De libero arbitrio*, III, c. 18, n. 50, ed. Green (CCSL 29), p. 304.6-11.
5. RICCARDUS FITZRALPH, *Lectura in Sententias*, I, q. 10, a. 2, Paris 15853, f. 59rb.
6. ANSELMUS CANTUARIENSIS, *De casu diaboli*, c. 5, ed. Schmitt, p. 242.28-243.3.
7. RICCARDUS FITZRALPH, *Lectura in Sententias*, I, q. 10, a. 2, Paris 15853, f. 59rb-va.

est, non potuit dilexisse, sequitur quod necessario et inevitabiliter peccavit, quia inevitabiliter pro illo tempore intermedio fecit contra praeceptum.

[11→10] Sed[1] tu dices quod isto casu posito, si tale praeceptum fuisset datum
E 49va angelo vel primo homini, tunc habebit primum actum voluntatis | sine medio, videlicet in tempore immediate se habente ad instans creationis; nec tunc erit dare primum instans positionis huius actus dilectionis, posito isto casu etc.

[12→11] Contra[2] : ponatur quod unus alius angelus non impediatur ab actu dilectionis pro illo primo instanti in quo producitur, ac per consequens quod eliciat actum in illo primo instanti. Constat quod isti duo actus istorum duorum angelorum, quorum unus elicitur in instanti et alter in tempore, sunt eiusdem speciei – patet, quia sunt respectu eiusdem subiecti – et naturaliter producuntur, ergo producuntur productionibus eiusdem speciei. Ergo si unus producitur in tempore, et alius, et si unus producitur in instanti, et alius, quia omne accidens essentiale alicui individuo eiusdem speciei est essentiale cuilibet individuo eiusdem speciei, sicut patet II *De caelo*, commento 49[3].

[13] Praeterea[4], si esset dare primum instans actus voluntatis, in quo videlicet instanti fieret actus dilectionis totus simul quantum ad eius generationem, tunc sequitur quod aliquis posset mereri in instanti. Et tunc ulterius sequeretur quod essent duo merita penitus aequalia omnibus paribus ex parte utriusque merentis, quorum meritorum unum fieret in tempore et aliud in instanti. Consequens est impossibile, quia tunc nihil prodesset continuare aliquod meritum. Prima consequentia probatur, quia si ponatur quod duo merentur, ita quod unus in instanti et alius per unam integram horam, aliis omnibus se habentibus uniformiter et aequaliter ex parte utriusque merentis – puta cum aequali conatu, similiter cum aequali caritate, et cum aequali intensione actuum, et ita de singulis aliis – tunc sic : meritum factum in hora est maius; et non in infinitum, quia tunc esset meritum infinitum (patet, quia quicquid excedit aliquod finitum in infinitum est infinitum); ergo excedit in aliqua proportione finita[j] illud meritum quod fit in instanti. Sit ergo, gratia exempli, quod in duplo sit talis processus. Pono tunc tertium hominem, qui cum omnibus similibus condicionibus illis duobus prioribus mereatur per medietatem unius horae : tunc meritum illius est in duplo minus quam meritum per duplum tempus; ergo meritum eius est aequale merito illius qui meretur in instanti. Quod autem meritum illius tertii hominis sit in duplo minus quam meritum illius secundi, et meritum illius secundi in duplo[k] maius quam meritum primi, patet, quia meritum secundi et in prima medietate horae est aequale merito illius tertii, et pari ratione meritum ipsius in secunda medietate horae est similiter aequale merito illius tertii, ergo meritum illius in tota hora est duplum.

(j) finita] infinita *a.c. E* || (k) duplo] mia *add. sed del. E*

1. RICCARDUS FITZRALPH, *Lectura in Sententias*, I, q. 10, a. 2, Paris 15853, f. 59va.
2. RICCARDUS FITZRALPH, *Lectura in Sententias*, I, q. 10, a. 2, Paris 15853, f. 59va.
3. *Recte* AVERROES, *Commentum super libro De coelo et mundo*, II, comm. 59, transl. Michael Scotus, p. 387, Cologne : Digital Averroes Research Environment : https://dare.uni-koeln.de/app/fulltexts/FT19.
4. RICCARDUS FITZRALPH, *Lectura in Sententias*, I, q. 10, a. 2, Paris 15853, f. 59va-b.

Consequentia patet, ut videtur. Assumptum probo, videlicet quod meritum secundi pro prima medietate horae <sit aequale> (et loquor hic de aequalitate quantum ad praemia eis debita) merito totali tertii : quia si iste secundus habuisset aliquam interruptionem inter istas medietates horae in qua meretur, tunc manifestum est quod meritum eius in utraque medietate esset aequale totali merito alterius, scilicet tertii ; sed nunc suum meritum est tantum quantum foret si esset interruptum, quia est cum condicionibus similibus totaliter ; ergo etc.

[14→13] Sed[1] tu dices quod non sequitur, quia maior difficultas est elicere duos actus similes in duobus temporibus diversis quam continuare unum actum per duplum unius illorum temporum.

[15→14] Sed[2] istud non obstat, posito quod illi qui merentur sint[l] angeli vel homines pro statu innocentiae. Tunc enim eliciendo illum actum nullam patientur difficultatem, et ita de aliis procedit argumentum etc.

[16] Praeterea[3], si actus dilectionis meritorius vel demeritorius possit fieri in instanti quantum ad eius totalem generationem, sequitur quod aliquis angelus possit tantum peccare pro aliquo determinato[m] tempore quod Deus non posset[n] pro toto posse suo punire ipsum sufficienter de peccato suo, et ita aliquod peccatum remaneret de necessitate impunitum, et per consequens totum universum esset deordinatum, quia debitus ordo universi est quod peccatum puniatur, sicut deducit Anselmus, I libro *Cur Deus homo*, capitulo 12°[4] ; sed haec omnia sunt absurda. Probo consequentiam : constat enim quod angelus est finitae naturae, ergo ad recipiendum poenam habet finitam capacitatem, et per consequens potest dari poena ita magna quod maiorem non posset angelus recipere, videlicet poena maior et excedens quam sit ultimata poena cuius angelus est capax. Sit ergo illa poena ita magna quam non potest angelus recipere *a*. Tunc arguo : constat quod aliqua est proportio poenae *a* ad poenam determinatam angelo pro peccato facto in instanti. Patet, quia utraque est finita. Sit ergo decupla proportio. Tunc ultra : quocumque tempore accepto, potest angelus in illo tempore decies peccare ita graviter sicut fecit in instanti uno ; ergo potest in quocumque et in quantocumque parvo tempore mereri decem tales poenas, et per consequens in quocumque tempore potest mereri poena *a* ; | sed non potest recipere poenam *a*, ut positum **E 49vb**
est ; quare etc. Quod autem iste angelus possit decies sic peccare patet, quia angeli non habent volubiles cogitationes, sicut patet XV *De Trinitate*, capitulo 41 et 71[5] ; ergo in quocumque tempore quantumcumque[p] parvo ipse <potest> velle aliquid et illud nolle et suam voluntatem dimittere, quia nullam difficultatem patitur in

(l) sint *coni.*] sicut *E* || (m) determinato] *iter. E* || (n) posset] pro tanto tempore *add. sed del. E* || (o) 12 *coni.*] ar *E* || (p) quantumcumque] pono *add. sed del. E*

1. Riccardus FitzRalph, *Lectura in Sententias*, I, q. 10, a. 2, Paris 15853, f. 59vb.
2. Riccardus FitzRalph, *Lectura in Sententias*, I, q. 10, a. 2, Paris 15853, f. 59vb.
3. Riccardus FitzRalph, *Lectura in Sententias*, I, q. 10, a. 2, Paris 15853, f. 59vb-60ra.
4. Anselmus Cantuariensis, *Cur Deus homo*, I, c. 12, ed. F. S. Schmitt (Opera Omnia 2), Edinburgh 1946, p. 69.11-13.
5. *Fortasse* Augustinus, *De Trinitate*, XV, c. 16, n. 26, ed. W. J. Mountain (CCSL 50A), Turnhout 1968, p. 500.18-501.34

volendo; quare[q] angelus habens libertatem arbitrii non confirmatus potest in quocumque tempore voluerit malam volitionem elicere, sicut acceptum est in argumento.

[17] Praeterea[1], si actus voluntatis potest fieri in instanti, ponatur in esse : sequitur quod angelus vel homo haberet meritum vel demeritum in instanti, et tunc ille qui continuaret unam bonam voluntatem per tempus uniformiter in omnibus condicionibus mereretur praemium infinitum intensive. Consequens est falsum, quia tunc Deus non posset ipsum sufficienter praemiare, quia ipse non potest capere praemium infinitum intensive. Probo quod, si meritum fiat in instanti[r], hoc sequatur : suppono quod *a* sit unum tempus in quo aliquis meretur continue. Tunc arguo : sicut pro primo instanti istius temporis *a* debetur isti merenti aliquod praemium praecise, ita pro quolibet instanti temporis *a* debetur sibi aliquod praemium. Aut ergo debetur sibi aequale praemium, et tunc sequitur quod pro omnibus debentur sibi praemia aequalia infinita, et per consequens aliquod praemium simpliciter infinitum debetur sibi pro omnibus instantibus. Aut pro primo instanti debetur sibi maius praemium semper quam pro aliquo posteriori vel econverso.

[18] Si[2] dicatur quod <pro> priori debeatur maius, tunc accepto aliquo instanti posteriori, puta medio instanti ipsius temporis *a*, constat quod pro illo praecise debetur sibi aliquod praemium – sit *b* – et pro quolibet praecedente illud instans debetur sibi maius praemium; et infinita praecedunt; ergo pro istis omnibus debentur praemia infinita quorum quodlibet est maius quam *b*, et per consequens pro illis omnibus debetur praemium infinitum.

[19] Si[3] dicatur quod pro quolibet instanti posteriori semper debeatur sibi maius praemium, tunc accipiatur medium instans : constat quod pro isto debetur aliquod praemium[s], et per consequens pro infinitis sequentibus debetur praemium infinitum.

[20→19] Sed[4] respondeo[t] quod pro primo instanti debetur praecise aliquod praemium et pro nullo instanti debetur sibi aliquod praemium praecise.

[21→20] Sed[5] contra[u] istam responsionem, sequitur quod posito casu possibili quod inaequaliter merentes aequaliter debeant praemiari. Probatio : posito quod Sortes continue mereatur in instanti, et in primo instanti eius et in ultimo simili et non ultra – et sit ultimum instans illius temporis *a* in quo meretur et non ultra *c* – et tunc assumatur ad gaudium. Ponatur tunc quod Plato[v] mereatur uniformiter in omnibus sicut Sortes praeter in instanti *c*, quia ponatur quod tunc nihil mereatur. Tunc arguo sic : praemium Sortis et Platonis erunt penitus aequalia vel praemium

(q) quare *coni.*] quod* *E* || (r) instanti] quia *add.* *E* || (s) premium *coni.*] instans *E* || (t) respondeo] respondetur *Opus correctum* || (u) contra *coni.*] quia *E* || (v) plato *coni.*] plura *E*

1. RICCARDUS FITZRALPH, *Lectura in Sententias*, I, q. 10, a. 2, Paris 15853, f. 60ra.
2. RICCARDUS FITZRALPH, *Lectura in Sententias*, I, q. 10, a. 2, Paris 15853, f. 60ra.
3. RICCARDUS FITZRALPH, *Lectura in Sententias*, I, q. 10, a. 2, Paris 15853, f. 60ra.
4. RICCARDUS FITZRALPH, *Lectura in Sententias*, I, q. 10, a. 2, Paris 15853, f. 60ra.
5. RICCARDUS FITZRALPH, *Lectura in Sententias*, I, q. 10, a. 2, Paris 15853, f. 60ra-b.

Sortis erit maius. Si praemium Sortis dicatur esse maius, ergo excedit praemium Platonis in aliquo divisibili, et illud divisibile debetur Sorti pro instans *c*. Et ita sequitur[w] quod pro aliquo instanti posteriori debetur aliquod praemium praecise, et per consequens pro quolibet, et habetur propositum.

[22] Si[1] vero dicatur quod habebunt praemia aequalia cum meruerunt inaequaliter, quia Sortes meruit in *c* quando Plato non meruit, ergo inaequaliter merentes habebunt praemia aequalia[x].

[23] Confirmatur[2] idem sub alia forma sic : tunc Sortes bene vellet[y] in instanti, et tamen hoc non sibi magis prodesset quam si non bene vellet, quod non potest capere ratio ; ergo sequitur quod pro *c* debetur praecise aliquod praemium, et per consequens pro alio instanti, et ita pro omnibus debetur praemium infinitum, dato quod pro[z] primo instanti debetur aliquod praemium.

[24] Praeterea[3] ad idem[4] : si in instanti haberet novum actum respectu alterius obiecti[a], mereretur, ergo nunc meretur, cum ita bona sit ista voluntas sicut et illa.

[25] Praeterea[5], si aliquis peccaret venialiter continuando actum suum uniformiter per aliquod tempus in cuius fine moreretur, sequitur quod pro quolibet instanti illius temporis debetur sibi aliqua poena in purgatorio, et ita pro omnibus illis deberentur sibi infinitae poenae, et per consequens semper esset in purgatorio. Et similiter potest argui ponendo quod suum peccatum sit mortale, quia pro isto debetur sibi poena aeterna et infinita intensive, quod est impossibile, quia tunc non posset punire sufficienter.

[26] Iterum[6], sequeretur quod secundum legem Ecclesiae pro aliquibus venialibus cum consimilibus circumstantiis deberetur maior poena quam pro maximo peccato mortali facto in uno instanti. Patet, quia pro veniali unius instantis debetur aliqua poena, ergo proportionabiliter pro aliquo veniali continuato in aliquo toto tempore[b] etc.

[27] Praeterea[7], si actus dilectionis potest esse in instanti, ergo angelus vel primus <homo> potuit demereri et peccare in aliquo uno indivisibili instanti. Et tunc posito quod ita de facto fuerit, sequitur quod meritum et demeritum sint immediata, ita quod inter ista nec fuerit instans nec tempus medium. Et tamen uterque istorum, cum stetit in iustitia, fuit semper sapiens, quando vero fuit in demerito et iniustitia fuit stultus. Sequitur quod inter sapientiam et stultitiam istorum non fuit aliquod medium, scilicet transitus de uno in alterum, qui transitus non fuit sapiens nec stultus. Consequens est falsum et contra Augustinum, III *De*

(w) sequitur] pro *add. sed del. E* || (x) aequalia *coni.*] inaequalia *E* || (y) vellet *coni.*] velle *E* || (z) pro *coni.*] prae *E* || (a) obiecti *coni.*] instantis *E* || (b) tempore] et5 *add. sed del. E*

---

1. Riccardus FitzRalph, *Lectura in Sententias*, I, q. 10, a. 2, Paris 15853, f. 60rb.
2. Riccardus FitzRalph, *Lectura in Sententias*, I, q. 10, a. 2, Paris 15853, f. 60rb.
3. Riccardus FitzRalph, *Lectura in Sententias*, I, q. 10, a. 2, Paris 15853, f. 60rb.
4. *Supra*, 22.
5. Riccardus FitzRalph, *Lectura in Sententias*, I, q. 10, a. 2, Paris 15853, f. 60rb.
6. Riccardus FitzRalph, *Lectura in Sententias*, I, q. 10, a. 2, Paris 15853, f. 60rb.
7. Riccardus FitzRalph, *Lectura in Sententias*, I, q. 10, a. 2, Paris 15853, f. 60rb-va.

E 50ra *libero arbitrio*, capitulo 4[1], ubi quaerit : « Numquid prius enim | homo stulte vel sapienter fecerit recedendo a Deo ? ». Et respondet quod nec sic nec sic, quia <inter> ista duo, ut ipse dicit, necessario est transitus medius qui nec est sapiens nec stultus, sicut inter somnium et vigiliam est medium, scilicet obdormitare et expergisci, quod medium nec est somnus nec vigilia. Hoc Augustinus. Ubi evidenter apparet quod, secundum <eum>, inter meritum et demeritum primi hominis fuit saltem aliquod instans in quo nec stulte[c] nec sapienter egit, et per consequens in isto instanti nihil voluit, et ita peccatum suum sive mala voluntas non fiebat in instanti.

[28] Praeterea[2], si actus <voluntatis fieret in instanti, sequeretur quod, quando voluntas educit se libere in actum> volitionis absque aliqua motione praecedente immediate quae sit causa volitionis, quod[d] tunc actio sive transmutatio subita esset per se terminus subitae actionis et motionis, et non esset finis alterius transmutationis successivae, quod est contra Commentatorem, VI *Physicorum*, commento 32[3], ubi dicit quod si transmutatio fuerit subita, impossibile est quod sit per se, sed semper est finis alterius transmutationis successivae.

[29] Praeterea[4], quod non sit aliquod primum instans in quo voluntas vult suam beatitudinem vel suum esse vel aliquid tale probatur[e], quia non est aliquod primum instans in quo intellectus cogitat illud volitum, ergo non est aliquod primum instans in quo voluntas velit primo illud volitum. Patet consequentia. Probo antecedens, quia aut talis cogitatio nova est libera, et tunc esset per se terminus mutationis absque hoc quod esset finis alterius mutationis successivae praecedentis, quod est contra Commentatorem, VI *Physicorum*[f][5], ut allegatum est[6]. Aut est naturaliter causata ab aliqua specie in imaginativa; et tunc arguo : suppono quod in imaginativa non sit aliqua minima species quae potest agere in intellectum. Patet, quia ponas illam : adhuc, si daretur, una alia minor posset movere eundem intellectum, licet tardius vel minus intenso; ergo illa non fuit minima. Iterum, suppono quod in imaginativa non sit aliqua maxima species quae potest agere in intellectum; tunc sic : si species in imaginativa agit nunc in intellectum, et certum est quod agit naturaliter, non libere, ergo nunc primo ista species est satis fortis ad agendum, quia si prius fuisset satis fortis, prius egisset; ergo nunc primo agit. Sequitur quod sit aliqua species minima sive debilissima in imaginativa quae potest agere in intellectum, cuius oppositum probatum est. Ergo hoc instans non est primum instans in quo species in imaginativa agit in intellectum, et per consequens non est aliquod primum instans in quo intellectus

(c) stulte] s *add. sed del. E* || (d) quod *coni.*] quia *E* || (e) probatur *coni.*] probatio *E* || (f) physicorum] a *add. sed del. E*

1. *Recte* Augustinus, *De libero arbitrio*, III, c. 24, n. 73, ed. Green (CCSL 29), p. 318.75-319.92.
2. Riccardus FitzRalph, *Lectura in Sententias*, I, q. 10, a. 2, Paris 15853, f. 60va.
3. Averroes, *Commentum super libro Physicorum*, VI, comm. 32, transl. Michael Scotus, f. 148rb.
4. Riccardus FitzRalph, *Lectura in Sententias*, I, q. 10, a. 2, Paris 15853, f. 65vb-66ra.
5. Averroes, *Commentum super libro Physicorum*, VI, comm. 32, transl. Michael Scotus, f. 148rb.
6. *Supra*, 28.

cogitat quando sua cogitatio fit naturaliter ab agente extrinseco. Nec est aliquod primum instans suae cogitationis quando libere cogitat, ut prius probatum est. Ergo nullius cogitationis actualis est aliquod primum instans.

[30] Praeterea[1], pro merito bono debetur augmentum caritatis, certum est in via ; cum ergo illius augmenti sit aliqua proportio ad caritatem Christi, sequitur quod in quocumque tempore iste homo posset acquirere tantam caritatem quantam habet Christus. Probatur consequentia, quia totiens potest in quocumque tempore sic subito velle, quotiens illud augmentum continetur in caritate Christi ; quare etc.

[31] Praeterea[2], sequitur quod obesset homini continuare actum meritorium, quia[g] pro tali actu debetur sibi certum praemium, et pro merito instantaneo debetur sibi certum praemium minus in certo numero. Sit[h] in decuplo minus. Cum ergo decem actus subito, immo centum, posset producere in tali tempore, ergo maius praemium acquireret quam continuando.

[32] Confirmatur[3], quia sequitur quod aliquis habens meritum summum per horam posset in eadem hora in decuplo plus mereri habendo diversos actus aliquorum obiectorum, et ita nullus deberet eligere continuare respectu unius obiecti[i] meritum per tempus in quo posset amare duo obiecta successive, quod falsum est, quia in hoc laudatur maxime felicitas a Philosopho, X *Ethicorum*, capitulo 8[4], quia est maxime continua.

[33] Praeterea[5], tunc sequeretur quod aliquis, ipso invito vel saltem necessario, esset otiosus habendo libertatem summam arbitrii : posito quod Deus in uno instanti sequestret voluntatem unius angeli vel alterius, tunc primo vellet in instanti immediato, <et> tunc in tempore medio esset otiosus.

[34] Posset[6] dici ad multa quae tacta sunt superius quod pro merito unius solius instanti nihil deberetur praecise.

[35] Contra[7] : tunc aliquis bene ageret et Deus nesciret ipsum praemiare[j], quia non est bonus propter futurum, sicut probat Augustinus in *Enchiridion*, capitulo 68[8] et X *Super Genesim*, capitulo 19[9] : tum quia diabolus non demeruisset, cum non fuerit nisi per instans in peccato ante obdurationem, sicut videtur dicere Magister, II *Sententiarum*, distinctione 5, capitulo 1[10]; tum quia aliquis intensissime in caritate amaret Deum et non mereretur, quod est inconveniens ; quare etc.

[36] Ista sunt argumenta pro una parte. | **E 50rb**

(g) quia *coni.*] quod *E* || (h) sit *coni.*] sic *E* || (i) obiecti *coni.*] instantis *E* || (j) praemiare *coni.*] praemiari *E*

1. Riccardus FitzRalph, *Lectura in Sententias*, I, q. 10, a. 2, Paris 15853, f. 60va.
2. Riccardus FitzRalph, *Lectura in Sententias*, I, q. 10, a. 2, Paris 15853, f. 60va.
3. Riccardus FitzRalph, *Lectura in Sententias*, I, q. 10, a. 2, Paris 15853, f. 60vb.
4. Aristoteles, *Ethica*, X, c. 8 : 1177a20, ed. Gauthier (AL XXVI. 1-3), p. 576.2021.
5. Riccardus FitzRalph, *Lectura in Sententias*, I, q. 10, a. 2, Paris 15853, f. 60va.
6. Riccardus FitzRalph, *Lectura in Sententias*, I, q. 10, a. 2, Paris 15853, f. 60va.
7. Riccardus FitzRalph, *Lectura in Sententias*, I, q. 10, a. 2, Paris 15853, f. 60va.
8. *Recte* Augustinus, *Enchiridion de fide, spe et caritate*, c. 25, n. 98, ed. Van den Hout, Evans, Bauer, Ruegg, O'Reilly, Vander Plaetse, et Beukers p. 101.18-22.
9. *Recte* Augustinus, *De Genesi ad litteram libri duodecim*, X, c. 16, n. 28, ed. J. Zycha (CSEL 28.1), Prague-Vienna-Leipzig 1894, p. 315-316.
10. Petrus Lombardus, *Sententiae*, II, d. 5, c. 1, ed. Brady, vol. 1, p. 351.12-26.

<QUOD ACTUS VOLUNTATIS FIAT SUBITO ET IN INSTANTI>

[37] Pro[1] opposita parte sunt argumenta multa. Unde arguo sic primo : probo quod actus voluntatis fiat in instanti et subito tota simul, quia intellectus quando deducit se de actu primo ad actum secundum intelligit subito, sicut patet III *De anima* a Philosopho et Commentatore, commento 28[2]. Dicunt enim expresse quod intellectio est actio perfecta et fit in instanti, nec illam praecedit aliqua actio diminuta ; ergo voluntas vult subito. Patet consequentia, quia voluntas est ita activa et ita potens ad agendum et non minus abstracta ab impedimento et resistentia quam intellectus ; quare etc.

[38] Iterum[3], volitio sequitur comprehensionem sicut umbra sequitur corpus, XII *Metaphysicae*, commento 14[4] ; ergo voluntas sive actus voluntatis est in eadem mensura sicut comprehensio ex parte intellectus.

[39] Praeterea[5], visio sensus particularis fit subito in instanti, ergo volitio fit subito in instanti. Patet antecedens per Philosophum, III *De anima* et Commentatorem, 28 commento[6]. Et hoc ipsum dicit Commentator, X *Ethicorum*, capitulo 4[7]. Patet etiam consequentia, tum quia voluntas est non minoris facilitatis ad actum suum quam potentia visiva ad suum. Tum etiam quia voluntas copulat virtutem visivam cum obiecto visibili, aliter non[k] videret, sicut dicit Augustinus, XI *De Trinitate* per totum[8], et II *De libro arbitrio*, capitulo 8[9] ; sed voluntas non copulat aliqua nisi per actum suum ; ergo[l] quandocumque homo videt, voluntas habet actum eius.

[40] Praeterea[10], si visio fit in instanti, sequitur quod volitio fiet in instanti.

[41] Praeterea[11], agens corporale, sicut agens luminosum, agit subito, sicut patet VI *Physicorum*, commento 32[12], et II *De anima*[13], et in *De sensu et sensato*[14] ;

(k) non] si *add. sed del. E* || (l) ergo] quq *add. sed del. E*

1. RICCARDUS FITZRALPH, *Lectura in Sententias*, I, q. 10, a. 2, Paris 15853, f. 64vb.

2. AVERROES, *Commentarium magnum in Aristotelis De anima libros*, III, comm. 28, ed. Crawford, p. 467.

3. RICCARDUS FITZRALPH, *Lectura in Sententias*, I, q. 10, a. 2, Paris 15853, f. 64vb.

4. *Recte* AVERROES, *Commentum super libros Metaphysicorum*, XII, comm. 39, ed. Iuntina II, 1562, f. 322vaG.

5. RICCARDUS FITZRALPH, *Lectura in Sententias*, I, q. 10, a. 2, Paris 15853, f. 64vb.

6. AVERROES, *Commentarium magnum in Aristotelis De anima libros*, III, comm. 28, ed. Crawford, p. 467.

7. MICHAEL EPHESIUS, *In Ethica Nicomachea*, X, c. 3, ed. Paul et Mercken, p. 359-360, 365-366.

8. *Vide*, e.g., AUGUSTINUS, *De Trinitate*, XI, c. 2, n. 5, p. 339, ed. Mountain (CCSL 50A) ; c. 3. n. 6, p. 340-341 ; c. 4, n. 7, p. 341-343 ; c. 5, n. 8, p. 345 ; c. 7, n. 12, p. 348-349 ; c. 8, n. 15, p. 351-352 ; c. 9, n. 16, p. 353 ; c. 11, n. 18, p. 355.

9. *Recte* AUGUSTINUS, *De libero arbitrio*, II, c. 4, n. 10, ed. Green (CCSL 29), p. 243.1-14.

10. RICCARDUS FITZRALPH, *Lectura in Sententias*, I, q. 10, a. 2, Paris 15853, f. 64va.

11. RICCARDUS FITZRALPH, *Lectura in Sententias*, I, q. 10, a. 2, Paris 15853, f. 64va.

12. AVERROES, *Commentum super libro Physicorum*, VI, comm. 32, transl. Michael Scotus, f. 148rb.

13. ARISTOTELES, *De anima*, II, c. 7 : 418b20-26.

14. ARISTOTELES, *De sensu et sensato*, c. 6 : 446b25-447a10.

ergo voluntas multo magis agit subito, cum habeat minorem resistentiam, et specialiter voluntas angelica.

[42] Praeterea[1], delectatio in voluntate fit subito, ergo volitio. Patet consequentia, quia delectatio non est sine volitione sicut nec tristitia sine nolitione. Antecedens patet, X *Ethicorum*, capitulo 4[2], ubi Aristoteles declarat quod delectatio est actio perfecta et fit in indivisibili et non in tempore.

[43] Praeterea[3], Christus in primo instanti suae conceptionis habuit summum meritum, sicut declarat Magister, libro III, distinctione 10[4], et est sententia Gregorii, homilia 10[5]; sed impossibile est quod sit meritum sine actu voluntatis; ergo actus voluntatis fit subito.

[44] Praeterea[6], si volitio non fieret in instanti[m], tunc esset possibile quod aliquis videret Deum clare in primo instanti sui esse et tamen non amaret ipsum, et per consequens quod aliquis haberet excellentem delectationem sine actu voluntatis, quod est impossibile. Patet consequentia, quia ad claram visionem Dei sequitur necessario delectatio excellens, sicut patet per Augustinum, libro I *De doctrina Christiana*, capitulo 38[7], et allegat eum Magister, I libro, distinctione 1, capitulo 8[8], ubi dicit Augustinus quod cum adest quod[n] diligitur delectationem secum gerat necesse est. Patet etiam per Commentatorem, XII *Metaphysicae*, commento 3[9], ubi dicit quod voluntas sequitur apprehensionem sicut umbra corpus; sed umbra[o] sequitur corpus pro eodem instanti; quare etc.

[45] Praeterea[10], si volitio non fiat in instanti ad imperium voluntatis, sequitur quod intellectio erit magis in potestate voluntatis quam ipsa volitio. Consequens est contra Augustinum, II *De libero arbitrio*, capitulo 14[11], et libro III, capitulo 3[12], ubi dicit quod « nihil est tam in nostra potestate sicut ipsa voluntas ».

[46] Praeterea[13], suppono quod diabolus postquam peccavit non fuit per tempus absque obduratione, sed statim obduratus est, alias potuisset paenitere, sicut videtur sentire Augustinus, Anselmus, et Magister. Et tunc arguo sic : si diabolus non peccavit in instanti sed in tempore, ita quod sua mala volitio non habuit primum instans sicut nec tunc, sequitur quod numquam libere peccavit,

(m) instanti] tunc *add. sed del. E* || (n) quod] quia *a.c. E* || (o) umbra] in *add. sed del. E*

1. RICCARDUS FITZRALPH, *Lectura in Sententias*, I, q. 10, a. 2, Paris 15853, f. 64vb.
2. ARISTOTELES, *Ethica*, X, c. 4 : 1174b10, ed. Gauthier (AL XXVI. 1-3), p. 570.3-9.
3. RICCARDUS FITZRALPH, *Lectura in Sententias*, I, q. 10, a. 2, Paris 15853, f. 64vb-65ra.
4. PETRUS LOMBARDUS, *Sententiae*, III, d. 18, c. 2, ed. Brady, vol. 2, p. 113.1-17.
5. GREGORIUS MAGNUS, *Homiliae in Hiezechihelem prophetam*, I, hom. 6, n. 8, ed. Adriaen (CCSL 142), p. 71.
6. RICCARDUS FITZRALPH, *Lectura in Sententias*, I, q. 10, a. 2, Paris 15853, f. 65ra.
7. AUGUSTINUS, *De doctrina Christiana*, I, c. 33, n. 37, ed. Martin (CCSL 32), p. 27.21-22.
8. *Recte* PETRUS LOMBARDUS, *Sententiae*, I, d. 1, c. 3, ed. Brady, vol. 1, p. 58.6-7.
9. *Recte* AVERROES, *Commentum super libros Metaphysicorum*, XII, comm. 39, ed. Iuntina II, 1562, f. 322vaG.
10. RICCARDUS FITZRALPH, *Lectura in Sententias*, I, q. 10, a. 2, Paris 15853, f. 65ra.
11. *Recte* AUGUSTINUS, *De libero arbitrio*, I, c. 12, n. 26, ed. Green (CCSL 29), p. 228.54-55.
12. AUGUSTINUS, *De libero arbitrio*, III, c. 3, n. 7, ed. Green (CCSL 29), p. 279.63-64.
13. RICCARDUS FITZRALPH, *Lectura in Sententias*, I, q. 10, a. 2, Paris 15853, f. 65ra.

immo non peccavit nisi quando fuit induratus, et per consequens non libere peccavit, ut videtur.

[47] Praeterea[1], secundum Augustinus, III *De libero arbitrio*, capitulo 12[2], non intervallo temporis etiam puncto temporis fuit sine poena; sed si non fuit aliquod primum instans in quo peccavit, sequitur quod eius peccatum non praecesserit eius poenam tempore nec instanti, et per consequens suum peccatum non fuit causa efficiens suae poenae. Consequens est manifeste falsum. Patet consequentia, quia causa efficiens praecedit necessario suum effectum in esse, sicut dicit Aristoteles, *Metaphysicae* XII, in textu commenti 17[3]. Et IX *Metaphysicae*, commento 13[4], dicit quod agens necessario praecedit effectum suum tempore.

[48] Praeterea[5], tunc sequeretur quod angelus vel etiam Christus non posset se movere subito in loco. Patet, quia non potest Christus se movere in loco nisi per suammet voluntatem humanam; sed, per te, voluntas humana non potest subito elicere actum suum in Christo; ergo nec potest Christus subito se movere in loco, nam voluntas in Christo et in aliis hominibus est eiusdem rationis et eiusdem speciei, et ideo si in aliis hominibus non potest voluntas elicere actum suum, ergo nec in Christo.

[49] Praeterea[6], si non sit dare primum instans peccati, sequitur quod sit dare ultimum instans caritatis, quia caritas non corrumpitur nisi per malam volitionem[p]. Et ita sequitur quod quando res permanens corrumpitur, in medio instanti inter
**E 50va** tempus esse et tempus non-esse | res non est, et econverso quando res generatur.

[50] Praeterea[7], si non sit aliquod primum instans ipsius actus voluntatis, sequitur posito casu possibili quod angelus peccavit et non prius fuit bonus. Consequens est contra Augustinum, sicut deductum est in primo argumento ad partem oppositam[8]. Consequentia probatur : posito quod Deus creet unum angelum sicut creat formas generatas cum motu, puta formas substantiales elementorum, ita quod non sit aliquod primum instans illius angeli; et ponatur quod Deus simul concreet cognitionem perfectam, et det sibi praeceptum de diligendo Deum quam citius poterit. Hoc facto, constat quod angelus potest habere bonam voluntatem secundum praeceptum sibi datum, ergo simul cum suo esse poterit habere bonam voluntatem, et pari ratione simul cum suo esse poterit habere malam voluntatem, quia ita libere potest producere malam voluntatem sicut bonam, et ita sequitur quod sit[q] possibile quod iste angelus non prius habuit

(p) volitionem *coni.*] vo[tam] *E* || (q) sit *coni.*] fit *E*

1. Riccardus FitzRalph, *Lectura in Sententias*, I, q. 10, a. 2, Paris 15853, f. 65ra-b.
2. Augustinus, *De libero arbitrio*, III, c. 15, n. 43, ed. Green (CCSL 29), p. 301.58-65.
3. *Recte* Averroes, *Commentum super libros Metaphysicorum*, XII, comm. 16, ed. Iuntina II, 1562, f. 302rbF-vaH.
4. Averroes, *Commentum super libros Metaphysicorum*, IX, comm. 13, ed. Iuntina II, 1562, f. 239rb-240rb.
5. Riccardus FitzRalph, *Lectura in Sententias*, I, q. 10, a. 2, Paris 15853, f. 65rb.
6. Riccardus FitzRalph, *Lectura in Sententias*, I, q. 10, a. 2, Paris 15853, f. 65rb.
7. Riccardus FitzRalph, *Lectura in Sententias*, I, q. 10, a. 2, Paris 15853, f. 65rb-va.
8. *Supra*, 3-4.

naturam bonam quam peccatum, quod est contra Augustinum, XI *De civitate Dei*, capitulo 17[1] etc.

[51] Praeterea[2], si[r] non sit dare aliquod primum instans peccati, sequitur quod idem simul peccabit, quod est contradictio. Probatur consequentia : ponatur quod iniungatur alicui poenitentia vel quod detur praeceptum vel quod cadat sub voto de incipiendo aliquem bonum actum in aliquo determinato instanti, puta in instanti *a*, et quod ipse gratis omittat actum illum incipere pro illo instanti. Quaero tunc a te : pro qua mensura ipse peccavit peccato omissionis ? Quia si dicas quod praecise in instanti *a*, ergo peccatum est in instanti, et habetur propositum. Si autem dicas quod post instans *a*, patet quod istud est falsum[s], quia non est sibi iniunctum quod actum illum incipiat post instans *a*, et ita pro quocumque signo post instans *a*, ista propositio est falsa : « Iste peccat nunc primo ». Et quia, per te, etiam falsa est pro solo[t] instanti *a*, ergo sequitur quod iste peccavit ex quo praeceptum omisit, et tamen quod numquam peccavit, quia numquam de praesenti verum fuit dicere « Iste peccat », et ita sequuntur contradictoria ; quare etc.

[52] Praeterea[3], omnis creatura fuit prius[u] aliquo modo in cognitione angeli quam in se ipsa, et tamen omnis creatura fuit facta simul, IV *Super Genesim*, capitulo 34[4] ; sed angelus cum cognovit laudabat Deum, et laus est actus voluntatis ; ergo in primo instanti habuit actum voluntatis.

## RESPONDEO PRIMO AD ARGUMENTA STATIM SUPERIUS TACTA[v]

[53] Respondeo[5] primo ad argumenta statim superius posita quae probant quod actus voluntatis fiat in instanti. Est tamen advertendum quod intellectio, volitio, sensatio, et delectatio dicuntur perfici subito et in instanti non quia quodlibet eorum generetur et intendatur quantum ad totum suum esse quod habetur subito in instanti – immo potest quodlibet eorum generari et intendi successive in tempore, sicut suo modo forma caloris[w] in aqua, licet non ita perceptibiliter, apponatur de tempore – sed quodlibet eorum dicitur fieri et perfici subito in instanti quia quando esse completum et totaliter intensum cuiuslibet istorum fuerit in aliquo instanti terminante tempus suae factionis, tunc anima et potentia habens eum quiescit. Unde totalis et completiva perfectio intellectionis et cuiuslibet eorum quattuor fit in quiete vel cum quiete subiecti habentis eam. Ita quies subiecti et instans ultimatae perfectionis cuiuslibet[x] illorum stant simul. Sed non sic est de forma

(r) si] l *add. sed del. E* || (s) falsum *coni.*] falsam *E* || (t) solo] t° *add. sed del. E* || (u) prius] p *add. sed del. E* || (v) responsio – tacta] *mg. E* || (w) caloris *coni.*] coloris *E* || (x) cuiuslibet *coni.*] cuius *E*

1. *Recte* AUGUSTINUS, *De civitate Dei*, XI, c. 15, ed. Dombart et Kalb (CCSL 48), p. 335-336 ; c. 17, p. 336-337.
2. RICCARDUS FITZRALPH, *Lectura in Sententias*, I, q. 10, a. 2, Paris 15853, f. 65rb.
3. RICCARDUS FITZRALPH, *Lectura in Sententias*, I, q. 10, a. 2, Paris 15853, f. 65va.
4. *Recte* AUGUSTINUS, *De Genesi ad litteram libri duodecim*, IV, c. 22, n. 39, ed. Zycha (CSEL 28.1), p. 121-122 ; c. 24, n. 41, p. 123-124 ; c. 32, n. 49-50, p. 129-131.
5. RICCARDUS FITZRALPH, *Lectura in Sententias*, I, q. 10, a. 2, Paris 15853, f. 66rbva.

quae proprie acquiritur per motum et alterationem, sicut est calor in aqua, immo ultimata perfectio formae alterabilis in subiecto coniungitur in ultimo instanti quo habetur ultimum complementum motui praecedenti in tantum quod alteratio non est quando cessat motus. Nam forma alterabilis intenditur et perficitur per motum ; sed intellectio et volitio et sensatio et delectatio perficitur magis per quietem ; tamen non sequitur « ergo subito in instanti », immo potest perfici et fieri cum quiete in tempore.

[54] Et[1] ista est ratio Aristotelis, X *Ethicorum*, capitulo 4[2], ad ostendendum quod delectatio non est motus nec est vera generatio sicut nec visio, quia delectatio est perfecta in instanti sicut visio. Similiter Philosophus et Commentator, VII *Physicorum*, commento 17[3], dicunt, probantes quod in virtutibus moralibus non est motus, quia virtutes sunt perfectiones et consistit in indivisibili pro quanto esse perfectum ipsarum[y] virtutum consistunt in quiete et in indivisibili, scilicet instanti. Et isto modo loquuntur Aristoteles et Commentator, III *De anima*, commento 28[4], ubi dicunt quod intellectio et similiter visio sunt actiones perfectae et fiunt in non-tempore, nec eas praecedit actio diminuta. Hoc est quia sunt perfectae in suis speciebus in instanti. Nec tunc requirunt actionem successivam immediate praecedentem, sed sunt in perfecta quiete animae et corporis, et tunc maxime sunt perfectae.

[55→37] His praemissis, respondeo. Ad primam[5] rationem, cum dicitur, « quando intellectus educit se de potentia ad actum secundum » etc., dico quod intellectus non sic intelligit quod sit aliquod primum instans in quo intelligat, sed tamen sua intellectio[z] completur et perficitur in intellectu, et sic est de visione
**E 50vb** | et volitione. Et ideo non oportet quod si aliqua illarum actionum sit in suo esse perfecto, quod tunc necessario habeat aliquam operationem imperfectam, puta motum verum immediate praecedentem ; immo post perfectam omnium naturalium sive corporalium transmutationem, sunt istae actiones in suo esse perfectae, sicut dicit Aristoteles, VII *Physicorum*, et Commentator, commento 10[6]. Et hoc intelligunt cum dicunt quod illas actiones non praecedit actio diminuta, scilicet necessario et immediate.

(y) perfectum ipsarum] *tr. a.c. E* || (z) intellectio] l *add. sed del. E*

1. Riccardus FitzRalph, *Lectura in Sententias*, I, q. 10, a. 2, Paris 15853, f. 66va.
2. Aristoteles, *Ethica*, X, c. 4 : 1174b10, ed. Gauthier (AL XXVI. 1-3), p. 570.3-9.
3. Averroes, *Commentum super libro Physicorum*, VII, comm. 18, transl. Michael Scotus, f. 175ra-b.
4. Averroes, *Commentarium magnum in Aristotelis De Anima libros*, III, comm. 28, ed. Crawford, p. 467.48-57.
5. Riccardus FitzRalph, *Lectura in Sententias*, I, q. 10, a. 2, Paris 15853, f. 66va.
6. Averroes, *Commentum super libro Physicorum*, VII, comm. 20, transl. Michael Scotus, f. 175vb-176vb.

[56→41] Ad illud[1] vero quod tangitur, quod voluntas in volendo non habet resistentiam etc., et etiam specialiter in angelis, propter quod videtur posse concludi quod voluntas suam volitionem non eliciat successive, sed simul et subito in instanti, potest dici quod sive volitio producatur successive sicut qualitas alterabilis, quod potest rationabiliter sustineri in hominibus, sive non producatur successive, sed sit perfecta pro quocumque instanti sui esse, sicut rationabiliter est dicendum in angelis, dico tamen quod non est aliquod primum instans volitionis, sed semper generatur cum tempore. Unde hoc quod[a] voluntas non habet resistentiam, non arguit quod volitio sit in instanti.

[57] Utrum[2] autem ex hoc sequatur quod nulla volitio fiat successive, ita quod eius generatio non fiat per partem qualitativam ante partem, sicut formae alterabiles generantur, dico quod non oportet, quia possibile est quod lumen in aliquo medio intenditur per tempus ex hoc quod aliqua nubes interposita inter solem et illud medium continue subtiliatur, et tamen hoc non fit propter resistentiam in medio ad receptionem luminis, sicut multi dicunt. Similiter, voluntas potest velle suum volitum intensius et remissius, et hoc libere, saltem usque ad aliquem gradum, et tamen non erit intensio propter resistentiam. Unde patet quod non oportet successionem semper habere resistentiam coniunctam, et maxime in agente libero.

[58→39] Ad secundum[3], cum dicitur « visio » etc.[b], dico quod visio completur et perficitur in instanti, et hoc intelligit Aristoteles ubi allegatur, nec tamen est aliquod primum instans in quo visus videt, nec in quo voluntas vult.

[59→41] Ad tertium[4] dico quod illuminatio alicuius medii potest esse in instanti, sed hoc est per accidens, quia illuminatio ista est finis alicuius mutationis successivae. Sed de volitione non est sic, et ideo non est simile.

[60→42] Ad quartum[5] dicendum quod Aristoteles intelligit quod delectatio est in suo perfecto esse in instanti, non tamen intelligit quod sit aliquod primum instans in quo voluntas delectatur.

[61→43] Ad quintum[6] posset dici quod Christus habuit summum meritum in primo instanti suae conceptionis, et hoc non quidem elicitive a voluntate humana, sed a Deo per creationem. Et si tu dicas, « Ergo non fuit meritum Christi », potest dici quod non sequitur, quia talis actus producebatur a toto Christo, qui non solum erat homo, sed Deus, et recipiebatur in toto Christo ratione animae in qua fiebat ; et ideo adhuc erat meritum Christi.

(a) quod] q *add. sed del. E* || (b) etc.] respondeo *add. sed del. E*

1. Riccardus FitzRalph, *Lectura in Sententias*, I, q. 10, a. 2, Paris 15853, f. 66va-b.
2. Riccardus FitzRalph, *Lectura in Sententias*, I, q. 10, a. 2, Paris 15853, f. 66vb.
3. Riccardus FitzRalph, *Lectura in Sententias*, I, q. 10, a. 2, Paris 15853, f. 66vb.
4. Riccardus FitzRalph, *Lectura in Sententias*, I, q. 10, a. 2, Paris 15853, f. 67ra.
5. Riccardus FitzRalph, *Lectura in Sententias*, I, q. 10, a. 2, Paris 15853, f. 67ra.
6. Riccardus FitzRalph, *Lectura in Sententias*, I, q. 10, a. 2, Paris 15853, f. 67ra.

[62→44] Ad sextum[1] dicendum quod Augustinus loquitur de diligi in actu secundo, quia tunc gerit secum delectationem. Sed ego dico quod actus diligendi non fit in aliquo uno primo instanti, sed in aliquo tempore in cuius ultimo instanti habet esse completum.

[63→45] Ad septimum[2] patet. Dico enim quod intellectio fit in instanti pro quanto perficitur in instanti, et etiam concedo de volitione.

[64→46] Ad octavum[3] potest dici quod diabolus stetit per morulam antequam actum aliquem volitionis haberet.

[65] Quaere de aliis in Rober Yber[c].

[66→51] Ad argumentum de *a*[4], potest primo dici quod illud argumentum non magis probat quod volitio fiat in instanti quam in tempore, quia potest similis casus poni in utroque, puta quod iniungeretur Sorti quod ipse haberet unam certam volitionem subitam ante *a*, et quod ipse omitteret eam producere ; tunc sequeretur eam contradictio. Probatio : quia Sortes peccavit. Patet, quia[d] omisit illud quod erat sibi iniunctum. Secundo sequitur quod non peccavit, quia nec in *a* nec ante *a*. Patet : non quidem in *a*, quia non tenebatur habere illam volitionem in *a*. Iterum, nec ante *a*, quia in nullo instanti ante *a* tenebatur habere, ergo in nullo instanti ante *a* Sortes omisit facere illud quod debuit, et per consequens non peccavit ante *a*.

[67] Pro solutione istius argumenti, ubi est quasi infinita, quaere in quaestionibus[e] de divisione et compositione continui, quia ibi tractavi istam materiam etc.[5]

(c) rober yber] *pro* reportatione Hybernici ? || (d) quia *coni.*] qui *E* || (e) quaestionibus *coni.*] qustionibus *E*

1. Riccardus FitzRalph, *Lectura in Sententias*, I, q. 10, a. 2, Paris 15853, f. 67rb.
2. Riccardus FitzRalph, *Lectura in Sententias*, I, q. 10, a. 2, Paris 15853, f. 67va.
3. Riccardus FitzRalph, *Lectura in Sententias*, I, q. 10, a. 2, Paris 15853, f. 67va.
4. Riccardus FitzRalph, *Lectura in Sententias*, I, q. 10, a. 2, Paris 15853, f. 68ra-b.
5. Non invenimus.

# INDEX NOMINUM

### Ancient and Medieval Authors



### Modern Authors

## TABLE OF CONTENTS

APPENDIX

**RICCARDUS FITZRALPH**
**UTRUM ACTUS VOLUNTATIS FIAT SUBITO IN INSTANTI VEL FIAT IN TEMPORE**

Dépôt légal : mars 2025 - N° imprimeur : 032581137

*Imprimé en France par Présence Graphique - Monts.*